THE GREEKS AND THE GOOD LIFE

THE GREEKS
AND THE
GOOD LIFE

PROCEEDINGS
of the
NINTH ANNUAL PHILOSOPHY SYMPOSIUM
CALIFORNIA STATE UNIVERSITY, FULLERTON

edited by

DAVID J. DEPEW

A Publication of
California State University, Fullerton

Distributed by
Hackett Publishing Company
Indianapolis, Indiana

For further information, please address the publisher:

California State University, Fullerton
Department of Philosophy
Fullerton, California 92634

Cover Design by Claire and Craig Ihara

Library of Congress Cataloging in Publication Data
The Greeks and the good life.

"Revisions of ten papers constituting the ninth annual philosophy symposium at California State University, Fullerton, held March 1979."
1. Ethics, Greek--Congresses. I. Depew, David J. , 1942-
BJ161.G73   170'.938   80-20440
ISBN 0-937622-00-1
ISBN 0-937622-01-X (pbk.)

Please direct all book orders
to the distributor,
HACKETT PUBLISHING COMPANY, INC.
P.O. Box 55573
Indianapolis, Indiana 46205

CONTENTS

ACKNOWLEDGMENTS

The publication of this volume was made possible by a grant from the Partners in Excellence Program at California State University, Fullerton, made available through the good offices of President L. Donald Shields. A matching grant was generously provided by Mr. and Mrs. George Klimek. The publication also owes a great deal to the cooperation of the Hackett Publishing Company, and to its president Mr. William Hackett.

Design and typesetting were done through the Oral History Program at California State University, Fullerton. The editor wishes to express appreciation to the Program's director, Dr. Lawrence de Graaf, for his cooperation; and to the Program's excellent and helpful staff, especially Mrs. Shirley Stephenson and the resourceful Mr. Russ Hartill. The technical advice of Mr. James Rogers on behalf of the Hackett Publishing Company was also indispensible in this connection.

The origin of the volume was the Ninth Annual Philosophy Symposium, held March 6-9, 1979, at California State University, Fullerton. Financial support for that endeavor was provided by the Departmental Associations Council, the Philosophy Club, the Faculty of the Department of Philosophy, and President L. Donald Shields, all of California State University, Fullerton. To the students who served on the Symposium Committee and on Student Discussion Panels go warm thanks, as also to the faculty moderators of those panels, Dr. J. Michael Russell and Mr. Peter Dill.

The entire process from symposium planning to publication was smoothed by the thoughtful assistance of Mrs. Elaine Weidner, secretary of the Department of Philosophy, and her staff, particularly Ms. Phoung T. Nguyen. In various ways thanks are due to the following for giving initial impetus to the publication project: Mr. Duane Day, Director of Development, CSUF; Dean Donald A. Schweitzer, School of Humanities and Social Sciences; Dr.

John Cronquist, of the Department of Philosophy; and Dr. James Hullett of the Hackett Publishing Company. The cooperation of Ivan Richardson, Vice-President for Administration, CSUF, is also gratefully acknowledged. The contributors to the volume were uniformly generous with their time and energy during the symposium and in preparing their manuscripts for publication. The entire effort owes a great deal especially to Dr. Julius Moravcsik's participation and unflagging support. The Faculty of the Department of Philosophy all gave much of themselves throughout. The cover is the work of Claire and Craig Ihara, who, with Myrtali Anagnostopoulos, also did valuable work on the interior design and graphics.

Above all, the editor wishes to express his special gratitude to Russ Hartill; and to Diana Klimek, who had a large part in organizing the symposium and supporting it through to publication.

THE GREEKS AND THE GOOD LIFE:

AN INTRODUCTION

DAVID J. DEPEW

I

The papers collected in this volume are revisions of
lectures given at the Ninth Annual Philosophy Symposium, at
California State University, Fullerton, in Spring 1979. This
symposium series has attempted over the last decade to
devise ways in which philosophical interchange among
experts can be conducted in close interaction with a
well-prepared undergraduate audience. In view of this goal,
choice of symposia topics is of considerable importance, and
casts light on the selection of "The Greeks and the Good
Life" in the present instance. Greek ethical theory, and its
relevance to our own moral situation and thinking, is a
subject that brings us into contact with texts that are
accessible enough to provide beginners with an entry point
into the procedures of ethical self-clarification. This fact
underlies the traditional role of such texts in introductory
philosophy classes. At the same time, they are so powerful
that they continue to enrich and enchant even the most
sophisticated of philosophical minds.

There are many things that unite us with the Greeks. There
are also many things that divide us. This theme of closeness

and separation between ancients and moderns provides one key to the shared concerns of the papers collected here. About half of the papers deal with what might appear to be a pleasantly surprising source of unity. The powerful techniques of modern philosophical analysis, when deployed on the writings of Aristotle and Plato, reveal thinkers of great ability and results by no means outdated or crude. In the light of this fact reconstructions of their conceptual analyses, and the structure of their arguments, by both formal and informal techniques, becomes a most rewarding enterprise. As we shall see, however, these exercises often tend ironically to throw into relief differences which nonetheless stubbornly stand between ourselves and these strange and attractive ancient people.

The theme of difference and distance is also addressed in a number of papers which begin by acknowledging that we reach back to the Greeks across religious and intellectual traditions which appear to be at odds with the basic assumptions of classical culture. These traditions exercise much influence over us, though we are often lamentably unreflective about the distorting effect they have on our assessments of Greek thought. There is a need, then, when considering the relevance of Greek ethics to our own moral thinking, to systematically think through this problem. Thus the theme "Greeks and Christians" is never far from the concerns of many of these papers. Further, explicit attention is paid to a theme that might be called "Greeks and Germans." Seminal thinkers and scholars in the nineteenth century, particularly in Germany, became vividly convinced of a conflict between Greek and Christian world-views, while acknowledging attraction to components of each of them. The desire to generate a synthesis and reconciliation between the two traditions, and hence a new ethical vision suited to an emerging modern world, deeply affected thinkers as influential in the twentieth century as Marx, Nietzsche and Freud; and has affected interpretations of ancient Greek thought prevalent in our own time. Yet these received pictures, while often highly suggestive, can also stand in the way of the very synthesis that their creators were in search of. A case in point is the common view that our own ethical commitment to the cooperative virtues and to human mutuality finds a deeper resonance in Christian than in Greek thought. A closer look suggests that the Greeks have much to teach us about cooperation, and how to think about it. Thus where we might have expected differences, on the basis of typical post-Romantic views about the Greeks, we may well find a happy and instructive source of unity.

In the following pages I shall attempt to forge some links between these themes and various papers in the volume.

II

The effort of modern analytic philosophy to achieve elucidations of the concepts which structure our shared experience has found especially in Aristotle a predecessor, a co-worker, and--given his remarkable perspicuity--a guide. This is not entirely fortuitous. For many of the pioneers of analysis, among them Ryle and Austin, developed important components of their programs in conjunction with traditional Oxford study of Aristotle. Meanwhile, modern logic, when deployed on the classical texts, reveals unexpected strength and subtlety of argument. This richness has to some extent been obscured because standard accounts of these arguments, canonical since the Middle Ages, have been encoded in a Procrustean bed of what was taken, ironically, to be Aristotelian logic. These two thrusts in recent study of ancient philosophy have conjoined in the last several decades to generate a still emerging revision of our picture of Aristotle, Plato and Hellenistic sectarian philosophy. Many of the papers in this volume are contributions to this effort. But, as noted above, this process is as likely to turn up considerations uncongenial to our ways of thinking as concordant with them.

A case in point is Aristotle's notion of *eudaimonia*, conventionally translated 'happiness.' Is there one concept here for which the Greeks used the term '*eudaimonia*' and for which we use the term 'happiness'? Or does the Greek notion so differ from the notion of happiness that we should employ another word to translate it ('flourishing' is a current favorite, though 'success' has also been suggested) and should acknowledge that Aristotle's analysis of this 'flourishing' explicates an idea that we no longer share? The latter alternative is initially plausible. For Aristotle will not allow that there are many ways in which people can, in principle, become happy. Nor does he think that happiness is most surely attained when individuals are indifferently left to formulate a way of life that they believe best suits their own constitutions, situations and, in the end, preferences. We, on the other hand, hold just such views. We hold them, in fact, so firmly that the notion of a "free choice" with respect to "the pursuit of happiness" seems to be an inextricable *part* of our very idea of happiness. Aristotle, to the contrary, insists that only a "practically wise man" (*phronimos*) can tell what will conduce to his or anyone else's happiness, since, by definition, only such a man will know what behaviors (uniquely) satisfy the demands of *eudaimonia*.

Merrill Ring suggests, however, that this matter need not be left with a mere agreement to disagree. Perhaps Aristotle *is* talking about the same thing that we call happiness, and perhaps the traditional translation *is* well-grounded. For, in crucially important ways the terms 'happiness' and '*eudaimonia*', in their respective languages, perform the same functions. They both serve as a terminal explanation of why we do what we do, and they both give us a principle for evaluating and ordering those doings. How then are we to account for the differences? In this connection, Ring begins to distinguish between "concepts," which we share with the Greeks, and "conceptions," including many cultural and ideological assumptions, which we might well not. Thus Steven Smith, in a paper intended as an introduction to the issues of the symposium, distinguishes between six different "conceptions" of the good life. If Ring's argument is sound, all of these refer to the same thing, though what they have to say about it differs markedly. Moreover, Ring is inclined to believe that his adjudication of the issue is not one which we, under a latter day pressure, impose on it. For he holds that Aristotle himself is aware of, and argues in terms of, just such a distinction as that between "concept" and "conception." Would such a view also lead us back to Aristotle's opinion that there can be only one correct conception of happiness or the good life? It is indeed possible that some conceptions cohere more closely with fundamental features of the concept to which they refer than others. Thus, for instance, Smith attempts to give reasons which tend to favor some conceptions of the good life over others. It would not follow from this, however, that we must in the end award the prize to a single conception. We might do well, in fact, to find a path between an inappropriate dogmatism on one side and an equally inappropriate relativism on the other. Both Smith and Ring seem to take this line.

The tension between concept and conception is explored further in Georgios Anagnostopoulos' paper. Anagnostopoulos concentrates on one of Aristotle's most important but most baffling ethical arguments, an argument in which he seeks to establish *his* conception of happiness by discovering the "function of a man." Aristotle eventually concludes that happiness is a lifetime's realization of rationality. This is "the good of man." But how does inquiring into the "function of a man" help get us to this conclusion? And what, in any case, can it possibly mean to ask about the "function" of a man? Aristotle is not arguing that man plays a role in some larger whole, or is useful to some other kind of being, nor that his "good" is just to play these roles and serve these purposes. For as Anagnostopoulos demonstrates, Aristotle does not use the term "good" to ascribe a property to man, as surface grammar or traditional logic might suggest. Rather "good" indicates, somewhat adverbially, when a being is performing, or has performed, the characteristic work (*ergon*, function) of its sort *well*. Anagnostopoulos argues that this "attributive" sense of the term good, and other key terms, can tell us why Aristotle thinks he needs the "function argument." It also testifies once more to Aristotle's conceptual and logical sophistication. Nonetheless, even after this has been seen, we must still confront Aristotle's apparent *assumption* that man has *one* characteristic "work." This appears to derive from a picture of the *cosmos* in which living beings are distributed along a range of ontological niches in such a way that each kind of being is assumed to possess one capacity, the exercise of which constitutes its *ergon*. Once more a subtle conceptual analysis meets head on a "globular" picture that brings us up short.

Even if we get past this difficulty, we are left with the necessity of relating all the various things that human beings "rationally" do into a unity sufficient to qualify as the *ergon* of man. This issue has of late been the focus of an intense scholarly debate in which the relation between human *theoretical* activity and human *practical* activity in Aristotle's ethics has been variously construed. For his part, Anagnostopoulos feels that while the function argument does not commit Aristotle to choosing between these dimensions as, strictly speaking, *the ergon* of man, it certainly pushes him a bit further toward considering the necessity for such a choice and toward opting for theoretical activity. Others, however, and especially John Cooper in his *Reason and Human Good in Aristotle*, have argued that this commitment to theoretical reason is only fitfully and sporadically made, and a more "inclusive" conception of happiness is characteristic of the Aristotelian texts as a whole.

Charles M. Young's paper explores an important issue in this debate. It shows what in the case of one specific moral virtue--courage--Aristotle *could* mean by "rationality in action." This is important to get clear about. For since in some basic way the exercise of rationality is clearly central to Aristotle's vision of proper human functioning, it is tempting from this fact alone to infer the inferiority of the practical life, the life of the exercise of moral virtue, in point of "rationality." For moral virtue can be easily construed as embedded into good character in the form of a *pre-logical*, quasi-autonomic action and response system, somewhat after the fashion of modern behaviorism. And in fact there are aspects of Aristotle's own theory of moral virtue, and its acquisition by habituation, that point in this direction. But this impression to some extent derives from the fact that when Aristotle is describing the moral virtues he somewhat abstracts from that perspective in which they are viewed as an exercise of reason. Young sets out to remedy this gap by showing reason at work in a situation demanding what Aristotle takes to be courage, and in a man fully prepared to act appropriately. One implication of his argument is that it would be unwise to opt for the theoretical life as uniquely fulfilling the conditions Aristotle sets down for happiness, at least on the basis of a faulty underestimation of the role of reason in the active life itself.

The same virtue, courage, which provides Young with a test case for examining the relation between moral virtue and reason provides Eugene Garver with an opportunity to examine the relation Aristotle envisions between virtuous activity and pleasure. For Aristotle pleasure is closely tied to the performance of excellent activities. He variously thinks of it as an accompaniment to such activities, as identical with them, and as perfecting or completing them. But on any of these views, if they are in fact different, the exercise of courage is likely to make trouble. For, as Aristotle himself acknowledges, courage is painful. In his treatment of this problem, Garver is careful to point out that many proposed solutions come to grief because they involve doing violence to one or another element of Aristotle's complexly balanced conceptual network. Thus, for example, if we hold that the pleasure proper to courage attaches to the courageous act seen as having already been successfully accomplished, we are willy-nilly taking the *actual* exercise of the virtue as mere means to an end that lies beyond itself. Aristotle is quite insistent, however, that completely virtuous activity is something done for its own sake. Garver's own suggestion is that we need not think of Aristotle's perfected virtue as requiring that the passions, in his view largely fear in this case, be completely absorbed into a virtuous disposition. For negative feelings must, in some sense, still be there if virtuous activity is to *be* the overcoming of them; and this is consistent with the pleasure proper to that activity itself.

III

The role of pleasure in Greek ethics leads us to a consideration of egoism and to the charge, articulated by Christian apologists like Augustine, that classical moral theory is undermined by that egoism. The papers of Gerasimos Santas and David Glidden have something to say about this issue, the one dealing with the pre-Aristotelian views of Plato, the other the post-Aristotelian theory of Epicurus. (We shall see that Bernd Magnus and Julius Moravcsik also address this topic.) The main thrust of Santas' paper is to show how Plato's theory of love in the *Symposium*, despite its apparently rhapsodic character, is a highly structured argument. The theory rests, however, on definite assumptions, and notably on the frank admission that love is egoistic. It is centered on the needs of the lover rather than those of the beloved. It becomes clear, however, that Plato's theory, though egoistic, does not suggest a shrivelled narcissism and hostility to others. For it does not rest on a correspondingly shrivelled and hostile conception of the ego. Thus Plato's account of *erōs* is to be firmly distinguished from Christian *agapē* in at least two respects. First, it accepts, while the latter rejects, an egoistic model of love. Secondly, it does not presuppose, as the latter does, that the claims of the ego tend to be morally repugnant. Indeed, Plato's conception of the ego as "desiring good things" suggests a self whose *erōs* drives it to progressively open itself to an ever widening range of   fulfilling and stabilizing objects.

Aristotle's views are not dissimilar to these, except that stress is laid on the self's activity more than on the sense of receptivity that predominates in the thought of Plato. But by the time we arrive in the Hellenistic world of Epicurus there are undeniably radical changes. Withdrawal of the wise soul into concern with its own psychological states, rather than with either worldly or trans-worldly objects, is countenanced. This undoubtedly provided room for the Christian apologists who found in Hellenistic sectarian philosophy the true upshot of all classical culture to accuse the Epicureans of narcissism and self-indulgence. Moreover, the qualified defense of Epicurean views given by Enlightenment critics of Christianity often assumes this very interpretation, while adding epistemological considerations that seem to take Epicureanism in the direction of relativism and even solipsism. David Glidden's paper argues, however, that these received views ignore several important distinctions made in the Epicurean texts themselves. First, Epicurus distinguishes between formulating strategies for living well, the traditional concern of moral philosophy, and measuring success in living well–largely a matter of empirical psychology. Thus Glidden believes he is in a position to show that Epicurus is not contradictory when he alternately holds that *phronēsis*, moral insight, and pleasure are the good. Moral insight *is* indeed what is most basically required from the point of view of a philosophical theory of morals; while from the psychological point of view success *is* (as Aristotle himself would admit) most reliably measured by considerations centering on pleasures and pains. Epicurus' concentration on the latter sphere merely underscores his insistence that the demands of moral theory be made as concordant with the possibilities and limits of the organism as possible, if *eudaimonia* is to be at all attainable. Thus Glidden goes on to show that Epicurus' theory is very close· to that of Freud. Secondly, Glidden believes that Epicurus does not treat perceptions about states of affairs in the world in a way that typically leads to relativism and subjectivism. Only feelings of pleasure and pain are that firmly brought within the circle of the ego. Nevertheless, all this does severely modify some basic insistences of classical Greek ethics. For it assumes what both Plato and Aristotle would deny: that pleasure and pain can be described and assessed independently of what a person is taking pleasure or pain in. The need that Epicurus thus expresses to measure psychological states in relative independence of definable situations testifies to the fact that his more complex and unhappy world throws up moral problems of a complexity that renders Plato's and Aristotle's assurances about what actions do and do not conduce to *eudaimonia* less than reliable. Nonetheless, Glidden's interpretation also shows that Epicurus is still working in terms of, rather that reaction to, that very ideal of classical ethics which sees right action as the deployment of a rational strategy for dealing with the flux of experience. Pleasure here, as in the earlier philosophical tradition, is an indicator of how well one is doing, rather than, as Epicurean pleasures later appeared, an aestheticism that replaces morality.

IV

I turn now to the theme "Greeks and Germans," and so to the background of the idea that modern ethics should be a synthesis between classical culture and Christianity. The cult of Greece that was so pronounced a feature of Romantic German thought may, in part, be explained by the fact that pre-Bismarckean Germany was, like ancient "Hellas," a cultural rather than a political unity. Its leading thinkers and artists tried to take pride in this fact, imagining that where a nation-state did not exist a "republic of letters" might. Moreover, they sometimes fancied that their own small medieval cities might, if sufficiently modernized, provide a social environment built to proper human scale. They idealized the Renaissance city-states of Italy along these lines. And they characteristically believed that the basic theory of such states had been worked out by Aristotle, who spoke in the *Politics* of "leisure," in the sense of culture, as the end of the *polis*. All that was missing was the further insistence that all men and women, rather than some, could be, indeed must be, full participants in such a life. In the Christian sense of the infinite worth of the individual they found the proper corrective. In turn, the Christian world-view would find its complement in the classical insistence that a truly fulfilled human life need not await another world.

Philip Kain's paper points to the importance of Schiller's articulation of these themes for later thinkers in this tradition. Schiller attempted to develop hints thrown out by Kant in his last years, when the latter proposed in the *Critique of Judgment* that aesthetic sensibility can mitigate the tension between the lessons of science and the demands of morality. The first *Critique* had justified a science that threatened to absorb the individual into a merely mechanical order of things. The second *Critique* secured the autonomy of the self, but appeared to leave him struggling in isolation with a massive weight of responsibility. Aesthetic sensibility, however, could draw us together into a distinctively human and humanized world. Schiller, as Kain notes, enthusiastically began to fill in this sketch by articulating a revitalized social and political life, modelled after the Greeks, in which our mental and emotional faculties would be in balance, and we would once more be "at home in the world" and with other members of our kind. For his part, however, as Kain further reports, Hegel believed that Greek aesthetic life was impossible without a corresponding naïvete and unreflectiveness. Whatever might be recreated of it under modern conditions could only be acquired by bidding an elegaic farewell to Greek innocence. This would not be in the last analysis possible, as Schiller had hoped, in social life itself. It could only be reenacted in a thoroughly reflective theoretical life such as that envisioned in Hegel's own philosophy. It is with Marx's adventures with this "Greek Aesthetic Ideal," however, that Kain is most directly concerned. What is powerful about Marx, both early and late, is his insistence that the key to these problems lies in the quality of our laboring life, and thus in those spheres that Aristotle calls *poiesis*, production, and *praxis*, action, rather than in the philosophical *theoria* that inspired Hegel. But within the framework of this stable insistence, Kain argues that the young Marx tended toward Schiller's view that an aesthetic renewal will include a transformation of even the most basic work into an activity expressive in itself; while the older, and presumably wiser, Marx is said to share Hegel's more realistic perspective, and so to conclude that the aesthetically expressive dimension of life is restricted to a leisure time which lies beyond the realm of necessary labor. A panel of California State University, Fullerton students, in responding to Kain's paper during the symposium, suggested, however, that the differences between the younger and older Marx on this and related topics might not be as great as Kain holds them to be. This response has been included in this volume.

The Romantic view of ancient Greek life that Kain calls the "Greek Aesthetic Ideal," together with the insistence of its creators on the relevance of this ideal for a revitalized modern ethics, gave way in the latter half of the nineteenth century to a quite different picture. It is this picture, most clearly articulated by that shrewd classicist Nietzsche, that stands behind the concerns of Bernd Magnus' paper. Nietzsche's Greeks can appear as pessimistic, disenchanted, elitist and aristocratic as Schiller's appear happy, childlike and agreeably democratic. At the same time, Nietzsche's Christians seem less morally insightful than those of Kant and Hegel. For on Nietzsche's view, their deeper motivations do not lie in a profound new grasp of human self-worth, but in the psychological dirty linen of resentment and spite. (Here Nietzsche turns the tables on traditional Christian anti-classicism, portraying the Christians as the egoists.) Given such an initial gap between Greek and Christian, the much-heralded project of a modern synthesis between the two traditions seems more difficult, indeed, out of the question. On one view, in fact, Nietzsche's general project can be taken as an attack on the very idea of such a synthesis, and thus on a basic component of German Idealist culture. On this reading, Nietzsche would not hesitate to opt for Greeks over Christians--especially pre-Socratic Greeks--while in a parallel rejection of the traditional hope for synthesis, Kierkegaard can be represented as choosing the other alternative. Given such a context, Walter Kaufmann's notations on Nietzsche's *Uebermensch* or "Superman" concept cannot but appear significant. For Kaufmann likens such a man to Aristotle's great-souled or magnanimous man—whose pride would be decidedly suspicious to Christians—and intimates that Aristotle influenced Nietzsche on this point. But Magnus seeks to show that the central texts on the *Uebermensch* concept do not support either this analogy or influence. Indeed, on Magnus' reading, Nietzsche's portrait of the *Uebermensch* as combining "the Roman Caesar with Christ's soul," while bizarre, suggests that in some sense the traditional search for a synthesis between classicism and Christianity is still alive in Nietzsche's thought. What Nietzsche's image reflects is his conviction that such a synthesis will, in the nature of the case, be very difficult. It will make severe demands on genuinely ethical individuals, demands well-expressed by what Magnus has called an "existential imperative."

V

The contrast between Schiller's Greeks and Nietzsche's reflects shifts in opinion between the early and the late nineteenth century. A more disenchanted sense of Europe's cultural situation and possibilities began to set in as the century ended. This sense of disillusionment helps us to situate Nietzsche's views about the Greeks. It also, I think, bears on Glidden's case for a similarity between Epicurus and Freud. It is quite possible that such a famously disillusioned thinker as Freud, who was also steeped in German classical learning, might come to see in Epicurus one who, like himself, lived in times that put severe strains on earlier, naive assumptions and aspirations, and who felt that our only hope lies in reducing our illusions about ourselves. All this reminds us that interpretations of Greek life tend to reflect, and to be distorted by, much more immediate issues. The fact of the matter is that images of Greece have long tended to serve as symbols and tokens in modern European cultural debates. Hence, much that one generation wishes to say about the ancients appears to a later age to be largely retrospective projection. This indicates, on the one hand, how cautious we should be in pronouncing our own reconstructions to be definitive. On the other hand, it suggests that reflection on the Greeks is a useful and familiar tool in our ethical thinking. It might be a habit we should think twice about giving up.

It is in the context of these remarks that I would like to place Julius Moravcsik's important contribution to this volume. Moravcsik expresses the aspiration of many when he holds that our ethical ideas might well be renewed in a way that gives greater prominence, in a very dangerous and fragmented world indeed, to the cooperative virtues. If, however, given this aspiration, we continue to suppose that the Greeks have something to contribute, we must challenge the post-Nietzschean picture of the Greeks as at their best when gloriously elitist and competitive. It is, of course, commonly acknowledged, as Moravcsik points out, that Plato and Aristotle did try to move received Greek morality in the direction of cooperation over competition. Nietzsche himself, as Magnus has noted, laments this very fact, or something not unlike it. But what Moravcsik wishes particularly to focus attention on is Plato's and Aristotle's shared anaysis of what a moral theory is, and what it is supposed to do. For it is this analysis that makes their shift to cooperation possible, gives it much of its compelling character, and suggests how it might be used as a pattern for our own thinking.

We may begin by taking note of some points already raised by Steven Smith. In a world that encourages a plurality of conceptions of the good life to coexist, Smith points out, it may be thought that the core of morality "as such" lies in the set of social *rules* which allow people with differing substantive and "prudential" views about life to live in common and in mutual respect. In treating of this issue, Moravcsik points out how deeply this picture presupposes that the distinctively moral is a matter of following rules. Actions are deemed moral when they issue from these rules. But this view does not do justice, Moravcsik extensively argues, to our sense that what is paradigmatically moral—*particularly in our dealings with others*—rests on attitudes and sensitivities that resist formulation into rules of action. I think it could in fact be argued that when rule-following *is* taken as central such sensitivities and attitudes appear to be grounded in, and even reducible to, mere psychological and cultural givens. Their moral dimension may accordingly be dismissed as falling into the naturalistic fallacy: deriving ought from is. And this can further imply moral relativism once it is acknowledged that there is a good deal of actual variation among such "givens." These considerations soon reinforce, in turn, the idea that the moral must be located in the sphere of the rule governed. For only rules seem to express the degree of invariance and objectivity that we want in a conception of morality.

The fact of the matter is, however, as Moravcsik argues, that we cannot talk about morally relevant sensitivities and attitudes without speaking of ideals of human life and flourishing which we formulate and share. The formulation of such ideals, furthermore, is not entirely fixed by psychological or social givens, and thus is not reducible to them. Indeed, so strong an influence, conversely, do ideals of life have on psychological reactions and social behaviors that, as Plato and Aristotle clearly saw, our very emotional satisfactions and enjoyments–pleasures–are determined at least as much by our ideals as by any fixed drives. In this way, an "alternative pattern" for moral thinking begins to emerge. Sensitivities become central. The "moral" and the "prudential" may thus be seen as continuous. Accordingly, we do not simply have a reversal of the pattern of moral thinking we are questioning. The effort to identify non-rule-governed considerations as importantly moral does not entail that rule-governed areas, of various sorts, are conversely non-moral.

Moravcsik goes on to show that the "virtues" or "excellences" of which Plato and Aristotle spoke are explicable as such ideal-informed sensitivities. Indeed, the "alternative pattern" that Moravcsik lays out generally seems to articulate quite well what the classical Greek thinkers took to be the structure and aim of moral theorizing. The desire to advance an ethics of cooperation by reference to this pattern can, accordingly, find much to inspire it in the Greek philosophers. This may be a conclusion reached against initial expectations, and a source of unity between ourselves and the ancients that intervening traditions have obscured. If so, it is a happy surprise, and one we are compelled, I think, to follow up on.

The reader will find many more points of contact among the papers in the volume than those I have mentioned, and doubtless many points of agreement and disagreement that are not intimated in what I have said. It is as an invitation to such discoveries that these remarks have been advanced.

THE CONCEPT OF THE GOOD LIFE

STEVEN SMITH

What is it to live a good life? That we care about the answer to this question is not surprising. For if we choose to live rather than to die, we want our lives to be good ones. But we do not agree with one another as to what constitutes a good life; and our disagreement is often the cause of great suffering. Not only do we disagree with one another as to the nature of a good life; often we find that the answers we have given are unsatisfactory even for ourselves. This, too, may cause great suffering. By our own reckoning, we often go badly astray, in our pursuit of this or that elusive ideal. Yet we cannot let the matter rest, so long as we care about improving the quality of our lives. When we ask what it is to live a good life, we are concerned with what is, in many ways, the most important question of all.

My program here is as follows: I first distinguish two forms or dimensions of a good life, living rightly and living well. I briefly discuss the question of how living rightly and living well are related to one another, and indicate, without supporting argument, my own leanings on the matter. These preliminary remarks form the context for the central portion of my inquiry, an investigation of the good life in the sense of living well. I consider and evaluate six views of what it is to live the good life, and tentatively suggest a composite account that appears promising to me. I then return briefly to the connection between living rightly and living well, and close with some observations about the significance of self knowledge for the good life.

I

Living Rightly and Living Well. When we hear someone say "Look at Mary: she's really living a good life," what do we suppose the speaker to be saying about Mary? I think we are likely to assume that the speaker means one of two rather different things. On the one hand, the speaker may mean to assert that Mary is *living rightly;* that is, Mary behaves as one should behave; Mary is honest, responsible, prudent; Mary is decent and fair, a person of good character and integrity; Mary lives as she ought to live. On the other hand, the speaker may mean to assert that Mary is *living well;* that is, Mary enjoys life; Mary finds her life rewarding, satisfying, fulfilling; Mary is happy with her life; Mary is living as she wants to live. If our hypothetical speaker employs the definite rather than the indefinite article, and says "Mary is living *the* good life," we are perhaps more likely to understand the second of these two meanings, living well.

These two forms or aspects of a good life are happily not exclusive of one another, and our speaker may have them both in mind. Surely it is possible that Mary is both living rightly and living well. Nevertheless, I think we can sense an important distinction between them; furthermore, they often seem to occur separately from one another. We know of people who apparently are living well but not rightly; that is, they seem to be enjoying themselves greatly, and have, to an unusual degree, those things that most of us want from life, yet they exhibit little or no commitment to principles of right behavior and social responsibility. On the other hand, we also know of people who seem to be living rightly but not well: they live morally responsible, prudent, and admirable lives, yet are unhappy, even miserable much of the time. Living rightly seems to be neither a necessary nor a sufficient condition of living well. Many of our life decisions present themselves as choices between living rightly and living well. Too often, it seems, we can either do what we ought to do, or we can act to make our lives happier, more enjoyable, more fulfilled—but not both. When our options in life are understood in this manner, the prospect is discouraging. Morality becomes a dreary affair, at war with joy and self-fulfillment. And to be preoccupied with the personal enjoyment of life becomes slightly disreputable and egocentric; one ought to be concerned with other things. Living well is seen as a gratuitous matter, largely incidental to the serious business of governing one's life.

These are serious and important issues; and they have been, over the centuries, the subject of an immense amount of serious thought and writing. It can be plausibly argued that the relationship between living rightly and living well is the most important question in all of moral philosophy. Most major moral philosophers, from ancient times to the present, have asserted an essential connection between living rightly and living well, though the nature of the connection has been described in many different ways. Among the Greeks, Plato believed that one could become happy only by becoming just, and that the most evil person was also the most miserable.[1] On rather different grounds, Aristotle believed that a happy life was necessarily a virtuous life. He asserted that the state, "originating in the bare needs of life, (continues) in existence for the sake of a good life."[2] And Epicurus roundly declared that ". . . it is not possible to live pleasantly, without living prudently and honorably and justly, nor again, to live a life of prudence, honor, and justice without living pleasantly. For the virtues are by nature bound up with the pleasant life, and the pleasant life is inseparable from them."[3]

Philosophical piety aside, we cannot allow that these

claims settle the matter. The question of the relationship between living rightly and living well remains obscure and difficult, with many claims and counterclaims contending for our convictions. Although this question is not my central concern, it is of great importance for what I will have to say. Thus I think it well to state my own opinions on the matter, so that you may know where I stand. Living rightly and living well are not, in my view, independent alternatives that overlap only incidentally, but are essentially connected. I believe that the point of living rightly is to make it possible for all of us to live well. If, as Thomas Hobbes asserted, life without morality and its fruits is "solitary, poor, nasty, brutish and short," then life with morality should be social, rich, delightful, refined and long. I believe that morality should enrich our lives, not impoverish them; and I view living well not as an alternative to living rightly, but as its proper fruit.

I emphasize that these claims are offered without supporting argument or proof here. Nevertheless I pass on to another matter, one that seems to me to be prior and more fundamental. We cannot, I think, understand the relationship between living rightly and living well unless we have an adequate understanding of what it is to live rightly, and what it is to live well. And if the point of living rightly is to make it possible for us to live well, then before we can give an accurate account of the principles of living rightly, we need a better understanding of those goods that constitute that rationale for such principles. We must, in short, begin to understand what it is to live well.

II

Views of the Good Life. My primary concern here is, then, with the good life in the sense of living well. I want to explore with you some six views of what it is to live well, so that we may begin to evaluate them and refine our understanding. The views that I will examine are perhaps best understood as alternative descriptions of the conditions that constitute living well. I will not pretend to tell you what the good life is. On this question, my own position is relativistic or pluralistic: I believe that no substantive view of the good life in the sense of living well can be the appropriate, rational choice for all persons. Nevertheless, some of the views that I examine here seem to be to recommend themselves more strongly than others. I will try to make my opinions explicit, so that you may judge for yourselves.

As the first candidate for a view of the good life, I turn to what I will call the good life as *maximum gratification of desire*.   On this view, living well is primarily a matter of having whatever one wants to have and doing whatever one wants to do, regardless of the nature of one's own wants or desires. References to "the good life" in the popular media seem most commonly to have this view in mind. In one of its more extreme forms, the good life as maximum gratification of desire is viewed as a life of wealth, leisure, and luxury; one thinks of a yacht, private estates, a raft of Mercedes and Jaguars, winters in Acapulco, and so on. But a more modest and restrained version of this view can be discerned, according to which one need not be wealthy to live a good life, merely upper middle class. One does not need a yacht or a Jaguar, but perhaps one needs fine clothes, a large home, and ample leisure time.

Those of us who do not enjoy the good life as maximum gratification of desires are inclined to speak ill of it publicly but yearn for it in private. My own opinion is that more can be said for this view of the good life than our public piety allows, but less than our private behavior implies. Wealth and status confer power and freedom; and the uses of power and freedom are not always bad. Studies that ask persons of various socio-economic levels to assess their own levels of happiness suggest that on the whole, the wealthy, who are presumably more able to gratify their desires than are others, see themselves as more satisfied with their lives than do the poor---though this finding is subject to a variety of interpretations.[4] On the other hand, we frequently see, in ourselves and others, examples of self-indulgence that have become self-destructive; and we know of persons who can have almost anything they desire, yet whose lives are apparently miserable. Whether maximum gratification of desire constitutes the good life would seem to depend in large part upon what one's desires are.

A second candidate for an account of the good life is in reality a family of various views, united by a common formal feature. Following current philosophical convention, I call views of this kind *dominant-end* views of the good life. A dominant-end view of the good life arises when one selects, from the wide array of human goods, one dominant end or cluster of ends, to be pursued to the relative exclusion of other ends. Dickens' character of Ebenezer Scrooge exemplifies one version of a dominant-end view; in his single-minded pursuit of wealth, Scrooge has excluded nearly all other values. Other commonly pursued dominant ends are the exercise of power, the achievement of status, and the enjoyment of love.

I am inclined to believe that few persons who understand themselves well would wish to adopt a dominant-end view of the good life. Human needs are diverse and multifarious; and any life plan that systematically denies major dimensions of the human personality for the sake of a single goal or cluster of closely-related goals would seem to me to be an unlikely candidate for the good life. Indeed, I find similarities between dominant-end views, and certain kinds of serious addictions such as alcoholism, in which the desire for drink gradually replaces other healthy human desires.

A third family of views of the good life might be called *"purpose-in-life"* views. According to such views, what is most needed to make life meaningful is some overarching aim, some *telos,* that transcends one's life and provides a point or rationale for one's entire existence. One's life becomes a good one by contributing to an end that lies beyond it. For example: a faithful Marxist may believe that his or her life derives its meaning and value from its contribution to the eventual triumph of the classless society; and a devout Christian holds that human life becomes truly worthwhile only by conformity to God's will. Some thinkers, such as Viktor Frankl, urge only that life needs to have a purpose of some sort, without specifying what that purpose should be[5]; other schools of thought insist upon a particular purpose as the only correct one.   I do not wish to discount the question of a higher purpose for human life. But it is a different question, I believe, than the question of the nature of the good life. It appears to me that some persons consistently live their lives according to a well-defined and significant larger purpose, yet feel personally unfulfilled and unhappy. Conversely, I believe that some people live lives that are enjoyable, rewarding and overall, without orienting those lives around an overarching theme or purpose that transcends them. Lin Yutang reflects this latter view, when he writes that:

> The word 'purpose' suggests too much contriving and endeavor. The question that faces every man born into this world is not what should be his purpose, which he should set about to achieve, but just what to do with life, a life which is given him for a period of on the average fifty or sixty years? The answer that he should order his life so that he can find the greatest happiness in it is more a practical question, similar to that of how a man should spend his weekend, than a metaphysical proposition as to what is the mystic purpose of his life in the scheme of the universe.[6]

I do not know whether human life needs to have a purpose that transcends it. I do know that some of my students clearly feel that they must have some larger purpose for their lives as a whole, if those lives are to be truly satisfying, while other students just as clearly feel that no such purpose is necessary, in order for them to live good lives.

According to a fourth view of the good life, living well consists in *living up to one's major expectations;* to live the good life is to have realized one's serious aspirations to a relatively complete degree. If, for instance, my family life is as successful as I believe it is reasonable for me to expect, if my career advancement and income level are about what I had seriously hoped for, if I rate my level of sexual satisfaction as about par, if my home and other material possessions are pretty much what I have counted upon having, I will probably regard my life as a relatively good one. On this view, whether I am living the good life depends very much upon what my expectations and ambitions are. For instance, if my station in life is comparatively modest, but is all I have ever hoped for, I will feel relatively happy; on the other hand, if I have achieved unusual success in all of my major endeavors, but in fact yearn and hope for more than I have achieved or can reasonably hope to achieve, I may be miserable. It is this dimension of the good life that seems most directly tapped by self-report surveys of happiness, in which people rate their relative satisfaction with their lives. Happiness on this view is largely a function of a cognitive judgment that the real conforms to a reasonable ideal.

There seem to me to be powerful considerations that favor this view of the good life, but also serious grounds for questioning its adequacy. In its favor is the observation that we are unlikely to feel happy with our lives, if what we expect from life consistently eludes us--whereas if we demand for ourselves no more than we are able to achieve through reasonable and serious effort, we may find contentment. Greek and Roman stoicism exemplifies one version of this path to the good life: learn to desire only what is within your power, says Epictetus, and you will find freedom and happiness.[7]

While these considerations are persuasive to me, I am also impressed with what seem to me to be serious shortcomings of this view. It appears to me that the view of the good life as the conformity of one's life with one's major expectations suffers some of the same weaknesses as do dominant-end views of the good life. If I have set my goals in such a manner that by pursuing them, I systematically deny certain of my basic needs, the achievement of those goals may leave me empty and dissatisfied—a feeling that I may not fully understand. The main character in Tolstoy's story *The Death of Ivan Ilyich* would seem to exemplify this condition. Another instance of the problem has been dubbed "the paradox of the happy housewife": in many surveys of levels of happiness, housewives on the average report greater levels of happiness than do single women; yet the same housewives on the average also report a greater incidence of anxiety, despair, irrational fears, and other psychological symptoms than do their single counterparts.[8] It seems likely that in many such cases, while goals in life have been largely achieved, those goals do not sufficiently reflect true needs.

Conversely, persons whose aspirations are well beyond their actual state may nevertheless function well and enjoy life greatly. Fictional examples of this latter point are Dickens' characters of Bob Cratchit and Tiny Tim, both of whom aspire to a better way of life, but who seem to be living good lives nevertheless. My own view is that while conformity of one's life with one's major expectations is a significant dimension of the good life for most people, it is neither sufficient by itself nor even in all cases, strictly necessary.

The fifth view of the good life that I will consider seems to me to be a highly promising account. Relatively well-developed versions of it are found in the writings of Aristotle, Abraham Maslow and Carl Rogers, among others. According to this view, to live the good life is to achieve a process of relatively full functioning of one's total organism. Borrowing a felicitous term from John Cooper's fine study of Aristotle's ethics, I term this view of the good life *human flourishing.*[9]

The view of the good life as human flourishing rests upon an organic model of the human animal. According to this view, there is within each of us a set of natural potentials for healthy growth and activity. Some of these potentials are species-wide; others are unique to the individual. One grows toward the good life by progressively actualizing one's potential for full human functioning; the good life consists in the mature exercise of one's human talents, capacities, abilities, and so forth. Thus, if my body is healthy, active, well-developed; if my reasoning powers are trained and effective; if the emotional dimensions of my personality function in a healthy, life-supporting way; if my social skills are comfortable and well-developed; if I have effectively exploited my various talents, and so on; then I am living the good life. In Aristotelian terms, the various dimensions of my *psychē* are functioning in accordance with their appropriate virtues or excellences.

It is worth emphasizing that the good life as human flourishing is a process rather than an end-state. Aristotle speaks of an activity of the *psychē* or soul; Maslow of a process of self-actualizing; and Rogers, in a happy turn of phrase, observes that the good life is "a direction, not a destination."[10]

From where I stand, the view of the good life as human flourishing appears to be very nearly correct. Those moments and periods of my own life that I value most highly for their own sakes have been times that I was fully engaged in the free-flowing, healthy exercise of some dimension of my natural capacities: running, singing, loving, creating, exploring, and so on. A life that approached this level of functioning, not merely in rare and isolated moments, but as its normal, ongoing state, would seem to me to be a good life indeed.

Nevertheless, I think there are important deficiencies in this account as it stands. For one, to say that the good life consists in human flourishing is to say very little about what actually constitutes full human functioning, how one achieves that process, and how one distinguishes it from imitations. These issues are complicated by the fact that what constitutes full functioning will vary in many respects from one person to the next.

The view of the good life as human flourishing seems to me incomplete in another important respect. Whether an organism is able to flourish is a function not merely of the state of the organism itself, but also of the environment in which it exists. A healthy plant withers and dies, if it is deprived of water and nutrients. Likewise, Maslow's self-actualizing persons could not be said to be living the good life if they were deprived of food, shelter, friends, and so on. Considerations such as these led Aristotle to conclude that a certain degree of good fortune was necessary, in order for human flourishing to occur.[11] If one's fundamental human needs are not met, then one cannot live the good life.

I come, then, to a sixth view of the good life, according to which the good life consists in the *satisfaction of need*. On this kind of view, genuine needs are viewed as more or less objective demands of the organism, rather than merely as products of culture or arbitrary desire; and to live well is to be relatively successful in meeting one's needs. A developed view of the good life as satisfaction of need requires an account of the various types of human need, how they are related to one another, which ones are more urgent or fundamental, and so on. Maslow's theory of motivation, with its hierarchy of human needs, provides one such account.[12]

The good life as need-satisfaction is, in fact, closely related to the good life as human flourishing. One way of understanding the notion of flourishing or functioning well is to see it as a state of maximum effectiveness in meeting real needs. A flourishing plant seeks out water, nutrients and sunlight efficiently, and makes the best possible use of what it acquires. Likewise, persons who are functioning well are able to acquire what they need from life more efficiently than are others. John Cooper argues persuasively that this is how Aristotle understands the concept of flourishing: Cooper writes that for Aristotle, "to flourish is not actually to possess a full portion of all the basic good things, but rather to be living in accordance with principles that are rationally calculated to secure them."[13]

If human flourishing requires an adequate level of satisfaction of needs, it does not follow that the proper way to achieve the process of flourishing is simply to surround oneself with all of those things that are capable of satisfying one's needs. A plant that is diseased cannot make proper use of the nutrients that are available to it; likewise, if I am undisciplined, emotionally disturbed, or otherwise unbalanced or diseased, I cannot make appropriate use of all of the goods that are available to me. Thus, if functioning well requires the satisfaction of need, it is also true that effective satisfaction of need requires that one function well. Probably the most effective means to achieve satisfaction of my needs is to enhance my capacity to function. Aristotle's view of this point is again nicely summarized by Cooper: "The correct ultimate end to pursue is not the collection of first-order goods themselves but the maintenance of the pattern of control designed to bring about their attainment."[14] And "the overriding concern of a virtuous person's life is with . . . the fitness to achieve success rather than success itself."[15] Put simply: achieving the good life is less a result of manipulating one's environment, than it is a consequence of developing oneself.

I believe that a view of the good life as satisfaction of need often underlies other alternative accounts of the good life; and the ways that these alternative accounts diverge from it are instructive. For instance, the view that the good life consists in maximum gratification of desire takes much of its plausibility from the fact that needs manifest themselves in conciousness as desires. Thus, we may feel that by gratifying our desires, we will meet all of our needs. In fact, however, our desires usually diverge significantly from our true needs. We desire things that we do not need, and we need things that we do not desire. The result is that we pursue things that are ultimately unrewarding; we seek satisfaction in ways that do not satisfy. Epicurus, who is often wrongly identified as an advocate of self-indulgent gratification of desire, in fact saw this problem quite clearly. He wrote, "Of desires some are natural, others vain, and of the natural some are necessary and others merely natural; and of the necessary some are necessary for happiness, others for the repose of the body, and others for very life."[16] Much of Epicurus' advice may be construed as urging the education and discipline of desire so as to bring it into conformity with true need.

I have suggested a similar line of objection to several other views of the good life. Dominant-end views may ignore certain needs for the sake of some overriding goal. Likewise, living in accordance with a particular purpose in life is in itself no assurance that one's needs are being met. And achieving one's major aspirations may turn out to be unsatisfying, if those aspirations do not adequately reflect one's true needs.

The six views that I have discussed here by no means exhaust the list of plausible candidates for a view of the good life. In particular, most of my discussion has centered around what might be called organic or naturalistic models of what it is to live well. But a number of historically prominent accounts maintain that the good life can be achieved only by somehow rising above or conquering the demands of our organism, and achieving a higher state that has little to do with organic functioning. Some of these accounts qualify as purpose-in-life or dominant-end views; others exemplify quite different approaches altogether. It is not clear to me, for instance, how to classify certain Oriental views such as Buddhism and Taoism, both of which strike me as powerful and attractive. Nevertheless, my own thinking continues to take shape along naturalistic lines.

III

Concluding Remarks. If living well consists in human flourishing and need-satisfaction, what is implied for the relationship of living rightly and living well? In my own thinking about this question, I find that I am guided by organic analogies. I would like to share one of these analogies with you. Perhaps because I was born and raised on an Iowa farm, my favorite model is that of a field of corn. Individual stalks of corn, growing haphazardly on untended ground, are likely to be overcome by weeds. And lone cornstalks in an open field will probably not survive the forces of wind, rain and predators. Corn does not survive well in a "state of nature." If the stalks grow next to one another, however, they provide mutual support and protection. But it would also not do to sow the seeds too thickly; for when they are crowded together, the individual plants compete for sunlight, water and nutrients, and most do not achieve their full growth. Moreover, without orderly rows it becomes difficult to cultivate the ground and thus remove the weeds that threaten to sap strength from the corn. What is needed for ideal growth and flourishing are carefully spaced plants that gain strength and protection from standing together, but that also allow one another sufficient space to flourish freely.

Perhaps the point of my metaphor is obvious. Humans, too, gain strength and effectiveness in numbers; only within society can we reach our full stature as human beings. But if collective living is to provide the conditions for human flourishing, it must be ordered by principles of restraint and respect, so that conflict is minimized and cooperation is promoted. Principles of right behavior provide the framework and means by which individual good may be maximized; the point of morality is the good life for all.

In closing, I want to speculate briefly with you about another factor that seems to me to be of central importance in any serious effort to achieve the good life. While I have not explicitly discussed it here, it is implicit in much of what I have said. That factor is self-knowledge. Nietzsche wrote that "We knowers are unknown to ourselves."[17] If I am ignorant of major dimensions of myself; if I have suppressed parts of myself, in order to pursue external goals; if I am unaware of my genuine needs, my potentials, my creative impules; then I am likely to wander upon unproductive paths, and fall short of what I could be. But if I learn to see beneath the encrustations of culture and social expectation, to look inside with what Jung called "the natural mind"; if I learn to heed not only the counsels of my reason, but also the murmurings of my deeper nature; if I become increasingly transparent to myself, integrated, whole--then perhaps I will find my way to a higher level of functioning and a fuller expression of my being.

Socrates declared that the unexamined life is not worth living. That has always seemed a hard saying to me. Are persons who do not have the habit of self-examination doomed to live worthless lives? But I believe that Socrates intended a different point. If I carefully examine my life, and come to a better understanding of my needs, my potentials, my *daimōn*–the person within that I most truly am–then my life can be immensely better than it might otherwise be. And if I can make my life better, richer, more productive, more fulfilled, what interest do I have in my old way of living? For a merely adequate life is not worth living, if one can live a genuinely good life.

Notes

1. See *The Republic*, Book IX, esp. pp. 586-591.

2. *Politics*, Book I, Chapter 2, 1252b28-30 (Jowett translation); in *Introduction to Aristotle*, ed. by Richard McKeon (New York: The Modern Library, 1947), p. 555.

3. *Letter to Menoeceus* in *Epicurus: the Extant Remains*, translated by Cyril Bailey (Oxford: Clarendon Press, 1926), p. 91.

4. Phillip Shaver and Jonathan Freedman, "Your Pursuit of Happiness," *Psychology Today*, August 1976 (Vol. 10, No. 3), p. 26.

5. Victor Frankl, *Man's Search for Meaning: An Introduction to Logotherapy* (New York: Pocket Books, 1963). See esp. pp. 171, 173f.

6. Lin Yutang, *The Importance of Living* (New York: The John Day Co., 1937), p. 123.

7. *The Manual of Epictetus*, Section One, in *Epictetus: The Discourses and Manual*, translated by P.E. Matheson (Oxford: Clarendon Press, 1916), p. 213.

8. Shaver and Freedman, *op. cit.*, p. 29.

9. John M. Cooper, *Reason and Human Good in Aristotle* (Cambridge, Mass.: Harvard University Press, 1975), p. 89.

10. Carl R. Rogers, *On Becoming a Person* (Boston: Houghton Mifflin Co., 1961), p. 186.

11. *Nicomachean Ethics*, Book I, Chapter 10.

12. See Abraham Maslow, *Motivation and Personality*, Second Edition (New York: Harper and Row, 1954, 1970), Chapter 4.

13. Cooper, *op. cit.*, p. 125.

14. *Ibid.*

15. *Ibid*, p. 126.

16. *Letter to Menoeceus* in *Epicurus: the Extant Remains*, p. 87.

17. Friedrich Nietzsche, *The Birth of Tragedy and the Genealogy of Morals*, translated by Francis Golffing (Garden City, New York: Doubleday Anchor, 1956), p. 149.

PLATO ON LOVE, BEAUTY
AND THE GOOD

GERASIMOS SANTAS

The literature on love is immense. Over the centuries love
in its various forms has been defined, described, depicted and
eulogized by poets, men of letters, theologians, philosophers,
psychologists, anthropologists, and even biologists. Several
historical and comparative studies have tried to distinguish
different concepts of love, the most familiar categories
perhaps being familial love, Platonic love, Christian love,
courtly and romantic love, and sexual love. Not all writers on
the topic can of course be said to have given us theories of
love; Sappho's love poems, for example, are delicate and
insightful, but it would probably be a misunderstanding to
interpret them as intended to present a theory of love. Aside
from empirically oriented studies in the last half century,
perhaps two of the clearest examples of writers who have
given us systematic theories of love are Plato and Freud.
Recent work on Plato has rekindled interest in his theory of
love; several works offer us partial exegeses and assessments
of the theory. Yet, a systematic and accurate exposition of
the theory, an essential preliminary to serious assessments

and comparisons, does not exist. As a result, serious disagreements remain not only on matters of detail but also on the essential features of the theory and on evaluations of it. My primary aim in this study is such a reconstruction. Eventually, in a larger study, I attempt to understand and assess the theory by comparison to rival theories such as Freud's and recent empirical studies.

I begin with two kinds of preliminaries: linguistic and conceptual considerations, and the contexts to which a theory of love belongs. Then I reconstruct Plato's theory in detail, and finally I broach briefly some criticisms in the light of the reconstruction.

I

Linguistic Preliminaries. In English the word 'love' seems to cover a fairly wide variety of feelings, attitudes, and behavior. We pick out some part of this variety by conjoining 'love' with some modifying word or phrase, such as 'parental love', 'sexual love', 'divine love', and so on. The single word common to all these cases creates an assumption that all these varieties have something in common or a common core or source. This linguistic situation, congenial as it might have been to Plato, did not exist in ancient Greek. Instead, three different words, *eros, philia* and *agapē*, and the corresponding verbs, were used to pick out different, perhaps overlapping, portions of this variety. *Eros* and *philia* are widely used by Plato, while *agapē* is the word in the New Testament to signify the kind of love Christ taught about. In the *Symposium* and the *Phaedrus* Plato investigates the concept of *eros*, while *philia* is Socratically discussed in the *Lysis* and some account of it is given in the *Republic*. Here we shall concentrate on his theory of *eros* in the *Symposium*.

In view of these linguistic complications and to avoid gross confusions, it is useful to discuss briefly two questions: first, what is the distinction between *eros* and *philia*? and second, what are the relations between the Greek '*eros*', '*philia*', '*agapē*' and the English 'love'? As Vlastos notes (*Platonic*

Studies p. 4, note 4), *eros* signifies something "more intense, more passionate" than *philia*, something "more closely tied to the sexual drive." He adds that "for non-incestuous familial love one would have to turn to *philia* in lieu of *eros.*" And we may add that for friendship both Plato and Aristotle use *philia* rather than *eros*. In sum, we might say that *philia* was used standardly to refer to the three kinds of familial love–parental, filial, and sibling–and to friendship. *Eros* on the other hand, was used to refer to relations among persons in which sexual feeling or desire was involved. This is fully confirmed by the use of *eros* by all the speakers in the *Symposium* (as well as the *Phaedrus*), except Euryximachus and Diotima. The physician elevates *eros* into a cosmic force such that both terms of the relation can be animate or inanimate objects, and the connection to sexual feeling is lost; and Diotima extends the range of the objects of *eros* to inanimate objects. But both extentions seem to be within the context of theories and to deviate from standard pre-theoretical uses of the term. (The use of *agapē* in Plato does not seem to represent a significantly distinct concept, as it does in the New Testament; in the latter work it seems to signify the love of God for men, of men for God, and of men for each other--a concept apparently modeled after familial love.)

In view of these rough considerations, we can perhaps say, in answer to our second question, that *eros, philia*, and *agapē* were used in ancient Greek to pick out portions of the feelings, attitudes and behavior that in English are picked out by conjoining 'love' with some modifying word or phrase. This situation can perhaps be roughly summarized by the following chart:

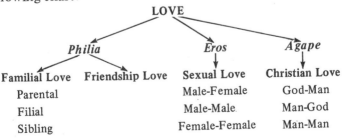

LOVE			
Philia		*Eros*	*Agape*
Familial Love	**Friendship Love**	**Sexual Love**	**Christian Love**
Parental		Male-Female	God-Man
Filial		Male-Male	Man-God
Sibling		Female-Female	Man-Man

It should be noted that this is very rough and does not capture the complexities of usage. Numerous qualifications would be necessary, among which we might note the following: first, with the possible exceptions of *agapē* in the New Testament, the relations the chart captures are pre-theoretical; second, *eros, philia* and *agapē* might overlap in various ways; and third, the chart does not attempt to capture the meanings or connotations of the four terms but only to indicate their extensions. In the context of our remarks, the chart is hopefully of some use in avoiding gross confusions that can arise from the fact that we are dealing with two languages and several cultures.

II

The Contexts of a Theory of Love. There are at least two wider settings in which it is useful to place a theory of love, both for understanding and assessing it: the cultural setting of the writer, and other theories of love.

The cultural setting of the writer is important perhaps primarily because some of the attitudes and behavior that a writer may take as characteristic of love or as data for his theory may be culture-bound. Social controls over courting and mating behavior, incidence and attitudes toward homosexuality, perceptions of beauty, the state of psychobiological knowledge—all these may vary with culture and time and all may influence importantly a theory constructed by a given writer. To investigate the culture setting of Plato's theory, one would have to look into the concepts of *eros* in various writers—Homer, Hesiod, the lyric poets, the dramatists, as well as customs and legislations about erotic behavior. We cannot do all this here of course. Fortunately, Plato himself provides some of the cultural setting for his theory in the *Symposium* itself in the speeches of Phaedrus, Pausanias, Euryximachus, Aristophanes, Agathon, and even Alcibiades. Plato's own theory, put in the mouth of Diotima and Socrates, is set within the context of the other speeches. These speakers describe and rely on myths, attitudes, and customs about *eros*, bring out important connections between *eros* and sexual desire, and *eros* and beauty, and give us ranges and characterizations of the objects of *eros*. Plato takes over some elements from these speeches without argument; for example, he adopts the connection between *eros* and beauty from Agathon and makes it an essential element in his own theory. In other cases, his own theory is set in conscious contrast to characterizations of *eros* by other speakers; for example, to the theory of Aristophanes. We shall mention some of these similarities and contrasts when they seem helpful.

The second context in which it is useful to place a theory of love, comparisons to other such theories, is important in assessing a given theory; such comparisons also help us to get a theoretical grasp of what a theory of love is, of the questions such a theory may reasonably be expected to answer, and of what counts as data for such theory. Thus a comparison of Plato's theory with Freud's and with some recent, empirically oriented studies, would enhance our understanding of all these things. We have neither space nor time to do all these things here. I will confine myself to constructing a list of questions that a theory of love may reasonably be expected to answer. The list is reasonable or non-arbitrary in at least the sense that it contains questions that various writers and theorists have thought important and have tried to answer.[1]

Love is presumably a relation with at least two terms, something that loves, the lover, and something that is loved, the beloved or the "object of love." This is true of *eros,* as Plato notes (199D), of *philia,* and of *agapē.* Moreover, it is fairly clear that love, *eros*, and *agapē* are non-symmetrical, non-transitive, and non-reflective relations. (*Philia*, at least in the case of friendship, may well be thought to be symmetrical, but we can ignore this here). The first question that arises is about the field of the relation:

Q1 What sorts of things can love and what sorts can be loved?

We note in passing that writers disagree on the answer to this question, but all treat the case of human-human as central and all suppose that the lover is a being capable of thought and feeling (except Euryximachus). In the *Symposium* Plato takes up three important cases: animal-animal, human-human, and human-inanimate object.[2]

Love is not indiscriminate: it is presumed to begin or at least to involve choice or selection of object by the lover. Accordingly, a second important question is:

Q2 How does a lover choose or select a beloved?

We note in passing that Plato does not explicitly raise this question, but his theory—the definitions and the ladder of love—contains answers to it, and so does the theory of Aristophanes. Freud and recent psychological studies explicitly attempt to answer it.[3]

A third important question concerns the origins, sources, or casual conditions of love. We may perhaps phrase it in general:

Q3 What are the causes of love?

Biological and psychological needs of various sorts are cited by writers in answer to this question. Plato provides some necessary, causal conditions for it, and some teleological explanations of erotic behavior.[4]

A correlative general question is often discussed in the literature:

Q4 What are the (characteristic) effects of love?

Plato raises this question explicitly in terms of the *erga* of *eros*. Writers disagree on the answers, especially on whether love is always beneficial and benevolent.

A fifth question, often discussed, is:

Q5 What is the relation between love and sexual desire?

There is much disagreement on whether sexual desire is always a component in love. The answer may of course be different for *eros, philia* and *agapē*. This question Plato does not raise explicitly but it is perhaps an important one to raise in this theory, since for him the objects of *eros* range from human beings to inanimate objects and abstract entities.[5]

Another controversial question in the literature has been:

Q6 Is love always or essentially egoistic or egocentric?

Plato does not explicitly raise this question, but his theory seems to contain a positive answer to it and has been much criticized on that account. Again, the answer may be different for *eros, philia* and *agapē*.[6]

A very central, Socratic question of course is:

Q7 What is love?

Plato raises this question explicitly about *eros*. We may understand his question, I think, as calling for some sort of definition or analysis of the concept, or at least for some central and general characterization of *eros*, which is true of all cases of *eros* and in some sense explanatory of them.[7]

Finally, a normative question has often been discussed:

Q8 Are some kinds of love better than others?

Theorists often try to rank evaluatively different kinds of love. Plato does so explicitly in his ladder of *eros*, Freud speaks of "normal love", Maslow of "healthy love", others of "genuine love" or "true love." [8]

I do not of course claim that this list of questions is exhaustive;[9] it contains, I think, most of the central and important questions about love, and a theory that does not answer several of them may well be thought to be incomplete. Also, writers do not always tell us whether they conceived these questions as empirical, conceptual, or

normative; we may perhaps reasonably suppose that Q1 and
Q7 are partly conceptual, and that all the rest are empirical
questions, except for the last which seems to be clearly
normative. In any case, the list perhaps gives us a rough idea
of what a theory of love is expected to accomplish.

III

Reconstruction of Plato's Theory. As I construct it, Plato's
theory contains four main parts: *A.* Plato's deficiency and
egoistic models of desire are applied to *eros. B.* A definition
of generic *eros* is constructed on the basis of *A* and other
elements. *C.* A definition of specific *eros* is reconstructed by
me on the basis of elements in the text. *D.* A ladder of *eros* is
constructed–the normative part of Plato's theory.

I proceed by listing the propositions that constitute Plato's
theory of *eros* and mark them by the letter 'E'. Propositions
on which Plato relies in his theory but are not explicitly
about *eros* (propositions that are part of his metaphysics,
epistemology, ethics, or moral psychology) I mark by the
letter 'P'. Some propositions Plato lays down without
argument, some he takes over from previous speakers; here I
indicate the source. Other propositions he derives from
propositions previously laid down or derived; these are
preceded by the word 'Hence'. If I supply a proposition I
mark it by the letter 'S'. In accompanying comments I
attempt to supply context and to raise problematic
questions. After I finish the reconstruction, I broach some
critical questions.

*A. The Deficiency and Egoistic Models of Desire Applied
to Eros.* Socrates begins his speech by remarking that he
thought they were supposed to say what is true about *eros,*
rather than pile up fine praises whether they were true or
not, as Agathon has done. (198d, 199b) He himself will try
to say only what is true. But he approves Agathon's
introduction in which he said that he would try to show first
what *eros* is and second what are his works (our questions Q4

and Q7; 199c), and Socrates takes these to be the basic questions to be answered. (201e) He proceeds to criticize Agathon for claiming both that Eros is always set on (is desire for) the beautiful and also that Eros is beautiful. By applying the deficiency model of desire to Eros, Socrates shows that these two claims are inconsistent. (Throughout, I think, 'Eros' signifies the god or daimon Eros and is symbolic of the lover, while '*eros*' signifies love or the lover in so far as he loves. 204c)

E1 Eros is *eros* of something. (199e)
E2 Eros desires that of which it is *eros*. (200a)
P1 Of necessity, a desiring subject desires something it lacks, and when it does not lack something it does not desire it. (200ab)

P1 is the proposition I have called the "deficiency model of desire."[10] Socrates gives several examples and makes an important qualification. A tall or strong man, a healthy or wealthy man, cannot desire to be tall, strong, healthy, or wealthy. However, a man who is or has these things may desire to also be or have them in the future, or to continue to have them, or to have them always. This qualification is apparently necessary to avoid the seeming paradox that would otherwise obtain from the conjunction of E2 and P1, namely that a man could not love the things he had or would cease to love the things he loved as soon as he made them his own or came to have them. Socrates now puts together the results of E2, P1, and Agathon's view that love is only of beauty or beautiful things:

E3 Hence, Eros lacks that which it loves. (from E2 & P1)
E4 Eros loves and desires beauty or beautiful things only. (201a) (from Agathon)
E5 Hence, Eros lacks beauty or beautiful things, and thus Eros is not beautiful. (201b) (from E3 and E4)

P1 deduces the necessarily deficient character of human being from the temporary character of having: always have only in the present

From E5 and a new proposition laid down without argument, namely,

P2 Good things are also beautiful things (201c)

Socrates infers

E6 Hence, Eros also lacks good things. (20lc)

And at the end of the very next paragraph Socrates claims to have shown by the above arguments that

E7 Hence, Eros is neither beautiful nor good.[11] (201e)

This completes the application of the deficiency model of desire to erotic love. In sum, Plato holds that only beautiful or good things can be objects of *eros* (or at any rate, only things thought or perceived by the lover to be good or beautiful), and that lack or deficiency of good or beautiful things is a necessary condition of erotic love.

Socrates now introduces Diotima as the wise woman who taught him all these things about Eros. He asked Diotima whether Eros, since he is not beautiful and good, is ugly and bad. She explains that just as there is an intermediate condition between knowledge and ignorance, true belief, so there is a third condition between beauty and ugliness, and good and bad, and that Eros is in this intermediate condition. Later she adds that since wisdom is about beautiful things, Eros is also a lover of wisdom. (204b) In an interesting sidelight Diotima gives Socrates proof that Eros cannot be a god. The proof is that all gods are happy and beautiful, that those are happy who possess good and beautiful things, and that since Eros has been admitted to lack good and beautiful things, Eros cannot be a god. The proof is interesting because it follows from the conclusion that a god cannot (erotically) love, or that a god cannot be an erotic lover! This shows clearly enough that eros as characterized here is importantly different from Christian *agapē*. A Christian would presumably deny that his God is deficient in beauty or goodness and yet he would also say that his God loves (*agapecally*) his children. The explanation of this difference between *eros* and *agapē* is probably that the deficiency model of desire does not apply to *agapē*, or that the objects of *agapē* need not be or thought to be beautiful or good, or both. The explanation may be different for the three types of Christian *agapē*, parental, filial, and sibling.

In a mythical interlude Diotima relates a myth about Eros. Briefly, Eros is characterized as a *daimōn*, a spirit between the divine and the human, poor in lacking good and beautiful things and wisdom, but aware of his lack and resourceful in pursuing these. He communicates divine things to humans and conversely. The myth climaxes with a proof that Eros is a lover of wisdom, a philosopher! (204b) The myth is consistent with Plato's theory, Eros being symbolic of the lover in the theory, and perhaps it foreshadows the ladder of love in which love enables one to get in touch with divine things, the Form Beauty, and became a philosopher.

Socrates now asks: if this is what Eros is, what is its use to mankind? (204c) Diotima switches from Eros to *eros* and raises two new questions about *eros* of beautiful things:

'The lover of beautiful things, what does he love?'
'That they may be his,' I replied.
'But your answer craves a further query,' she said, 'such as this:
What will he have who gets beautiful things?'
This question I declared I was quite unable to answer
offhand. (204d)

Diotima now drops her two questions about *eros* of beautiful things—they are taken up again when she discusses specific *eros*—and raises two parallel questions about *eros* of good things, which Socrates finds easy to answer:

'Well,' she proceeded, 'imagine that the object is changed, and the inquiry is made about the good instead

of the beautiful. Come, Socrates, I say, the lover of good
things, what does he love?'
'That they may be his,' I replied.
'And what will he have who gets good things?'
'I find this easier to answer,' I said; 'he will be happy.'
'Yes,' she said, 'the happy are happy by the possession of
good things, and we have no more need to ask for what
end a man wants to be happy: the answer is final.'
(204e-205a)

We may perhaps better understand Diotima's questions by
distinguishing between "the object" and "the aim" of *eros,* as
Freud distinguishes between the object and the aim of the
sexual instinct. The object is that from which the attraction
emanates, the aim that toward which *eros* strives.[12] And we
may express the propositions to which Diotima and Socrates
agree as follows:

E8 The lover of good things loves the good things to be his
   for the sake of his own happiness.

It is this proposition that expresses what I shall call the
egocentric or egoistic model of *eros: eros* of good things is
egoistic relative to the two aims of possession by the lover of
the things loved and of the lover's own happiness.

B. The Construction of the Definition of Generic Eros.
With the switch from *eros* of beautiful things to *eros* of good
things we have entered the passage where the definition of
the latter is constructed. Let us first look at the distinction
between the two kinds of *eros.*

Having agreed on E8, Diotima and Socrates also agree that
the desire and love for good things and happiness is common
to all men (205ab); yet, she remarks, not all men are said to
love (*eran*); some are said to love and some not, a situation
that Socrates finds puzzling. The explanation for this, she
says, is that "we have singled out a certain form of *eros,* and
applying thereto the name of the whole, we call it *eros.*

(205b) She adds that there are other names we abuse in this way, and gives an illustration: poetry (*poiēsis*) is the art that causes the composition or making of anything (shoes, buildings, statues, tragedies) and all its practitioners are poets; but not all these are *commonly called* poetry and poets, but only the business of music and meters is called poetry and only its practitioners poets. Generically, poetry is all these things, but common linguistic practice gives the name of the whole to only a part of it. Presumably, this common linguistic use is an abuse because it hides the whole-part or genus-species relation that holds between poetry in general and the part of it concerned with music and metres. Similarly, Diotima continues, generically (*to men kephalaion*) eros is all desire for good things and happiness, but those who pursue him in a variety of ways--in money making, sports, philosophy--are not said to love (*eran*) and are not called lovers (*erastai*), whereas those who pursue him in one particular form are given the name of the whole, are said to love and are called lovers. (205d) This too is a linguistic abuse, presumably for similar reasons. We have then, in Plato's theory, generic *eros, eros* of good things, and specific *eros* (or, as I sometimes shall call it, *eros* proper), *eros* of beautiful things. Plato is consciously extending the use of *eros* beyond what he considers common linguistic use; the linguistic use he refers to is that of all the previous speakers, except Euryximachus, who use *eros* only for sexual love.

After a dig at Aristophanes (in whose theory, in marked contrast to Plato's, the object of *eros* is one's other half in the original human condition and the aim of *eros* is union or reunion of the two halves),[13] Diotima now proceeds rapidly to construct the definition of generic *eros* on the basis of E8 and a new element she introduces without argument:

E9 Men love the good to be theirs *forever.* (206a)

Putting together E8 and E9 she defines generic *eros*:

E10 (Generically) *eros* is for the good to be one's own forever. (206a)

We may note briefly that generic *eros* as defined here, satisfies the deficiency and egoistic models, that the distinction between aim and object is implicit in the definition, and that there is implicit reference to happiness. We shall remark on the new element, E9, shortly.

C. The Construction of the Definition of Specific or Eros Proper. Right after the definition of generic *eros* has been constructed and has received Socrates' emphatic approval, Diotima asks:

Now if *eros* is always for this, she proceeded, what is the method of those who pursue it, and what is the behavior whose eagerness and straining would be called *eros*? What is actually its characteristic work (*ergon*)? (206b)

I think the phrase "would be called *eros*" signals that Diotima is now asking about that part of generic *eros* to which alone common linguistic practice gives the name *eros*; in short about what we have called specific or *eros* proper. Socrates does not know the answer, and she answers:

E11 The characteristic work (*ergon*) of *eros* (proper) is the begetting of offspring on a beautiful thing by means of body or soul. (206b)

Socrates does not understand and she elaborates. All men, she says, are "pregnant in body or soul" and at a certain age "our nature desires to beget"; we cannot beget on the ugly but only on the beautiful. The conjunction of man and woman is such begetting, and this pregnancy and begetting is something divine and immortal in the mortal animal. In almost lyric language she describes the role of the beautiful in begetting:

...when the pregnant approaches the beautiful it becomes not only gracious but so exhilarated that it flows over with begetting and bringing forth.... When a person is big and teeming ripe he feels himself in sore flutter for the beautiful, because its possessor can relieve him of his heavy pangs. (206d-e)

Right after this, Diotima makes a correction in the reply Socrates had given back at 204d, when they were talking about *eros* of the beautiful and Diotima had asked: "The lover of beautiful things, what does he love?" Socrates had replied, "That they may be his." She now says:

For you were wrong, Socrates, in supposing that *eros* is of the beautiful. What then is it? It is of begetting and engendering on the beautiful. (206e) [14]

Here, unlike the case of generic *eros,* it is the beautiful rather than the good that is the attracting object; and unlike the former case where possession of the good was the aim, here the aim is not to possess the beautiful but to generate offspring on it—a point already implicit in Ell.

Diotima now asks further: Why (is *eros*) of (for) this begetting?

Because this is something ever-existing and immortal in our mortal life. From what has been admitted, it is necessary that we desire immortality no less than the good, if *eros* is for the good to be one's own forever. Of necessity it follows from this definition that *eros* is also of immortality. (207a)

Here Diotima has made two moves: she infers the proposition that *eros* is (among other things) desire for immortality from the definition of generic *eros*; and she claims that this desire for immortality explains the (desire for) begetting offspring on a beautiful object, which is characteristic of *eros* proper. Let us consider briefly these two moves.

The inference seems appropriate, in the sense that if *eros* proper is a part or species of generic *eros* it will have all the features that are definitionally true of generic *eros*; while presumably the desire to beget on a beautiful object will be the distinguishing mark of *eros* proper. The inference, though, is logically faulty to a puzzling degree. One fault has to do with the scope of *aei* (forever, always) in the definition of generic *eros*. If someone told us that he wanted to have some good forever, say, health, wealth, knowledge, or happiness, we would naturally understand him to mean by "forever", "during his whole lifetime." But this clearly does not amount to immortality in any of the senses which Plato subsequently defines. Aside and independently of this fault, the inference apparently detaches *aei* from the definition and treats it as if this expression can signify a separate aim—and this too seems puzzling. Expressions such as "to have good things forever" or "to be happy always" can be used to signify aims, but "always" and "forever" do not seem to be expressions that can by themselves signify aims. How then we infer from someone's wanting to be happy always that he has two aims, to be happy and to be immortal? Laying aside these puzzles, we can state the proposition derived as follows:

E12 *Eros* is also desire for (the lover's own) immortality.

Let us now consider Diotima's second move. At 207a she makes more explicit her previous question ("Why is *eros* of begetting?"). What is the cause of this *eros* and desire (to beget offspring on a beautiful object)? What is to be explained is the desire for and the begetting of offspring, which she takes to be a fact and we take as a characteristic of *eros* proper. She constructs the explanation by appealing to E12, to a definition of immortality (208b) and to certain facts about mortal nature, animal and human (207d-208c). In so far as this explanation is satisfactory, we may regard it as confirmatory of E12 which now plays the role of an explanatory hypothesis.

Diotima begins with the case of animals: she describes the behavior of mating and rearing offspring and asks for the cause of it. (207b) Socrates does not know the answer and she gives it at 207cd, intending to cover both the case of animals and humans, though humans so act on the promptings of reason while presumably animals act from instinct:

> Well then, she said, if you believe that *eros* is bent on what we have repeatedly admitted, you may cease to wonder. For here too [the case of humans as well as animals], on the same principle as before, the mortal nature ever seeks, as best it can to be immortal. In one way only can it succeed, and that is by generation; since so it can leave behind it a new creature in place of the old.

She proceeds to argue that all mortals change with respect to all their properties, whether of body (hair, flesh, bones, blood), or soul (manners, habits, opinions, desires, pains, pleasures, fears). This is so, she claims, even with respect to knowledge:

> ...with regard to the possession of sciences, not merely do some of them grow and others perish, so that neither in what we know are we ever the same persons; but a like fate attends each single sort of knowledge. What we call learning implies that our knowledge is departing; since forgetfulness is an egress of knowledge, while learning substitutes a fresh one in place of that which departs, and so preserves our knowledge enough to make it seem the same.... Every mortal thing is preserved in this way; not by being always the same in all respects like the divine, but by replacing what goes off or is antiquated with something fresh in the semblance of the original. Through this device, Socrates, a mortal thing partakes of immortality, both in its body and all other aspects; by no other means can it be done. So do not wonder if

everything naturally values its own offshoot; since all are beset by this behavior and love for the sake of immortality.(208ab)[15]

In these passages we have the following elements: a definition of divine immortality; the claim that no mortal, animal or human, can become immortal in this sense; the claim that a mortal can partake of this immortality as far as possible only by begetting offspring and thus replacing itself in the semblance of itself; and the claim that given these facts E12 explains the mating and begetting and offspring-rearing behavior characteristic of *eros* proper. We can perhaps cast Diotima's explanation in the form of an argument:

E12 *Eros* is desire for immortality and all animals have this desire.

P3 A thing is divinely immortal if and only if for any property it has at any one time it has the very same property at all times.

P4 All animals change with respect to all their properties.

P5 Hence, no animal can ever be divinely immortal.

P6 During their lifetimes and through change animals continue to exist as "the same animals" in the sense of giving up properties or parts and replacing them by them by similar properties or parts.

P7 Animals approach or to some degree partake of divine immortality by begetting offspring similar to themselves and thus replacing themselves after death. (A process conceived somewhat analogously to the way they remain "the same" during life.)

E13 Hence, animals become erotically disposed, beget and

rear offspring for the sake of partaking in immortality in so as it is possible for them to do so.

It is on the basis of this explanation, of E11 and E12, and of the role of the beautiful described above, that I reconstruct a definition of *eros* proper:

SE14 Specifically, *eros* is desire for begetting offspring on a beautiful object by means of body or soul for the sake of the lover's own immortality.

I wish to note at once that this definition does not occur in the text. But I claim that all the elements in it and their relations are clearly in the text, and I have expounded Diotima's views in detail to secure this claim.

Several things are noteworthy about *eros* proper as defined here. It is constituted by two desires, the desire to beget offspring, and the desire for the lover's immortality. Both desires satisfy the deficiency model, and the desire for immortality satifies the egoistic model. *Eros* is presumably beneficial to the lover in so far as immortality is something good. This *eros* may also be beneficial to the offspring, at least in cases where the offspring is a sentient being, animal or human; but concern and care of the offspring is conceived as a means to the lover's own immortality. Since the lover's own immortality is the final aim of this *eros, eros* proper can appropriately be said to be egoistic. We shall see shortly that this is fully confirmed by Diotima's subsequent explanations. Second, the definition contains an implicit reference to the relation between the two desires, or between begetting offspring and immortality: a means-end relation. In humans this relation is cognized by reason, as Diotima remarks; in animals presumably by instinct. Third, possession of the beautiful object referred to in the definition is not the aim of either desire; rather, its role seems to be as the attracting object which sparks or releases the desire to beget. Later, in the ladder of *eros,* beautiful objects seem to assume the role as well of model for the creation of offspring. Thus, the

structure of *eros* proper seems different from that of generic
eros: in the latter it is the good rather than the beautiful that
is the attracting object--or perhaps happiness--and it is
possession of it, not generation or creation, that is the aim.
Finally, in the explanation we have reconstructed, the desire
for immortality assumes a new role, independent of its faulty
derivation from generic *eros*: even if this derivation is
mistaken, as it probably is, the hypothesis of the desire for
immortality may have genuine validity in so far as it explains
the behavior of courting, mating, and offspring-rearing
behavior in animals and humans. In modern biological
theories, representation of an individual, animal or human, in
succeeding generations is taken as explanatory of mating and
breeding behavior. To be sure, such explanations are now cast
in an evolutionary rather than a teleological model. Plato's
explanation can perhaps be viewed as the teleological
analogue of such explanations, and in the case of humans, at
any rate, it is not obviously without value.

So far (208c), Diotima has been speaking mainly of
begetting biological offspring, but Plato could hardly have
confined *eros* proper to such cases: for the male-male *eros*
(and even female-female) was a widely recognized cultural
phenomenon and previous speakers took up such cases as
prominent, even the best, cases of *eros*; and of course in such
cases there is no biological offspring. Diotima now takes up
these other cases, where the offspring is not biological but
rather actions and *logoi* of various sorts, such as discourses,
poems, constitutions, the arts, crafts, and sciences.
(208c-209e) As the range of "offspring" expands, so does the
range of "beautiful objects" that attract the lover, from
bodies to souls, and so on. In all these new cases her
explanations contain the same elements as before and
confirm the view that *eros* proper (as well as generic *eros*) is
essentially egoistic.

At 208c Socrates professes some skepticism about such
explanations and Diotima tries to convince him by piling case
upon case of lovers who acted and created for the sake of
their own immortality. They all had *eros* for "winning a

name and laying up fame immortal for all time to come."
(208c) Alcestis would not have died for Admetus
(female-male *eros*) nor Achilles for Patroclus (male-male *eros*)
"had they not expected to win an immortal memory for
virtue." (208d)

> I hold it is for immortal virtue and such illustrious fame
> as this that they do all they do, and so much the more in
> proportion to their excellence. They love (*erosin*) the
> immortal. (208c)

These two cases are noteworthy, for they might normally be
cited to show not only the great motivating power of *eros*
but also its non-egoistic nature, since they seem to be cases
where the lovers sacrificed their very lives for their beloveds.
But Diotima clearly implies that the lovers so acted as to
secure "immortal fame" for themselves and that they would
not have so acted had they not expected to secure this. She
goes on to cite a number of other cases of creations of *logoi*–
the poems of Homer and Hesiod, the constitutions of Solon
and Lycurgus–explaining them all on the same principles. She
apparently takes all these to confirm the structure of *eros*
proper, and the desire for immortality to be explanatory of
them. The expansion of the range of cases of *eros* proper is
clearly preparatory to the ladder of *eros*–the last and
normative part of Plato's theory to which we now turn.

D. The Ladder of Eros. The ladder of love is normative in
the sense that it ranks cases of *eros* from less to more
valuable, and of course describes an ascent to the most
valuable. I do not have space here to reconstruct the ladder in
detail, and in any case this has been done accurately by
Moravcsik. Rather, after some preliminaries, I will discuss a
question that, so far as I know, has not been adequately
discussed in the literature: what are Plato's criteria for
ranking cases of *eros?*
First, the preliminaries:
(1) I take the ladder to be about *eros* proper rather than

generic *eros*. This seems clear from the fact that at every step of the ladder we have creation of offspring, and the fact that it is the Form Beauty rather than the Form of the Good that we find at the top of the ladder; and both of these are characteristic of *eros* proper. That the Form of Beauty is at the top is essential to the theory according to our reconstruction. The Form of Beauty is at the top not only because it is divinely immortal (after all, all Forms are), but also because of the role of beauty in the structure of *eros* proper: it is the perception or thought of an object as beautiful that releases the desire to create. As Vlastos puts it, it is "the sense of beauty" that sparks creation in all the diverse cases Plato subsumes under *eros* proper. (*Platonic Studies*, pp. 27-28)

(2) We must distinguish between steps in the ladder and ascents from step to step. If our reconstruction is correct, we should expect to find all the elements of *eros* proper at each step: a lover, a beautiful object, begetting offspring on that object, and the aim of the lover for his own immortality for the sake of which the begetting takes place. We do in fact find all these elements at each step, except the aim of immortality; but at the top step Diotima brings in this element in a full way and ends the description of the ladder with it. (211e-212b) Recognition of this element in Plato's theory will perhaps serve as a corrective to understanding it. Recent studies, not making the distinction between object and aim, either underestimate this element (Vlastos) or do not recognize it at all (Moravcsik).[16] This element is essential to the theory, and it is important since it is relative to it that *eros* proper can appropriately be said to be egoistic. *Eros* proper is also beauty-directed, or, as Vlastos puts it for at least the top of the ladder, "idiocentric". But this is not a competing characterization with "egoistic". Platonic *eros* is both idiocentric (relative to its object) and egoistic (relative to its aim). The issue of egoism belongs with the aim, not the object.

(3) The lover's ascent from step to step involves a change of attracting object and of offspring. The ascent is initiated

and directed by reason: it is by "perceiving" a new object as beautiful or by "seeing" the beauty common to several objects, or by "perceiving" a new kind of beauty (beauty of soul), that the lover ascends from one step to another and creates different offspring. Moravcsik has, I think, described this intellectual process well (see especially pp. 288-290). As reason "perceives" a new beautiful object, the lover becomes attracted to it and wants to create new offspring after the new beauty. In this sense reason initiates the ascent, and emotion and creation follow reason. And this is very Platonic indeed.

We come now to our main question: what are Plato's criteria for ranking evaluatively different kinds of *eros*? In a passage before the ladder soul-*eros* is ranked above body-*eros*. Speaking of soul-lovers Diotima says:

> Equally with him he shares the nurturing of what is begotten, so that men in this condition enjoy a far fuller community with each other than that which comes with children, and enjoy a far surer friendship (*philia*), since the children of their union are more beautiful and more immortal. (209c)

Here soul-*eros* is ranked above body-*eros* on the ground that soul-lovers have a fuller community and a far surer friendship than body lovers; and this in turn on the ground that the offspring of soul-lovers is more beautiful and more immortal. It would seem then that greater degrees of beauty and immortality in the offspring make for better *eros* as we go up the ladder. In so far as the offspring is modeled after the attracting beautiful object, presumably degrees of beauty and immortality in the offspring will reflect degrees of beauty and immortality in that object. And in so far as degrees of beauty and immortality in the offspring reflect the lover, its creator, he too as he goes up the ladder will presumably become more and more beautiful and immortal.

Two questions arise here. First, how are we to construe degrees of immortality and beauty? Second, why should greater degrees of immortality and beauty make *eros* better? It is fairly easy to construe degrees of immortality. In the ladder only Beauty itself, being a Form, is divinely immortal; all the other attracting objects below it, being non-Forms, wax and wane, increase and decrease, come into being and perish. (211ab). These attracting objects are more or less like the divinely immortal Beauty in lasting more or less; the poems of Homer, for example, had already lasted longer than any biological offspring, so they are more immortal than biological offspring and more like, in that respect, to the divinely immortal Beauty. Degrees of beauty are perhaps more difficult to interpret. The only clue that Plato gives us here is in the description of Beauty itself as being beautiful without qualification:

> It is not beautiful in part and ugly in part, nor is it beautiful at one time and not at another, nor beautiful in comparison with one thing and ugly with another, nor is it so affected by position so as to seem beautiful to some and ugly to others. (211a)

So presumably the attracting beautiful objects below the top are beautiful with one or more of these qualifications and are less beautiful in this sense. This is probably Plato's view. The double characterization of Beauty itself, as at once divinely immortal and beautiful without qualification, provides the ideal standard by which degrees of lesser immortality and beauty are to be judged.

But why should Plato suppose that greater degrees of beauty and immortality, in the attracting object and the offspring, make *eros* better? Two answers already hinted at or suggested by the theory seem insufficient. The first is hinted by the passage just quoted (209c). Soul-*eros*, where a lover is attracted by the beauty of another's soul and creates a poem, or a constitution about justice, is ranked above body-*eros* on the ground that since the offspring of their love is more beautiful and more immortal, the lovers enjoy "a far fuller community" and a "far surer friendship" than biological lovers. Granting the benefits of such community and friendship, this answer does not seem general enough to cover all of the ladder, and especially the top. For at the top of the ladder the attracting object is not a human being but an abstract entity, a Form, and no other human being besides the lover need be involved in such a case of *eros*; community and friendship need not come into it at all, and yet this is the best kind of *eros*. The second answer, internal to the theory, is general enough but does not by itself go far enough. According to the theory we have reconstructed, in every case of *eros* proper the lover's final aim is his own immortality. And according to the ladder, as the lover ascends from step to step he realizes his aim more and more, since he is attracted to more immortal objects and creates more immortal offspring; and at the top of the ladder he realizes this aim as much as it is possible for humans to realize it. So, relative to realizing the final aim of *eros* proper, the lover is better off as he goes up the ladder, and best off at the top. I think that this answer does not go far enough because it does not reveal sufficiently Plato's criteria for the ranking: for I think that generally for Plato we are not necessarily better off achieving what we want or aim at unless what we want or aim at is good to begin with. I wish therefore to supplement this answer by bringing in Plato's theory of the Form of the Good in the *Republic*, at least as interpreted by me in a recent paper. ("The Form of the Good in Plato's *Republic*," *Philosophical Inquiry*, 1980) The theory shows the connection, for Plato, between the two characterizations of Beauty itself in the *Symposium*–being divinely immortal and beautiful without qualification--and his concept of goodness.

Briefly, the theory of the Form of the Good assumes that Plato (at least in the middle dialogues, and especially in the *Symposium* and *Republic*) conceived of the Forms not as properties or attributes, but as ideal or paradigmatic exemplars complete with non-Pauline self-predication. On this assumption, the Form Beauty is beautiful, the Form Circle a circle, the Form Bed a bed, and so on. Within this assumption, the theory distinguishes between proper and ideal (or formal) attributes of Forms. In the case of Beauty, being beautiful is a proper attribute of that Form, i.e. an attribute that Form has by virtue of being the particular Form it is. But being (divinely) immortal is an ideal attribute of that Form, i.e. an attribute that Form has by virtue of being a Form. In addition, being always beautiful, being beautiful in all parts (or aspects) of itself, being beautiful to all who apprehend it no matter from where, all these are also ideal attributes of the Form Beauty, in the sense that the Form Beauty has them by virtue of both being a Form and the particular Form it is. Given these distinctions, the theory of the Form of the Good asserts that the Form of the Good is the formal cause of all the other Forms having their ideal attributes, or that all the other Forms have their ideal attributes by virtue of participating in the Form of the Good. The ideal attributes of all the other Forms are proper attributes of the Form of the Good; or, the Form of the Good consists of the ideality of the Forms. So conceived, each Form other than the Form of the Good is the best object of its kind, and it is such by virtue of participating (fully) in the Form of the Good. The attributive goodness (goodness of kind) of a sensible object is accounted for by participation (to some degree) in the ideal attributes of the Form of its kind, and through such participation, also participation (to some degree) in the Form of the Good. According to the Theory of Forms, a sensible is F by virtue of participating in the proper attributes of the Form the F. According to the theory of the Form of the Good, a sensible F is a good F (to some degree) by virtue of participating (or resembling) (to some degree) in the ideal attributes of the Form the F: for in so far as it participates in the ideal attributes of the Form the F it also participates in the Form of the Good, since the F has its ideal attributes by virtue of participating in the Form of the Good. Applying the theory of the Form of the Good to the ladder of *eros* we obtain the desired correlation between degrees of immortality and beauty and degrees of goodness. As we go up the ladder, the attracting object participates more and more in the ideal attributes of Beauty itself, being divinely immortal and being beautiful without qualification; and since Beauty itself has these attributes by virtue of participating in the Form of the Good, the attracting object thereby participates more and more in the Form of the Good. In so far as the offspring is modeled after the attracting object, the same characterizations obtain for the offspring. And in so far as the offspring reflects the lover, its creator, the lover too, as he ascends the ladder, becomes more and more immortal beautiful, and hence good.

We may end this section by noting that the application of the theory of the Form of the Good to the case of *eros* proper and the ladder of love does not imply a conflation of the two theories. The theory of the Form of the Good is general and applies to all the Forms. The two theories are related but distinct. The distinction between them enables us to throw some light perhaps on the distinction between generic *eros* and *eros* proper. *Eros* proper is concerned with the concept of beauty, has as its ultimate object (not aim) the Form Beauty, and its distinctive mark is creation of offspring in the image of Beauty. Generic *eros*, on the other hand, is concerned with the notion of goodness and has as its ultimate object the Form of the Good. The ladder for generic *eros* would presumably be the divided line of the *Republic,* which does have the Form of the Good at the top. And when the philosophers of the *Republic* are called lovers (*erastai*) it is probably meant that they are generic lovers. The distinction between generic *eros* and *eros* proper in the *Symposium* suggests that in that work at least Plato has some distinctions going between beauty and goodness, and that he thought of goodness as the more abstract notion; and this coheres well with our application of the theory of the Form of the Good to the ladder of love.[17] Whether he held to the distinction in the *Republic* and what the distinction exactly is is not clear. In any case, lacking a definition of beauty, as well as an explicit definition of goodness, Plato would have found it difficult to elucidate the distinction. What is clear in the *Symposium* is that the concepts constitutive of *eros* proper are desire, beauty, creativity, and immortality. It is probable, I think, that the primitive models for these concepts were the attraction for the physical beauty of bodies, the creation of biological offspring to which such attraction leads, and the notion that the function of such biological procreation is the representation of the individual in future generations. It was Plato's distinctive contribution to widen these models to the attraction of the beauty of soul and even of abstract entities, to the creation of arts and sciences, and to the immortality such creations bring. And by subsuming the typical Greek notion of *eros* under generic *eros* he seems to imply that love of beauty is to be subsumed under desire for the Good.

IV

Critical Questions. I do not have time or space here to discuss in detail even the main critical questions that arise about Plato's theory. I will confine myself to raising some critical questions and making some brief critical remarks.

Critical questions obviously arise about the deficiency model of desire applied to *eros*. It is not clear whether Plato means to assert some sort of *a priori* principle pertaining to the logic of the concept of desire, or some empirical proposition to the effect that some physiological or psychological deficiency is always among the causal conditions of desire and love. The explanatory value of the former is unclear, and the latter has been challenged by at least one empirical study, that of Maslow.

Critical questions also arise about the egoistic model of *eros*. Our reconstruction, and Diotima's explanations of the rearing and caring of offspring and of apparently altruistic acts of love, leave little doubt that Platonic *eros*, generic and proper, is essentially egoistic. Yet Plato's derivation of the egoistic desire for the lover's own immortality is faulty. And, so far as I know, the aim of immortality or some analogue of it appears as a component of love in modern, empirically oriented studies, only in cases of sexual love, where there can be biological offspring.

Is the desire to create offspring, biological or spiritual, an essential component of all cases of *eros* proper, as Plato supposes? There is probably an important grain of truth in the proposition that love and the perception of beauty often can spark the desire to create and that love is a great motivating power. But this is a lot weaker than what the theory asserts, that such desire is essential to *eros* proper, an element that enters the definition. It is one thing to suppose that love and the perception of beauty sometimes account for creativity, perhaps in many important cases, but quite another to make the desire to create an essential component of love. I have not found the latter either in the other theories of love Plato recounts nor in modern empirical studies.

Plato's theory also contains an important grain of truth on the question of selection of object by the lover. In all modern theories I have found the assumption that love begins with the perception of something attractive in the object (usually, a person). In Plato's theory the analogue is that *eros* begins with the perception of something as good (generic *eros*) or beautiful (*eros* proper). But here Plato's theory lacks important details. How such perceptions arise, how they vary with culture and the development of the individual--all these are important details for any theory of selection. And the distinction and the interplay between goodness and beauty also remain relatively unclear in the theory.

We may also remark on two remarkable features of Plato's theory--remarkable relative to his culture, relative to other theories of love, and remarkable also in the sense that they may endanger the coherence of his theory.

One of these is the apparently connotative extention of the Greek concept of *eros* to generic *eros*. We saw that Plato is aware that the Greeks would not have called his generic *eros eros* at all. Perhaps the philosophical motivation for Plato's move is the subsumption of *eros* under desire for the Good and the construction of a unified and grand moral psychology. In Plato's middle dialogues it would seem that the Good is the most attractive and beneficial object there is or can be, and the desire for it the most dominant human motivation. To subsume eros–an admittedly powerful human motivation–under desire for the Good is perhaps an attempt to show that there is no separate and competing motivation other than desire for the Good. The question arises, though, whether the Greeks were not correct in not calling desire for the Good (generic eros) eros. Can all cases of erotic love be subsumed under desire for the Good? Are beauty and goodness related as the theory requires? Can't there be erotic love of a person with a beautiful body and a cruel and malicious soul?

The second remarkable feature of Plato's theory is the denotative extention of the objects of eros proper from persons to inanimate objects and abstract entities. This is remarkable relative to Plato's culture, as can be seen from the other speeches where the object of eros is another human being. It is also remarkable relative to other theories of love. In modern empirical studies of erotic love the object is invariably a human being; exceptions are viewed as "deviations" requiring elaborate explanation. In English we can speak of "love of country", "love of money", and so on, but it would be strange to suppose that this is erotic love, for the connection to the sexual component of erotic love is nowhere in sight. Similar remarks would seem to apply for the Platonic case of eros (proper) of the beauty of a constitution, a mathematical system, or Beauty itself. The question, therefore, arises whether as we go up the ladder of eros the concept of eros has not beeen essentially changed. To be sure, Plato brings in all the elements of the definition at all steps of the ladder; but given the radical changes in attracting object and offspring as we go up the ladder, this may be illusory and insufficient to forestall the objection that Plato has changed the subject. This may perhaps be glimpsed in two observations. First, eros of persons is clearly a non-symmetrical relation: it makes sense to ask whether such eros is returned by the beloved; this question can have a true positive answer or a negative one. But *eros* of inanimate objects seems clearly asymmetric; the question makes no sense. Second, in the case of *eros* of persons, it makes sense to ask whether the lover has certain feelings or attitudes toward his beloved: for example, whether he has care and affection for his or her beloved: for example, whether he has respect for him or her, whether his *eros* is benevolent--these are some of the elements that Vlastos builds into what he calls the "highest type of interpersonal love." But it seems to make no sense to ask these questions of the erotic lover of inanimate objects. It seems therefore unlikely that all the radically diverse cases Plato tries to bring under *eros* proper can satisfy the definition literally; the relations among them may be weaker, perhaps analogical, which can still be illuminating, guiding, and even inspiring. But in so far as Plato does not recognize this, and in so far as he takes *eros* of Beauty itself to be not only the highest type of *eros* but also as paradigmatic of the concept, his *eros* is--relative to its attracting object, not its aim--truly "idiocentric." Love of persons, erotic or otherwise, is ignored, or if brought in, peripheral to the concept and radically downgraded. As objects of *eros,* generic or proper, persons not only are loved only for their goodness or beauty, but no matter how beautiful or good in body or soul they always lose out to Beauty and the Good.[18]

Notes

1. My bibliography is a very small selection of works on the subject. The questions I list have been discussed, though not all of them by each writer, by Plato, Freud, and the writers in the Ellis Encyclopedia and the Montague anthology. See following bibliography.

2. This question is rarely discussed explicitly. Most writers assume that the human-human case is the case to be discussed; some consider the animal-animal case instructive (H.F. Harlow, "The Nature of Love" in Montague), while the human-inanimate object case is rare.

3. Freud and Grant discuss this question extensively, and Grant usefully reviews the main theories of selection.

4. Various variants of this question are extensively discussed in the contemporary literature; see especially Daly & Wilson, Ellis, and Montague.

5. This question has of course been much discussed since Freud, who seems to have supposed that all love has a sexual component.

6. This question has been discussed by Vlastos, Nygren, P.A. Sorokin in Ellis, W. McDougal in *Social Psychology,* and many others.

7. Besides Plato, many writers raise this question and attempt definitions; see Montague.

8. This question is implicit not only in the ladder of love, but also in the speech of Pausanias, in the speeches in the *Phaedrus,* in Freud, Maslow, and many other writers (e.g. P.M. Symods in Montague). Writers do not always manage to disentangle normative from conceptual or definitional considerations.

9. One important aspect of love I have left out of account here is the phenomenon of overestimation or overevaluation of the loved object by the lover. There is much discussion of this in accounts of courtly and romantic love, in Freud and subsequent writers. The causes and effects of overestimation are of course an important part of the study of love. It should perhaps be noted that Vlastos seems to claim that Platonic *eros* is not subject to overevaluation or overestimation, so characteristic of courtly and romantic love, and superior to the latter on that account (pp. 28-30). I think this is certainly true for Platonic *eros* at the top of the ladder, for it is not possible to overevaluate Beauty itself, but I do not see that it is necessarily true for lower steps.

10. This model is, I think, also at work in the *Lysis*, the *Philebus,* and the *Republic.* The view is probably subject to a variety of interpretations, but the subsequent inferences Plato makes render the application of the model to the case of *eros* clear enough.

11. These inferences are faulty on several grounds. Plato goes back and forth from "beauty" and "the Good" to "beautiful things" and "good things" in a confusing fashion: if one lacks beauty or goodness, then one is not beautiful or good, but if one lacks good or beautiful things it does not follow that one is not beautiful or good. We can try to repair the latter inference by supposing that Beauty and the Good are self-predicational. But even so questions of scope arise; one can desire and love and lack some beautiful or good things while at the same time having others.

12. Freud, *Three Contributions,* p. 553. It may seem anachronistic to apply the distinction to Plato, but I think it is implicit in his grammar, where the object is given by a genitive and the aim by an infinitive construction. The distinction is also necessary in order to understand Diotima's questions, "The lover of good things, what does he love?", and "The lover of beautiful things, what does he love?", where the object is already given in the questions, and what is asked for has to be the aim. The distinction also enables us to resolve the controversy between Nygren and Vlastos as to whether Platonic *eros* is "idiocentric" rather than "egocentric and acquisitive." (Vlastos, p. 30). Our reconstruction supports the answer that generic and *eros* proper are egoistic relative to their aims and idiocentric relative to their objects. Generic *eros*, but not *eros* proper, is also "acquisitive" in the sense that the aim is possession of the object by the lover. Freud makes powerful use of the distinction.

13. The distinction between object and aim is also implicit in Aristophanes' theory: the object of one's love is one's other half in the original human condition, the aim is union with it. Aristophanes' theory, though fanciful in its hypotheses, is I think a beautifully constructed theory of love in miniature: it contains explanatory hypotheses of erotic behavior, a definition of *eros*, interesting comments on the sexual component in *eros*, and an explanation of different kinds of love, homosexual and heterosexual. It even contains principles of selection of love object.

14. It is this move that Marcus has emphasized claiming that it represents a "radical change of perspective" and a "new picture" of love (pp. 255ff). Vlastos corrects this (p. 20, note 56) pointing out the connection to the definition of generic *eros*. It is true, as I consider below, that the desire for immortality is directly inferred from the definition of generic *eros*. I don't think, though, that "birth in beauty" follows from that definition or that Diotima claims this, as Vlastos thinks. We have rather a less direct inference through the new, independent proposition that only through begetting in beauty can mortals share in immortality. I reconstruct this inference below. This I think coheres well with the idea that *eros* proper is a part of or a species of a generic *eros*.

15. R.Bury (pp. 113, 117) points out that the idea that mortals, humans and animals, can partake of immortality by creation of offspring is also found in the *Laws* 773e and in Aristotle, *De Anima* 415a26ff. This is not divine immortality but immortality by replacement, and it has its analogue in modern biological, evolutionary

theory, in which procreation is seen as representation of the individual in future generations. It should be noted that the two kinds of immortality Plato talks about in the *Symposium*–divine immortality and immortality by replacement through creation of offspring–are different from the immortality of soul he talks about in the *Phaedo, Phaedrus* and *Republic.* The soul is said to be immortal, in these works, in the sense of being everlasting and having always at least two properties (supposing they are different properties), namely being self-moving and being alive. This is clearly not divine immortality, since it is compatible with the soul changing in other respects, and it is clearly not immortality by replacement through offspring since this does not entail everlastingness of one and the same entity. Moreover, immortality by replacement can be achieved only through creation of offspring, biological or spiritual, whereas the third kind of immortality (*Phaedo,* etc.) every soul has no matter what it does. The only puzzle here is that Plato has Diotima say that mortals can share in immortality *only* through replacement of offspring, which seems clearly incompatible with the doctrine of the *Phaedo* of the everlastingness of souls. Vicky Harper has pointed out to me that in the *Symposium* Diotima is speaking of *personal* immortality, whereas the arguments in the *Phaedo* may be interpreted as intended to show some sort of generic immortality. This is probably correct, and makes the two works consistent.

16. Moravcsik concentrates on reconstructing what I call ascents from step to step (he calls the ascents steps, and my steps levels). When one considers the fact that he does not reconstruct or even bring in at all the theory of *eros* within which the ladder belongs, his reconstruction of the ascent is remarkably accurate. He finds three kinds of "steps", steps of reason, steps of emotion, and steps of creation. Now these three kinds of things are found in every case of *eros* proper according to our reconstruction: the apprehension of beauty and the apprehension of the relation of creation to immortality would be reason-elements; the desire to create, the desire for immortality, and emotional attitudes to the attracting object would be emotion-elements, and the creation of offspring a creation-element. Moravcsik brings out nicely the interplay between reason and emotion in the ascent, and the fact that reason guides and directs the ascent. On our reconstruction, every case of *eros* at all four levels (our steps) involves reason, emotion, and creation. It is not clear to me that Moravcsik recognizes this. Comparisons with his paper are difficult because he has not reconstructed the rest of the theory.

17. I am really unclear at present on the distinction and relation between beauty and goodness in Plato. My present speculation is that he found it difficult to suppose either that not all good things are beautiful or that not all beautiful things are good. Now if the two Forms have the same participants, this amounts to extentional equivalence; this does not entail that the Forms are identical, and Plato is capable of understanding this, as the *Sophist* shows (where the Forms Sameness, Difference, and Being have the same participants but are nevertheless distinct). Perhaps he thought that though the two Forms have the same participants, Goodness is the more abstract notion and Beauty is to be defined in terms of it. The *Gorgias* and the *Hippias Major* perhaps provide some evidence for this view. All this would cohere well with our present interpretation, in which *eros* is part of generic *eros*, and the ladder of love part of the divided line.

18. This paper was read at the California State University, Fullerton Symposium on "The Greeks and the Good Life," and also as an invited paper at the APA meetings at Denver, 1979. I am much indebted to Prof. Vicky Harper's comments, and also to comments by Profs. David Depew, Robert Turnbull and Charles Young.

Bibliography

1. Bretlinger, J., ed., *The Symposium of Plato*, U. Mass. Press, 1970.

2. Bury, R. G., *The Symposium of Plato*, Cambridge, 1969.

3. Cornford, F. M., "The Doctrine of *Eros* in Plato's *Symposium*," in *The Unwritten Philosophy*, ed. W.K.C. Guthrie, Cambridge, 1950.

4. Daly, M. & Wilson, M., *Sex, Evolution & Behavior*, Duxbury, 1978.

5. Freud, S., *Three Contributions to the Theory of Sex*, in *The Basic Writings of S. Freud*, Random House, 1938.

6. Freud, S., *Three Contributions to the Psychology of Love*, in *On Creativity and the Unconscious*, Harper, 1958.

7. Grant, V. W., "Sexual Love" in *The Encyclopedia of Sexual Behavior*, ed. by Albert Ellis, Hawthorn Books, 1961, vol. 2.

8. Gould, T., *Platonic Love*, London, 1963.

9. Marcus, R. A., "The Dialectic of *Eros* in Plato's *Symposium*," in *Plato II*, ed. by G. Vlastos, Doubleday, 1970.

10. Maslow, A. H., "Love in Healthy People," in Montague, A., ed., *The Practice of Love*, Prentice Hall, 1975.

11. Moravcsik, J.M.E., "Reason and *Eros* in the 'Ascent'-Passage in the *Symposium*," in J. Anton, ed., *Essays in Ancient Greek Philosophy*, Albany, 1971.

12. Morgan, D. N., *Love: Plato, the Bible and Freud*, Prentice-Hall, 1964.

13. Nakhnikian, G., "Love in Human Reason," *Midwest Studies in Philosophy*, Vol. III, 1978.

14. Nygren, A., *Eros and Agapē*, Harper, 1969.

15. Rosen, S., *Plato's Symposium*, New Haven, 1968.

16. Singer, I., *The Nature of Love, Plato to Luther*, Random House, 1966.

17. Vlastos, G., "The Individual as Object of Love in Plato," in *Platonic Studies*, Princeton, 1973.

ARISTOTLE AND

THE CONCEPT OF HAPPINESS

MERRILL RING

When one reflects upon the ways we think and talk about people's lives, it is soon realized that the notion of happiness plays an important role in that thought and talk. In our inquiries into people's lives, our own as well as those of others, we are quite concerned to learn whether or not the person is (or was) happy. It would be well worth going on with this matter, becoming clear as to both the breadth and the depth of our concern with happiness. But that is not my project here and so I shall take it as given that happiness, or at least the thought of it, plays a significant part in our lives.[1]

Philosophers have noticed that state of affairs of course. They have, however, gone on to disagree sharply about how prominent a place happiness *should* be given in accounts of what is valuable. Many have held happiness to be the chief end of human life. Others have not only denied that, but have declared that a view of life which elevates happiness to a prominent spot is offensive.

Suppose that we were to take up this problem of what role happiness should have in human life. On beginning to look into that problem, one with a predilection for Plato might realize that there is another question which should be considered first. In the *Meno* Socrates says he cannot consider the question 'Can virtue be taught?' So too one might well think that questions about the proper role of happiness in human life must wait until we have clearly grasped what happiness is.

Philosophers, unfortunately, have not displayed a Socratic patience about this matter. They have generally rushed off to the larger question without waiting for the antecedent investigation. Very little has been said in works on moral philosophy on the topic of what happiness is.[2] Moreover, not only is the literature on the nature of happiness skimpy in extent, but it is also disappointing in quality. While the presumption should be that there are interesting and enlightening things to be said about happiness, very few such items turn up in existing work on happiness.[3]

One cannot pursue issues about happiness for very long without receiving numerous reminders that one must look into Aristotle. Those reminders are well taken. For one finds in Aristotle not only a major discussion of the role of happiness in human life, but also finds, if attentive to the problem and to the text, the most revealing comments on what happiness is to be found in the literature. Aristotle, then, seems to hold the key to commencing a satisfactory investigation of the nature of happiness.

If one turns from reading Aristotle to reading his commentators, those hopes are threatened. Many writings on the *Ethics* are committed to the view that one cannot learn anything, or at least not much of anything, about happiness from Aristotle. The argument for that view can be sketched as follows. Translators have translated the Greek word *'eudaimonia'* in the Aristotelian texts as 'happiness', thereby giving rise to the idea that Aristotle was examining the nature and role of happiness; such a translation, however, is not proper; *'eudaimonia'* does not mean the same as 'happiness'; hence, though there is a great deal of talk in Aristotle's work about *eudaimonia,* there is not talk about happiness; so we cannot learn anything about happiness from Aristotle's writings.

The moment has now arrived when I, the author, should tell the audience what the object of this paper is. Unhappily, that is somewhat difficult to do. The difficulty is that I have a set of aims not all of which are smoothly compatible. The long-term interest is in discussing the nature of happiness. To throw some light on happiness, I shall want to consider some of what Aristotle says about *eudaimonia*. But to so utilize Aristotle requires that I defend the view that Aristotle is talking about happiness when he talks about *eudaimonia*. To conduct such a defense requires being antecedently clear about what happiness is. Yet getting clear about *that* is the ultimate aim of the project, not its starting point.

In case it should be suspected that what I shall do cannot help but be hopelessly circular, let me suggest another picture which, of course, is in my favor. Wittgenstein produced a number of models of what philosophical problems are and of what it is to investigate such problems. One of those models runs like this. Think of the situation as if it were a library in which the books are scattered on the floor; and think of the philosophes's task as that of putting the books on the shelves in proper order. The only way to accomplish the task is to put some books in order; after that initial sort, others are added to and interpolated among the first group. Of course, where you place the initial volumes will not be the ultimate resting place for them. Regard what happens here in that light. Pieces of my task are interdependent in complex ways. The only procedure in such circumstances is to begin somewhere and work toward the final desired order.

The consequence of that plan is that I can begin more or less where I wish. Let me start by considering certain objections to the idea that we should take *'eudaimonia'* to mean 'happiness'. It should be noticed that this mode of proceeding rests on a conservative assumption. I shall presume that the traditional rendering of *'eudaimonia'* by 'happiness' is correct. The burden of proof shall rest with those who hold that the tradition is not correct. That means that I shall not be called upon to produce arguments for that reading, but rather shall be obligated to examine objections to the traditional understanding.

Aristotle did not invent the word *'eudaimonia'* (it was an ordinary Greek word) and he was not the first to concern himself with questions about *eudaimonia* in that larger context. That is, Aristotle's work grew out of a broad cultural and philosophical context. It might strike one that to help understand Aristotle on this matter it would be desirable to learn something about the notion of *eudaimonia* in that larger context. There is material available to provide such help in various concept studies produced by classical scholars.[4]

If, however, one turns to those scholarly works dealing with *'eudaimonia'*, one's first impression is that scholars do not think that *'eudaimonia'* means 'happiness' at all. What strikes one is that such works contain a large number of occurrences of the formula *'eudaimonia'* means (refers to, denotes, has the sense) 'X' where X is filled in with some term quite other than 'happiness'. It is claimed that in such-and-such a text *'eudaimonia'* meant Y while in another author or at another period of Greek history it meant Z, with neither Y nor Z being 'happiness'. This first impression, that *'eudaimonia'* is held not to mean 'happiness', is soon supplemented by the belief that it is a thesis of such scholarly works that *'eudaimonia'* changed its meaning several times in the course of Greek history. When the two impressions are combined it looks as if scholars are saying that, despite meaning several different things in its career, one meaning *'eudaimonia'* never did have was 'happiness'.

Thus it turns out that classical scholars are a source of the idea that *'eudaimonia'* is not to be translated as 'happiness'. Philosophers not possessed of philological expertise are likely to accept the apparent scholarly verdict as final and sigh, "Well, it seemed as if Aristotle was going to be of help in grasping the nature of happiness. But now it seems not: those who know have spoken against it." Further, I suspect that even those philosophers who do have philological expertise and who reject the traditional translation on philosophical grounds have nonetheless been influenced by the classicist's maneuvers. Consequently I shall take the scholarly objections seriously here.

At an early stage of my studies on this topic I held that there is a philological thesis about the meaning of 'eudaimonia'. At present it seems wrong to speak of a thesis. The works never seem to assert as a thesis that the meaning of the word underwent changes. Rather what we find is a sequence of claims: that at $time_1$ the word meant X, at $time_2$ it meant Y and at $time_3$ it meant Z. What the reader does is to infer from such claims that the word changed meaning--the authors, on the other hand, seem not to be much interested in making such an inference. The idea that there is a definite thesis put forward is further weakened by noticing concept studies of other notions, philological examinations of other philosophically interesting Greek terms. The pattern in those is essentially as we have seen it to be in the case of 'eudaimonia': it is said that word W meant X at $time_1$, Y at $time_2$, etc., but it seems unimportant to the authors to sum up by asserting that the word changed meaning frequently.

What dawned on me after noticing the recurrence of that pattern is that it is an illusion that there are philological theses about most interesting terms. Rather what we are faced with is a feature of the *practice* of philologists. The practice to which they are trained is to examine texts closely, noting the details of a word's usage in particular contexts and then to describe the results of that investigation by saying "Here word W means, refers to, X: there it means, has the sense, Y". It is not that they are out to prove a thesis about changes in the meaning of whatever particular word they are investigating. It is rather that they are trained to use the notion of meaning to express the results of their work. The occurrence of the philological formula "Here W means X, there it means Y" is not the outcome of critical reflection about meaning and about what it is to employ the phrase '...means————'. In classical studies, the use of that formula is the outcome of critical reflection about the usage of a particular word in particular contexts, with it being an institutional arrangement that differences in the usage of the word in different contexts are to be described as changes of meaning.

Turning back to 'eudaimonia', let us not be misled by scholarly writing that says 'eudaimonia' here means this and there means that. That is just how things are done in those scholarly works, that is just the conventional manner of reporting the results of one's investigation. We can reasonably wonder whether the differences in usage should legitimately be described as a difference in meaning. In my survey of the literature I have not yet encountered the kind of evidence which would establish that 'eudaimonia' underwent any changes of meaning. Possibly it did--the evidence, however, is not there.

I have so far omitted another curious feature of writings on 'eudaimonia', a feature that supports my thesis. Although one's first impression is that those works deny that 'eudaimonia' ever meant 'happiness', in fact they do allow that 'eudaimonia' is a word for happiness. Even more: strictly speaking the identification of eudaimonia with happiness is the very backbone of the classicist's work here. None of the claims that 'eudaimonia means X here and Y there' (where X and Y are not 'happiness') are taken as *falsifying* the basic formula 'eudaimonia' means 'happiness'. How should we explain the remarkable fact that assertions of the form 'eudaimonia means X' are made without the slightest sense that they contradict the larger claim that 'eudaimonia' is a word for happiness? I have suggested that the explanation is that philologists are trained to use the formula '....means————' to encapsulate the results of their research; that the manner of its use is such that we ought not regard it as a sober, reflective thesis that 'Z means X'. And because it is not that sort of assertion we can understand why instances of the formula are presented as if they did not contradict the fundamental principle that 'eudaimonia' means 'happiness'.

Having argued that talk of meaning is a reflex activity in classical studies, I shall now argue that it is an undesirable reflex and ought to be extinguished. That is, I will now attempt to show why it is seriously wrong-headed to utilize the meaning formula so generously. The following discussion, however, is of broader consequence than its bearings upon the philological 'objections' to the traditional translation of 'eudaimonia'; it forms the bridge to considering the philosophical status of the notion of *eudaimonia*.

The question to be asked is: How shall we decide between the following two theses; (a) the meaning of the word 'eudaimonia' changed (one or more times) in the course of Greek history; (b) the meaning of the word remained the same but the Greek *conception* of *eudaimonia* changed? There are several points to be noted before considering those theses. First, it seems that scholars are quite correct in holding that there were significant changes in what can, with more or less neutrality, be called the *usage* of the term 'eudaimonia'. The issue is whether those changes should be called changes of meaning or of *conception*. Secondly, I have introduced the idea of a conception of something (here of *eudaimonia*) without explanation. That explanation shall come later, though none of us are, of course, deeply in the dark about what a conception of something is. Thirdly, I shall not hesitate to utilize the rock-bottom scholarly claim that 'eudaimonia' is a word for happiness. The problem being addressed can be put 'Should we say that the meaning of the Greek term equivalent to "happiness" changed its meaning or was it the Greeks' conception of happiness which underwent alteration?' Lastly, I am counting on the idea of a 'conception of happiness' having an intuitively appropriate ring.

You have undoubtedly grasped that I shall hold that the changes which occurred were in the conception of *eudaimonia,* not in the meaning of the word. I have already claimed that there is little, if any, evidence that would support a claim of *meaning* change. What I intend to do now is to present some major shortcomings in any practice which adopts a principle of freely calling changes in the usage of a word 'changes in meaning'.

One of the major aims of philological research is to show how changes such as those surrounding 'eudaimonia' are significantly related to change in the social life of the speakers of the language. That the word 'eudaimonia' should have had, more or less successively, connection with such things as being favored by the gods, being prosperous, having social status, being wealthy, is intelligible as part of political, social and economic alterations in Greek life. But those connections are intelligible only if the changes are seen as changes in the conception of *eudaimonia,* of happiness. I can see no theoretically powerful way of relating changes in the meaning of words to socio-economic changes. Most meaning changes are the consequence of accidents, even misunderstandings. Consider the change in the borrowed Greek phrase (the) *hoi polloi.* In Greek and originally in English it meant '(the) many'—today many will say that it means 'the upper crust'. The change is remarkable. Or think of the ongoing change in the word 'validity' from meaning 'good argument' to 'true statement'. Such changes have no intelligible relation to differences in the way we live. On the other hand, it is altogether obvious that changes in our conceptions of things *are* consequences of social developments. In short, the purpose of understanding the nature and development of Greek society would be defeated if we think the changes discovered in the ancient texts are changes in meaning.

Think of the following analogy: philologists of the future, digging around in texts of the past 100 years and utilizing the same critical apparatus as is presently used, would conclude that the meaning of the word 'marriage' has changed. That not only would be false—our conception of marriage has altered and is continuing to alter but the meaning of the term has not changed--but, if taken seriously, would greatly impede investigation of how our manner of living and of being married changed. For the historian of the future will want the philologist's help in seeing how the changing conception of marriage and a changing social world mutually affected each other.

Another set of reasons for rejecting a generous resort to the idea of meaning change can be formulated by adapting arguments developed by G. E. Moore. In the first chapter of *Principia Ethica,* Moore produced two related arguments concerning the word 'good'. These have been labelled the trivialization argument and the open-question argument. Both are applicable to the present issue concerning *eudaimonia.* If the Greeks ever said something like '*eudaimonia* is due to the goodness of the gods' or '*eudaimonia* is wealth', etc., then they had best not also say '*eudaimonia*' means 'favored by the gods' or means 'is wealthy', etc. Or rather, if *we* want to allow the Greeks to have said those things about *eudaimonia,* then we, as philologists and philosophers, had better not claim that in Greek '*eudaimonia*' meant 'wealthy', etc. or we shall end up making their beliefs trivial. To put it more strongly, if we find evidence that the Greeks did hold things like '*eudaimonia* is being able to avoid the dark forces of the supernatural', then they *could not* have meant by '*eudaimonia*' 'being able to avoid the dark forces of the supernatural', etc. Again if it made sense for a Greek to ask, 'Is that all there is to *eudaimonia,* the favor of the gods?' or 'Is a life of money/social status/pleasure/etc. an *eudaimōn* life?', then it could not have been the case that '*eudaimonia*' meant any of those things. For if that is what the word meant, the questions are already closed and so their worries are unintelligible.

All this adaptation of Moore has consisted in 'if-then' statements. Yet it seems quite obvious that the 'if' clauses are satisfied. The Greeks did hold substantial theses about what leads to *eudaimonia,* they did wonder and dispute about in what *eudaimonia* consists. Consequently, we cannot say that '*eudaimonia*' meant any of the things it very frequently is said to have meant. To try to hold such views is to trivialize problems and views that were important.

It is now time to consider some objection to reading '*eudaimonia*' as 'happiness' which come from philosophers rather than from classicists. There is not the space available here to examine all of those, but the following passage from H. H. Joachim's commentary on the *Nicomachean Ethics* is representative of an important class of such objections:

> The general sense of the term (*eudaimonia*) is brought out by 'living well', 'doing well', which are here said to be equivalents. The English 'happiness' is too narrow; it suggests 'pleasure', or at any rate unduly emphasizes one element only in the Greek conception, that of satisfaction of our sentient nature. Another element in the conception, and to Plato and Aristotle a more important one, was the satisfaction of our nature as active beings, and this is emphasized in ['living well', 'doing well']. We shall see that the Greek conception involved yet another element, prosperity, and that some Greek thinkers, by laying stress on this, identified *eudaimonia* with... 'favor of fortune, good luck.' [5]

Joachim's argument against taking the Aristotelian *'eudaimonia'* as 'happiness' can be reconstructed as follows.

P1 The Greek conception of *eudaimonia* contains several elements, including pleasure.

P2 The English (?) conception of happiness contains only one element, pleasure.

C1 Hence, the English conception of happiness is narrower than the Greek conception of *eudaimonia*.

P3 The meaning of *'eudaimonia'* is located in the conception of *eudaimonia,* while the meaning of the English word 'happiness' resides in the conception of happiness; in general, the meaning or sense of a term is specified by citing the elements in the corresponding (?) conception.

C2 Hence, the Greek word *'eudaimonia'* and the English 'happiness' cannot have the same meaning.

C3 Hence, 'happiness' is not a proper translation of *eudaimonia.*

Laid out as above (and while the reconstruction may not

be wholly fair to Joachim it nonetheless reveals the crucial issues), it is obvious that the argment involves much more than a claim that 'happiness' does not quite catch the *flavor* of *'eudaimonia'*. The argument involves a 'theory of meaning' (premise 3), a thesis about happiness (premise 2) and a thesis about *eudaimonia* (premise 1). It is a philosopher's rejection of a translation, not a poet's or even a translator's. It is to be evaluated not by one's ear for the two languages but by philosophical criteria.

To evaluate it I shall sketch an alternative model of some relevant features of language and thought and shall then explore (all too briefly) how happiness and so too *eudaimonia* fit into the model. The outcome will be directly opposed to the type of view represented by Joachim.

Joachim implies that it is in the conception of a thing that we find the meaning of the corresponding term. I have already opposed that earlier by holding that a conception might change while the meaning of the relevant term might remain unchanged. Here I will repeat in a new terminology that meaning is not to be located in the conception of a thing. To talk about concepts is to talk (in a certain way) about meaning. Thus a distinction must be drawn between the *concept* of something and the *conception* of that thing. (Joachim's basic fault is not that he hooked meaning up to conception, but rather that he does not distinguish concept and conception.) We can speak of Suzie's, or Americans', or the 19th century's, conception of something, say motherhood or marriage. A concept of something, however, does not belong to Suzie or America or· to a time. What I shall be holding is that the concept of happiness and the concept of *eudaimonia* are the same--i.e. there is one concept 'for which' (!) the Greeks used one word and we use another--but that the Greeks had various conceptions of happiness at various times and we today have a conception which is different from those.

If one adopts the present terminology, there is a danger that someone will conclude that 'concept' means 'correct conception'. That is, someone will think that conceptions are approximations to the concept. But that is not generally so–the concept of happiness is quite one thing, the correct conception of happiness, should there be such a thing, is quite another. (There is one special case where the correct conception is related in that way to concept. Philosophers want to elucidate concepts–their attempted elucidations may be called a kind of conception; here a correct conception is one which captures the concept. But we can talk that way only because the special object of the philosopher's concern is the concept, only because we philosophers work to develop the correct conception of it.)

Because of that potential trouble, a still different terminology is desirable. We can talk about the *formal* features of a thing and the *content* of a thing. We might say that the content can vary in ways that the formal features cannot. The word 'formal' is used here because of such things as the following: one of the things that can be said about happiness is 'It makes sense to say "He is ————, so he is happy." ' The intelligibility of that form of words is a feature of happiness. The blank can be filled in with different *contents*. Different individuals, peoples and eras may fill it in, and have filled it in, differently. Of course there are formal limits to what can go in the blank–e.g. 'miserable' *cannot* be inserted there. In other words, grammar (in Wittgenstein's sense of 'grammar') shows the formal features of a thing. The content, on the other hand, of happiness (say) has to do with what counts as happiness-making characteristics of one's life, self or surroundings; and what counts is subject to variation and change.

In fairness, one further discussion should be entered here. The question 'What is happiness?' plays a dual role in thought. It can be a question about the concept, i.e. about the formal features of happiness. It can also be about how to conceive of happiness, about the content of the thing. (And the *form* of answer, 'Happiness is....', is appropriate to the question asked in either of those two manners.) When I said earlier that little has been said by philosophers about the nature of happiness, about what happiness is, I had in mind the question about the concept, not the similar sounding one about the conception. The latter has been asked (and answered differently) many times. (Snoopy's sayings such as 'Happiness is a warm blanket' or the Beatles' 'Happiness is a warm gun' are answers to the latter question, are citations of a conception of happiness.)

The question about the concept, the formal question, is the basic and primary one--the metaphysical question--the question about the nature of the thing, about its essence. The issue about conceptions is secondary, to some extent parasitic upon the answer to the first question. Answers given to 'What is happiness?' construed as answers to questions about the content of happiness may well be relativistic, given to change in time and in socio-economic conditions.

What is perhaps most difficult is to keep these matters separate. Few philosophers have--and not just on the topic of happiness. The issues rarely get sorted out so that in any given account we are likely to find both questions being confusedly discussed. Very little about happiness in its formal aspect has been said, however. Nonetheless, while Aristotle shares that duality of interest and never clearly gets the two issues sorted, he had more to say about the concept of happiness than other philosophers.

A general summary is in order here. Many of the objections to reading 'eudaimonia' as 'happiness' rest on an inadequate 'theory of meaning', in particular on a failure to distinguish between concept and conception.[6] For example, one of John Cooper's reasons for not taking 'happiness' as an adequate rendering of 'eudaimonia' is that for Aristotle children can be said to be eudaimōn only in a secondary and extended sense.[7] But it is certain, especially given Aristotle's way of arguing for that view, that that difference between 'eudaimōn' and 'happy' is a difference in conception and not a difference in the general logic of the two terms. Though failure to observe the distinction has hampered many discussions of the topic, other writers have seen the need to make some such distinction.[8] Yet even there the result has not been happy. The sorting has either been badly done

(Prichard) or very incompletely done and it has never been made central to the discussion of the relationship of *eudaimonia* to happiness. The moral of my discussion is that such a distinction must be squarely in the center of any adequate examination of the topic.

The next step is this. I have said that the concept of happiness entered into Greek thought and life via the word '*eudaimonia*'. What is now to be done is to start developing some formal features of *eudaimonia*/happiness which will be part of showing what it is—and which will also help to show skeptics that there is but one concept. Thirdly, I also want to use Aristotle to start working this out.

The beginning of the *Nicomachean Ethics* is concerned with questions about the highest good. In the fourth chapter of Book I, Aristotle asks 'What is the highest good?' The answer he immediately produces introduces *eudaimonia* into the discussion. "As to its name, there is agreement by most people; for both common people and educated men call it *eudaimonia*, and understand by that 'living well' and 'doing well'." (1095a17-19) That passage has been widely remarked. Still something fairly obvious has been overlooked in thinking about those lines. The chief object of interest has been that identification of *eudaimonia* as the highest good. That fits into my story but not today. I am interested in that part of the passage where Aristotle offers a report of what is meant by '*eudaimonia*' by (almost) everyone. He offers 'living well' and 'doing well' as simple, obvious renderings of *to eudaimonein,* being happy. Even this has not escaped attention: Joachim and others (I think in part Anscombe and Cooper) may have used this presentation of synonyms as a reason for denying that 'happiness' is an acceptable translation of '*eudaimonia*'. The grounds are that *we* would not give 'living well' and 'doing well' as obvious synonymous phrases for 'being happy'. About that we shall see.

What I especially want to call to your attention is the occurrence of the word 'well' in those two phrases given as synonymous with '*eudaimonia*'. (The Greek is '*eu*' in both places: *eu zēn* and *eu prattein*). They serve to bring out what we might have noticed from the etymology of *'eudaimonia'*: *eudaimonia* has to do with things being *well*. Let us step back and ask what that amounts to in philosophical terminology. It means that *eudaimonia* is an *evaluative concept*. When it was said that someone was *eudaimōn,* what was being offered was in some way an evaluation, an appraisal. To speak of someone as *eudaimōn* was not to describe but to assess. Moreover, since the word that is of interest here is living or doing or faring 'well', rather than 'poorly', the evaluation offered is favorable, positive.

Now it is quite obvious that, given everything else I have said, I shall claim that happiness is an evaluative concept, that when someone is said to be happy we are in some way offering a favorable evaluation.

I realize that many will find that claim perplexing if not false and that in the best of all possible papers a great deal of both clarification and argument is needed at this point. Sadly too little of that shall be forthcoming here.

It is not the part about the *favorable* nature of the evaluation that people will find troublesome. Most will readily concede that happiness and misery are impossible cohabitants, that people who find their lives painful or dull or boring are not happy. Rather it is the idea that happiness is at all evaluative that will be most troubling. So here, as a down payment on the needed discussion, let us look at a few features of our talk of happiness. We talk of a happy year in our lives, of being happy in our present job, happy with the arrangements for a meeting. All that talk goes with regarding that particular year, this job, those arrangements, as being *good*, as going or having gone, *well*; as being *right, proper,* etc. One is not happy in one's marriage if the marriage strikes you as being so-so, or disastrous.

As I mentioned earlier, so little work has been done on the concept of happiness that it is impossible to tell what a standard view of it is. If, however, I were to guess at what would typically be said about what happiness is, it would be that happiness is an inner state. Austin quite correctly points out that Pritchard's argument rests on identifying happiness with a feeling, a feeling of pleasure.[9] Similarly Cooper: "But it is not a good choice, since 'happiness' tends to be taken as referring exclusively to a subjective psychological state."[10] Philosophers are prone to turn things into inner conditions when they can't see what else to do with them. There are reasons, inadequate, of course, for talking of 'happiness' as the name of a certain inner state and some of these will be considered shortly. Here, however, let me point out that sometimes we have a difficult time answering the question, 'Are you happy?', a remarkable happenstance if happiness is just an inward state. Moreover, even more remarkably, when we are so asked, we do not, as would seem appropriate on this account, simply inspect ourselves to see whether we are happy. Instead we turn to our situations, our jobs, our marriage, financial circumstances, etc. And what do we do in considering them? My suggestion is that we assess how things are going there and that the answer about our happiness, whatever answer it is, is consequent upon that assessment.

At this point, it may seem somewhat plausible to concede that happiness is evaluative just like *eudaimonia,* but still to be struck by what look to be insurmountable differences. I will close this paper by considering two topics, an appreciation of which should help draw a number of themes together.

To speak of a concept as evaluative is to demand that there be something against which we measure relevant cases in order to evaluate them. In philosophical terminology we can say that there must be a *standard* (or standards) for evaluation. Earlier in the paper I talked considerably, but vaguely, about conceptions of happiness, about the content of happiness. Those conceptions turn out to be, for a notion such as happiness, what logically plays the role of standards. What we conceive happiness to be or to consist in is what we use to measure whether someone is happy, how happy, etc.

There are two large scale differences between our conceptions of happiness and that of Aristotle and of the Greeks generally, differences that look to be so large that we are inclined to think that *eudaimonia* and happiness cannot be the same thing. In the terminology I have offered, what Aristotle does is to argue that there is only *one legitimate standard of eudaimonia,* only one proper conception of what *eudaimonia* is. Aristotle argues that rational activity in conformity with excellence (or contemplation if you prefer Book X) is man's function or characteristic activity and is *thus* the good for man and is *thus* in what *eudaimonia* consists. In effect he argues that *human nature* allows only one *proper* standard of *eudaimonia,* though of course he sees people around him holding, both in theory and in practice, other standards.

One of the consequences of Aristotle's view that there is a uniquely correct idea of what an *eudaimōn* life is like is that, so armed, a person could tell other people whether they are *eudaimōn* or not *without regard to what the subject says or thinks about himself.* Hence, if you think a life of pleasure is the best life, and if you are succeeding in living that sort of life and so call yourself *eudaimōn,* an Aristotelian could come and tell you you are not happy no matter how you feel and what you say.

When we philosophers look at the text of Aristotle and do not see or do not see clearly the items I have pointed out, it will seem that *eudaimonia* and happiness are two quite distinct concepts. It will seem that for *eudaimonia* third person remarks--'He/she is *eudaimōn*'--have as great an authority as the first person 'I am *eudaimōn*'. When we look at happiness, that seems radically false. Only within narrowly circumscribed limits can anyone else override one's own claim that one is happy or unhappy. We do not go around to bright shining faces and say 'How unhappy you are'. Such a difference makes us want to say that happiness and *eudaimonia* are not the same thing.

If one realizes, however, that what we have to employ is the distinction between a concept and a conception and also the notion of an evaluative term and the standards connected with it, we can see quite another possibility. I would like to urge the following hypothesis. The relative authority of the third person 'He is *eudaimōn*' in Aristotle is a function of, not the concept, but the fact that Aristotle held there to be one and only one proper conception. Suppose that no one believes it is possible to say that there is only *one* proper standard of happiness. Suppose rather that we allow every individual to formulate a conception of a good life and to call themselves happy if their life measures up to the standard they themselves have formulated. A consequence shall be that, given that people do not articulate their conception fully, others are not in detail aware of how I propose to assess my life; hence, no one else shall be in a position to override my claims that I am happy or unhappy. If you genuinely believe that it is up to each individual to a) formulate a conception of a good life and b) assess for themselves how well their life meets that standard, and further that others have little information anyway about the other person's standards and life, you shall see that you are in no position to challenge another's claims about his or her own happiness.

What I am of course saying is that that is precisely how things are with us. We cannot believe (and here I do not mean 'we philosophers' but 'we citizens of 20th century liberal democracies') that any one standard of happiness is proper for everyone. We are individualistic and egalitarian with respect to the good life and happiness. That leads us as philosophers to think that happiness differs radically from the *eudaimonia* discussed by Aristotle. That is a mistake--the concepts are the same, the conceptions differ radically, not just in what one believes a happy life to consist in, but in the number of possibilities allowed.

Connected with that difference, there is a second, something further that disinclines us to see *eudaimonia* and happiness as one and the same. The difficulty can be put like this. 'On the whole the Greeks, including Aristotle, think of *eudaimonia* as consisting in externals, for example in wealth or status. But happiness is something inward--wealth isn't happiness though it can make some people happy. Happiness is a response, the feelings one has toward things, if one thinks them to be good things, etc. Since *eudaimonia* is not inward, it and happiness shouldn't be identified.'

The above objection plays a major role in suspicions about the proper translation of 'eudaimonia'. It has several roots, not all of which can be traced here. Very broadly, the main source is a fact: we, today, have a strong interest in the feelings and behavior of people who are happy; yet the idea of the *response* to assessing one's life as *eudaimōn* is almost entirely unmentioned by Aristotle. The differences are striking. However, that should not lead us to conclude that happiness is not at all the same as *eudaimonia.*

The greater the tendency to leave the standard to the individual's own formulation, the greater will be our concern, as a third party, with the behavior and feelings of others. Where there is a social consensus of what constitutes a good and happy life, then it is simple (relatively speaking) to determine whether a person is leading it. Or if I believe that there is only one proper conception of happiness, then I need not attend to how you feel and behave—all I need consider is the style of your life. In fact, given an Aristotelian belief, I may have to *discount* your feelings. If you sincerely and smilingly say you're happy and yet avoid participation in public affairs or are under the age of adulthood, the Aristotelian will deny that your cheerful countenance has any relevance to the issue at hand.

But when you are allowed to say in what your own happiness consists, we third parties must attend to your behavior and feelings. 'He is happy' starts losing its connection with the *speaker's* doing the assessing and becomes more and more a report. And such a report must be largely or importantly based on what you say and feel and how you look and act.

At this point another source of the claim that happiness, contrary to *eudaimonia,* is inward begins coming to the fore. Though the explanation of how this comes about is long, suppose that one's model of a good life shifts from something like wealth or public activity to something like peace, personal harmony, *ataraxia.* That is, think not only of the situation where the standard for evaluation is left up to individuals, but also of the different case where the standard involves one's response to the world. Both situations differ from the Greek world with which Aristotle was concerned in that both demand a greater interest in how you feel and act. Moreover, where one's goal becomes freedom from agitation, upset, etc., I, i.e. the individual himself, must have a greater concern with my own feelings. There is no other way of determining whether I am happy.

Still, this new situation does not establish that happiness is other than *eudaimonia.* In fact, since the transition to the ideal of quiet and inner peace began in the Greek world under the aegis of *eudaimonia,* one could offer that as a confirmation of my claim that the two are the same.

Look at the objection from another perspective. In Aristotle we find remarkably little concern with the feelings and behavior of individuals with respect to *eudaimonia.* The interest is overwhelmingly with the question 'What is a good life? How do such things as excellence, pleasure, wealth, etc. fit into a good life?' Now why should Aristotle not find much interest in how someone feels about his or her life? What we tend to forget is that whatever you think a good life consists in, you will respond, i.e. feel and act, appropriately if your life does (or does not) match that conception. The point, for Aristotle, is to find out what life is truly good. Further, we must recall to whom his work is addressed--to those who are capable of hitting the target, who are looking to do so. If Aristotle can get his readers to accept these standards, then, of course, they will feel appropriately if their lives satisfy the standards they have accepted. For Aristotle and his audience, it would have been pointless to dwell on that. The lack of such a concern shows nothing whatsoever about a distinction between *eudaimonia* and happiness. In that respect *eudaimonia* is just as inward as happiness.

The preceding is a sketch of an examination of the most general logical feature of *eudaimonia*/happiness and a few associated points. You should be as aware as I am that what I have accomplished is but a partial investigation of but one issue. There are an untold number of other formal features to be explored, including what is undoubtedly the logical feature which ranks second in importance to the matter already examined. Aristotle held that it is constitutive of the concept of *eudaimonia* that it makes sense to say of any activity X 'X is being pursued for the sake of *eudaimonia* but that it makes no sense to say *eudaimonia* is being pursued for the sake of X'. Unfortunately, time and space have grown short here. That investigation would involve, among other things, a consideration of the dispute about whether Aristotle takes *eudaimonia* to be a (so-called) 'dominant' or an 'inclusive' end. (The recognition that talk of *eudaimonia* is crucially related to evaluation will undercut that dispute, will show that neither party is exactly right nor wholly wrong.) Again, all that work and more remains to be done.[11]

Notes

1. The paper as read was a first draft of an attempt to put my thoughts down in some connected fashion. It is obvious *now* that the paper would be greatly improved by substantially shortening the first part (on philology) and vastly lengthening the present second half. I did not have that insight prior to writing and reading this paper. In fairness to the original audience I have not made those major structural changes which are clearly necessary. Alterations for publication have been minor. I have also let the text retain the marks of its origin as a paper intended to be read to an audience composed largely of students.

2. To understand this remark properly, see the distinction made later in the paper between two different ways of understanding the question 'What is Happiness?'.

3. A. Kenny, "Happiness", *Proceedings of the Aristotelian Society* LXVI (1965-66); R. Montague, "Happiness", *Proceedings of the Aristotelian Society* LXVII (1966-67); D.A. Lloyd Thomas, "Happiness", *The Philosophical Quarterly* 18 (1968); John Wilson, "Happiness", *Analysis* 29 (1968); Jean Austin, "Pleasure and Happiness", *Philosophy* 43 (1968); R. W. Simpson, "Happiness", *American Philosophical Quarterly* 12 (1975).

4. A very good recent work is Marianne McDonald, *Terms for Happiness in Euripides* (Göttingen: Vandenhoek and Ruprecht in Göttingen, 1978), especially Chapter 1 "Historical Background for Terms for Happiness" and the Introduction and Conclusion.

5. H. H. Joachim, *Aristotle: The Nicomachean Ethics, A Commentary*, ed. D. A. Rees (Oxford: Oxford University Press, 1951), p. 28.

6. For *similar* distinctions see H. L. A. Hart, *The Concept of Law* (Oxford University Press, 1961), p. 156ff; Julius Kovesi, *Moral Notions* (London: Routledge & Kegan Paul, 1967), Chapter 1; John Rawls, *A Theory of Justice* (Cambridge, Massachusetts: Harvard University Press, 1971), p. 5f; Alan R. White, "Conceptual Analysis", in *The Owl of Minerva*, ed. C. J. Bontempo and J. J. Odell (New York: McGraw Hill, 1975), pp. 113-114.

7. John M. Cooper, *Reason and   Human Good in Aristotle* (Cambridge, Massachusetts: Harvard University Press, 1975), p. 89.

8. See H.A. Prichard, "The Meaning of *Agathon* in the *Ethics* of Aristotle", *Philosophy* X, (1935), reprinted in *Moral Obligation* (Oxford: Oxford University Press, 1949), p.51; J.L. Austin, *"Agathon* and *Eudaimonia* in the *Ethics* of Aristotle", in J. M. E. Moravcsik, ed., *Aristotle: A Collection of Critical Essays* (Garden City, New York: Doubleday, 1967), pp. 275-276; J. L. Ackrill, *Aristotle on Eudaimonia*, The British Academy Dawes Hicks Lecture on Philosophy, 1974 (London: Oxford University Press, 1975), p.6; and of course the original in Aristotle himself, *N.E.* 1.4, 1094a 16-20.

9. Austin, *op. cit.,* p. 266.

10. Cooper, *loc. cit.*

11. In preparing this for publication I discovered a recent paper by Richard Kraut, "Two Conceptions of Happiness", *Philosophical Review* 88 (April, 1979) which, at least on first reading, takes a line very similar to that argued here, only does so in greater detail. I urge readers to consult it.

ARISTOTLE ON FUNCTION

AND THE ATTRIBUTIVE NATURE

OF THE GOOD

GEORGIOS ANAGNOSTOPOULOS

The importance of knowledge in relation to the conception of the good for man and the good life is attested in what survives about the very early stages of the Greek philosophical tradition.[1] Thus Diogenes reports that Anaxagoras neglected his wealth and belongings and that when his relatives complained and demanded an explanation for his neglect he told them to look after his belongings themselves and promptly gave his wealth to them in order to be able to live for study alone. Diogenes also tells us that when Anaxagoras was asked what he lived for he replied: "To observe and study the sun and the moon and the sky."[2] Similar anecdotes are recorded by Aristotle when he tells us that to the question concerning the happiest man Anaxagoras replied: "None of those whom you suppose but someone who would seem absurd to you."[3] Aristotle, of course, interprets this remark in a way that supports his own views, thus taking Anaxagoras to be saying that the happiest man is the one who is devoting his life to the pursuit of knowledge.

It should not however be concluded on the basis of

remarks such as the above that the dominant ideal in the Greek tradition was the theoretical life or that the Greeks in general conceived of the good in terms of the pursuit of knowledge. First of all there survive in the tradition along with those anecdotes that stress the role of knowledge in the philosophical conception of the good life anecdotes that reveal that such a view was not shared by the wider public. So Plato reports the story that Thales fell into a well while gazing in the sky and that he was mocked by a Thracian servant girl.[4] And being mocked by a Thracian girl is the lowest that one can sink, even lower than the deepest well. It is clear that these stories about Thales and similar ones about other thinkers reflect what the wider public thought about the pursuit of knowledge and what they took to be good: namely, that the knowledge the philosophers were after was useless and that the good life had little to do with it. This last point is brought out clearly in what Socrates and Plato tell us about the views of the many with regard to the good--that these in no way resemble the views of the philosophers. What especially comes to mind in this connection is what Socrates says about the attitudes of the many towards the philosophic life in the *Apology* and elsewhere, and the very pessimistic notes expressed in the *Republic* by Plato about the possibility of living the philosophic life amidst the many who neither understand it nor tolerate it. Similarly, Aristotle dismissed the opinions of the many with regard to the good, obviously because these opinions are removed the farthest from his own views about the good as the activity of contemplation or the theoretical life.

What has come down to us regarding the views of the early thinkers about the knowledge and the good is however problematic for other reasons as well. Most of what has come down to us is difficult to interpret, vague, or obscure. It is not clear for example if knowledge is only a means, and if so what kind of means, to the good, the latter being something distinguishable or distinct from it. And to compound the problems, most of these accounts about the early thinkers have come down to us primarily through the writings of later thinkers, thinkers who had clearly fixed opinions about the good life and they often attributed to their predecessors views that were similar to their own or interpreted obscure remarks of their predecessors in terms of their own views. It is most probable then that the views of the early thinkers about knowledge and the good are views that were formulated much later in the tradition. It is quite obvious for example that the obscure remark of Anaxagoras that the happiest man is someone who would seem absurd to most can mean several things, if it means anything at all. But Aristotle promptly interprets it as asserting precisely his own view, thus giving himself the honor of reproducing theories about happiness that seem absurd to most.

We have, however, clear evidence that Socrates and Plato assigned a central role to knowledge in their respective views on the good of man and the good life. In the Socratic dialogues Socrates is portrayed as one who never tires of arguing for the importance of knowledge in living the good life and its power for doing what is right. The knowledge however that Socrates was concerned with was primarily practical knowledge–knowledge of what is to be feared and not to be feared, of what is to be avoided and is not to be avoided, of what is pleasant and what is not pleasant, etc.– that is, knowledge of what is right to do or not to do. But we have no evidence, at least from what Plato says about Socrates, that he identified the good with knowledge, or the pursuit, or activity of knowledge itself. Tradition rather has it that it was Plato himself who introduced the idea of theoretical knowledge and connected it to a certain kind of life, the theoretical life, and in turn gave to this kind of life the highest place in an ordering of the various types of lives that are possible for humans. But Plato's views about the good are in no way easy to understand. We have the notoriously difficult passages about the good in the *Republic*, the suggestions that no account of the good can be articulated, as well as the opinion in the Platonic tradition that Plato gave lectures on the good that were never written down and possibly were never understood.[5] But although we cannot be altogether clear and certain as to what his views about the good were, it seems that he does not identify, at least in his mature works, the good with the activity of knowledge itself. There is no doubt, however, that the emphasis Plato put on theoretical knowledge and the role he assigned to it in relation to the good were the basis of the views of Aristotle, the philosopher in the Greek tradition who most clearly came to identify, at least sometimes, the human good, or happiness, with the activity of theoretical knowledge itself. But what is of more importance here is the role that the idea of function plays in Plato's and Aristotle's views on the good and in particular in Aristotle's tendency to identify the human good with the human function. I would like then to examine some aspects of this idea of function and try to explain in part why it plays such a central role in Aristotle's account of the good and of a number of related notions.

In Book I of the *N.E.* we find two lines of argument, or discussion, pertaining to Aristotle's account of the good. The first line of argument, which begins with the opening section of the *N.E.*, I shall call here "the desire argument or discussion." It examines the nature and structure of desires, wants, pursuits, aims, etc. and of the related notions of means, ends, degrees of finality and self-sufficiency of ends, etc. In the course of the desire argument Aristotle introduces and defines a number of concepts, such as the concept of a supreme (highest) good as that for the sake of which all else is done (the ultimate end of human pursuits, desires, wants, actions, etc.); the concept of the most final end as that which can only be pursued or desired for its own sake and not for the sake of anything else (it can never be a means), etc. Aristotle arrives at a number of conclusions in this discussion, but only the following are important for our purposes: a) there is some one end of human desires, pursuits or actions for the sake of which all else is desired, pursued or done, while it is not (and cannot) be desired,[6] pursued or done for the sake of anything else (the end of man); b) this is the good of man; c) and this is happiness (*eudaimonia*).

The second line of argument, or discussion, which I shall here call the "function argument," is an attempt to give an account of what happiness really consists of by explaining what the good of man is. This argument considers the relation between the function of something of a kind F, its being a good F, the excellence (virtue) of an F and the good of an F. On the basis of the function discussion Aristotle is able to give a schematic explanation of the good of man and, using what was supposedly established by the desire argument--namely, that happiness is the highest good--to give an account of human happiness in general terms. The familiar account he gives there is that the human good and happiness consist of the performance of the function of man in accordance with human excellence (virtue).

The complexity and difficulty of each of these two segments of the text are familiar to most of us. Some have found in these segments obvious fallacies. Thus, it has often been asserted that in the desire argument Aristotle commits some variant of the naturalistic fallacy or that he gives as real definitions what are only persuasive ones. Again, in the function argument he supposedly commits a number of fallacies in his attempt to prove that man has a function and equivocates in the final steps of the argument when he apparently moves from the good F to the good of F. I will not, however, be concerned here with evaluating the various criticisms scholars have raised against Aristotle's arguments, nor with giving new interpretations or criticisms of the arguments themselves. I will rather focus on the relation between the two lines of argument and in particular attempt to elucidate some of the reasons that might have partly led Aristotle to put forth the function argument altogether.

I, of course, am assuming here that the function argument is of some importance and was so viewed by Aristotle. The argument occurs in an expanded form in the *Eudemian Ethics* and is presupposed in the final sections of Book X of the *N.E.* in the discussion of human happiness and is indeed an essential part of that discussion. This opinion, however, has not been shared in some of the most important studies of

Aristotle's views on the human good. J. L. Austin once remarked that "that roundabout way of bringing into the discussion *psyché* (soul) and *ergon* (function) is a piece of unnecessary Aristotelian metaphysics." And John M. Cooper writes:

> Now what is disappointing about this argument...is that it is too abstract to be informative. It tells us at most only that the excellences, whatever these may turn out to be, are the essential condition of a flourishing life, but if one is in doubt, or in need of confirmation, as to precisely what states of mind and character are excellences, then the abstract statement in Aristotle's conclusion is not very interesting or helpful.[7]

Now, there is no doubt that the argument has problems that perhaps cannot be remedied. And I do not want to claim that the argument by itself fully explains or gives an account of the good and the excellences (virtues) of man. But I hope to show that, contrary to those who do not see the significance of the argument, the function argument, or some logically similar argument, was necessary given some of the underlying assumptions in Aristotle's thought, in order to account for a logical feature of the good that the desire argument alone could not account for.

The term Aristotle uses when he speaks of the good is *to agathon* (the good). This term is clearly a substantive in its grammatical form and is derived from the adjective *agathos* which, like most adjectives in Greek, has three distinctive morphemes corresponding to the three genders. But it is quite obvious that at least on the surface, the term in this connection is not used as an adjective. When the expression "x is an (the) *agathon*" is used, the standard rules governing gender agreement between adjective and what is modified by the adjective (a noun, noun-phrase) are not observed. Thus, irrespective of the gender of what takes the place of x in the above expression *agathon* is used. For instance, health (*hygieia*-feminine) is an *agathon*, wealth (*ploutos*-masculine) is an *agathon*, etc.

The phrase "y is an *agathon* (good)" is an incomplete one. The expression has really the form "x is an *agathon* (good) of y" when completed. This is indeed how Aristotle uses it in most of its occurrences. So he says that health is the good of the body, sight the good of the eye and in general he speaks of the good of an art and the good of man.[8] Quite often however the phrase is used in its incomplete form, without specifying what is to take the place of y, or whose good is in question, when it may not be necessary to do so. Thus, sometimes something is said to be a good, the implication being that it is a good for all things. But most often the incomplete form is used when it is obvious what is to take the place of y from the context, or the presupposed topic of discussion or investigation. And this is so in most of the occurrences of *agathon* in *N.E.* where it is obvious that the topic is the good of man or human good.[9]

Now to speak of the good of man, the good of the eye, the good of the body, etc., presupposes that one takes some one thing to be the good in each case. This is so in almost all the cases where Aristotle talks about the good of some y. He assumes without any discussion that a single thing is the good in each case and often tells us what he takes the good to be.[10] But in the case of man, however, he goes into considerable length to show that the good of man is some single thing.[11] To say or assume, however, that some one thing is the good of y does not imply that no other things are good for y. Aristotle repeatedly asserts that many different things (virtue, honor, wealth, etc.) are good for man, and that similarly other things than sight (the good of the eye) are good for an eye, etc.[12] The good of a certain kind, which he often calls "the proper good" of a thing, or kind of thing, is something which has a special place among the various things that are good for some thing or kind of thing.[13] And he views the things that are good *for* some y as the things that are pursued for the sake of *the* good of y or are the means to the good of y.[14] This relationship between the good of y and the things that are good for y is analogous to the architectonic structure of desires and pursuits and

means-ends that Aristotle elaborates in Book I of both the
N.E. and *E.E.* The main task of Aristotle in relation to the
good then is to explain what the nature of the good of man
is, i.e. what the good of a certain species is. And this can be
viewed as an instance of a general program which conceives
of the goods of the various species and envisages
investigations about the good of other species similar to the
one Aristotle carries on in the *Ethics.* Indeed Aristotle speaks
of the goods of other species in his ethical works. (*E.E.*
1217a27)

In addition to the above use of "good", however, Aristotle
uses the term as a straightforward adjective modifying a noun
that in most cases signifies a kind or a species. Thus he speaks
of a good man, a good horse, a good eye, a good flute-player,
etc. In saying though that the term is used as an adjective I
am merely saying that the surface grammar of the term is
that of an adjective.[15] This use of the term has an important
logical feature that was pointed out and discussed by
Geach.[16] According to Geach some expressions are used
predicatively while others are used attributively. "Yellow",
according to this view, is used predicatively in the sentence
"x is a yellow bird." For the following inference is valid:

> x is a yellow bird.
> A bird is an animal.
> x is a yellow animal.

In contrast to "yellow", "good" in "x is a good painter" is
used attributively. For the following inference is not valid:

> x is a good painter.
> A painter is a man.
> x is a good man.

This suggests that "good" unlike "yellow" is attached, or
glued, to the term that it modifies in the surface structure of
the statement. It is attached to a certain description (or
predicate expression) of the subject and characterizes, or

applies to, the subject under that description (or predicate expression). Thus "x is a good F" cannot be analyzed into, or does not have the logical form, "x is F and x is good." For this would clearly allow the unwanted inferences. From "x is a good F ⟷ x is F and x is good" and "x is F ⟷ x is H," we get "x is H and x is good" and therefore that "x is a good H." But "x is a yellow G" is analyzable, or has the logical form, "x is G and x is yellow."[17]

As a first step towards representing or analyzing expressions of the form "x is a good F" one might suggest treating "good" as a predicate applying to F or to x as characterized by F. So that "x is a good F" would be taken to have the form "good (F)x", which in turn shows that "good" is attached to the predicate or the way x is identified or characterized. We might view the application of "good" to a phrase "Fx", identifying or characterizing some kind, as a type of function that takes us to a description in terms of some feature(s) of F: good (F)x = f(F)x. This formal schema, and it is only a schema, captures some of the aspects of the notion of a good F. First, it blocks the unwanted inferences. For given "Gx" as another non-synonymous description and that (x) (Fx ⟷ Gx) we cannot infer that f(F)x ⟷ f(G)x, or good (F)x ⟷ good (G)x, and therefore cannot infer from the fact that something is a good F and F is a G, that it is a good G. Second, it represents in a way the pre-analytic intuition that the goodness of F is connected to some features of F or even to what makes something to be an F, an intuition that has been central in the recent discussions on the nature of goodness of some F and its relation to the criteria for being an F or the meaning of "F".[18] But it is quite obvious that this analysis does not take us very far, for it does not tell us what the relevant features of F are in connection with its goodness or of what features the goodness of F is a function and what kind of function it is. I would like then to turn to a proposal advanced recently, and as we shall see also by Aristotle, that preserves the insights of the above schematic analysis but clearly shows why "good" attaches to and is inseparable from the predicate and identifies the relevant features of F connected with its goodness.

Zeno Vendler has offered an analysis of expressions of the form "x is a good F" that I believe explains both the informal and formal facts about such expressions that we mentioned above–that "good" is attached to the predicate or noun that it modifies; that such expressions do not have the logical form "x is good and x is F"; and that certain inferences are not possible, whereas they are in the case of "yellow" and logically similar predicates.[19] Vendler has suggested that in a class of nouns that clearly signify something that has a function (functional nouns) there is a single verb associated with each such noun and "good", when modifying such nouns, is really functioning adverbially and thus modifies the associated verb.[20] So that "x is a good F" is a transformation of, has the semantic representation (or logical form or deep structure)

$$\text{x is a good F}_\Phi \longleftrightarrow \text{x is (an) F}_\Phi \quad \& \quad \Phi\text{'s well,}$$

where Φ is the verb associated with F and signifies the function of F. Indeed in the clearest, or paradigmatic, examples of functional nouns the associated verb is really the meaning of the noun and is obviously either morphologically identical with, or derived from, it: e.g. a cook, one who cooks; a painter, one who paints; writer, one who writes; hunter, one who hunts, etc.[21] And, incidentally, these cases seem to be the clearest cases of meaning one can come up with. We can now see why "x is a good F", unlike "yellow" in similar constructions, cannot be analyzed into "x is F and x is good," since "good" is really an adverb modifying the underlying verb appropriate to F and cannot, like all genuine adverbs, be detached from the verb. And we can also see why we cannot from "x is a good F" and the fact that F's are G's, (or even that x is F if and only if x is G) infer that "x is a good G." For clearly the verbs that underlie, or are associated with, "F" and "G" may be different:

$$\text{x is a good F}_\Phi \longleftrightarrow \text{Fx and x } \Phi\text{'s well}$$
$$\text{x is a good G}_\Psi \longleftrightarrow \text{Gx and x } \Psi\text{'s well.}$$

Now there is no doubt that Aristotle was aware of the attributive use of "good" (as well as "bad") in expressions of the form "x is (a) good F" ("x is a bad F"). This fact was understood by the traditional commentators and was expressed in their studies of the Aristotelian texts by pointing out that a man may be good (bad) *qua* lyre-player but not *qua* man and vice-versa; or a man may be good (bad) *qua* physician but not *qua* man, etc. So at *N.E.* 1148b8 he tells us "...just as we speak of someone as a bad (*kakōs*) doctor or bad actor whom we would not call simply (*haplōs*) 'bad'." This term "simply" (*haplōs*) is used by Aristotle to mark just this fact that something may be said to be true (or not) of something without qualification or with reference to what something is in terms of its essential nature. Here "good" ("bad") would apply without qualification when it is asserted of a man *qua* man and not qualified as doctor, actor, etc. It would be said "simply" (*haplōs*) when it applies to a man in relation to what he truly is, his essential nature. And again he says in *Met.* 1021b19 that "We speak of a complete scandal-monger and a complete thief; indeed we even call them ''good'' (*agathous*), i.e. a good thief and a good (*agathos*) scandal-monger." Aristotle is clear that we can't infer from x is a good F and x is G that x is a good G. The reason it can't be done in the example of the thief has nothing to do with morality. This is not a moral point but a logical one. For he goes on to speak of the proper (*oikeia*) excellence of each kind of thing (doctor, flute-player) that renders it a perfect (*teleion*) and good (*agathon*) thing of that kind. (*Hoion teleios iatros kai teleios aulētēs hotan kata to eidos tēs oikeias aretēs meden elleipōsin*).

But what is perhaps of greater importance here is the fact that Aristotle himself gives an analysis of "good F" (*agathos*) and a term which he takes to be synonymous with it--*spoudaios* (successful, efficient, excellent)[23]--which is identical with the analysis discussed above. At the beginning of the function argument he points out that in the case of things that have functions--and therefore in the case of functional nouns--the good (*to agathon*) and "the well" (*to eu*) may be found in their function. Let us leave aside questions about the good (*to agathon*) for the moment and focus instead on "the well" (*to eu*), for it is not obvious how one is to take this phrase in Aristotle's assertion about good and function. "The well" (*to eu*) is clearly a nominalized adverb which is sometimes used as being synonymous with "the good" (*to agathon*).[24] But to take it as synonymous with *to agathon* here would make Aristotle's assertion a redundant repetition. Hence the insight of some of the translators who presume the adverbial nature ("the well") as one of the components of Aristotle's assertion about the connection between good and function is a justifiable one.[25] For what he goes on to say here and elsewhere clearly shows that he thought the correct account of "a good F" (*agathos, spoudaios*) to be in terms of the verb associated with F which signifies its function and an adverbial modifier ("well"–*eu*–or some equivalent expression, such as *kalōs*, used in 1098a15).

So beginning at 1097b21 Aristotle considers a set of things which are paradigmatically functional: the flute player, sculptor, and in general all craftsmen (*kai panti technitē* 1097b26-27); builder, shoemaker (1097b29); eye, hand, foot, and other parts of the body--these may seem less functional than the previous examples, but Aristotle takes them to be like them[26] (1097b31-32). He then argues that the function of an F and a good (*spoudaion*) F is generically the same, Φ--e.g. the function of a lyre-player and a good (*spoudaios*) lyre-player is the same--playing the lyre (1098a10). And this is given as a general principle--*kai haplōs de tout epi pantōn* (1098a10-ll). The difference between a good lyre-player and a lyre-player is the difference of the excellence possessed by the former but not the latter and which results in the doing of the function well in the former case and simply doing the function in the latter--playing the lyre well and simply playing the lyre (*kitharistou men gar kitharidzein spoudaiou de to eu*) (1098a12-13). This tells us what the difference between an F and a good F is and that this difference consists in doing the function of F well (and this doing of the function of F well results from having the excellence–*aretē*–of F). Aristotle gives the same analysis when he considers the case of a good man, again asserting that the good (*spoudaios*) man does the appropriate activities of the soul well (*eu*) and rightly or properly (*kalōs*) (1098a15). And he gives later on an identical analysis of "a good eye" and "a good horse", which he clearly treats as instances of the general principle he asserts as explaining the excellence (*aretē*) of F and of being a good (*agathos, spoudaios*) F in terms of doing the function of F well: "All excellence has a twofold effect on the thing to which it belongs: it not only renders the thing itself good (*eu echon*), but it also causes it to perform its functions well (*to ergon autou eu apodidōsin*) (1106a15, Rackham's translation).

The preceding discussion shows that we have here a set of terms that Aristotle took to be interrelated and all to have the attributive character. For in addition to "good F", "the excellence (virtue) of F" and "the function of F" are attributive. It is clear that from "V is the (a) virtue of F" and "F is G" we cannot infer that "V is the (a) virtue of G." "V is the (a) virtue of F" is not analyzable into "V is the (a) virtue of x & x is F." Neither can we take the virtue of F as simply what belongs to F uniquely. That is,

$$V \text{ is the virtue of } F \longleftrightarrow (Vx \longleftrightarrow Fx).$$

For if there is a unique non-synonymous characterization of F's, "G", such that $(x) (Fx \longleftrightarrow Gx)$, unwanted inferences would be possible. From both analyses given above we could infer that V is the virtue of G. Expressions of the form "V is the virtue of..." attach, or are glued, to a description of a thing or kind of thing; they apply, or fail to apply, to something under a particular description. For just these reasons, I shall call occurrences such as the occurrence of "virtue" above "attributive" thus extending the use of this term beyond the context originally discussed by Geach.

There is no doubt that Aristotle took virtue to have the attributive character. He is clear for example that the virtue of a man is not the virtue he has by being a flute-player or by being an animal.[27] Indeed, the analysis he gives of virtue is in terms of function. In the passage quoted above he takes the virtue of F to be the necessary and sufficient conditions for doing the function of F well. To use his own example, if seeing is the function of an eye–"to see" is the verb associated with "eye"–vision (*opsis*) is the virtue of the eye--a power or faculty which is necessary and sufficient for seeing well.[28] And in general if Φ is the function of F and V is the virtue of F, Aristotle holds that:

$$V \text{ is the virtue of } F_{\Phi} \longleftrightarrow F_{\Phi} \; x \; \& \; (Vx \longleftrightarrow x \; \Phi\text{'s well}).$$

We see in Aristotle's analysis the agreement that must be preserved between the description or characterization of x as F and the associated or underlying verb (function), which in turn bars the unwanted inferences. The functional analysis of "...virtue of F" then, like the analysis of "good F", both explains what virtue is and captures the attributive character of the notion. And it can be seen easily that these two notions are equivalent--since the virtue, V, of an F is the necessary and sufficient condition for doing its function, Φ, well and some x is a good F if and only if x does Φ well it follows that

$$x \text{ is a good } F \longleftrightarrow x \text{ has the virtue of an } F.$$

Hence Aristotle's remark at 1106a15 that the virtue of F renders it a good F and makes it do its function well.

Now, if something can be characterized or identified in different ways and the excellences corresponding to the functions associated with such different characterizations or identifications would be distinct, in what way can we speak about the virtue of a certain kind? Clearly, Aristotle takes *one* description to give what is essential to a kind or species and the function correlated with the essential feature of a kind is really the function of that species. The virtue then of a certain kind would be just those conditions necessary and sufficient for doing the function of the species well.[29] In the case of man this cannot be the virtue of a flute-player, or builder, or an animal, or even a grammar-learning animal--the last being a unique characteristic of the species. What he calls "excellence of man" or "human excellence"[30] is correlated with the function of man *qua* man or the description that gives the nature or essence of man. And when we speak of the virtue (or vice) of some individual without any qualification, this is taken to mean the virtue (or vice) of that individual *qua* man. And this is the use that he designates as "speaking simply" (*haplōs*) of someone that he has a virtue (or vice), as we saw above.

The notion that Aristotle uses to give an analysis of "good F" and "virtue of F" and to account for their attributive character is that of the function of F, a notion that is central in his thought--as well as the thought of Plato--and that we especially associate with his biological and ethical-political treatises. I will not examine this notion in any detail here, but rather limit myself to a few comments that are essential to the main themes of the present discussion. Like the other notions explicated by it, the notion of function is itself attributive and Aristotle clearly took to be so. He points out that it does not follow from the fact that a doctor is a builder and the function of a builder is to build that the function of a doctor is to build.[31] And again, through the function argument of *N.E.* Aristotle presupposes the attributive character of the notion of function. For in this discussion he does not infer from the fact that the flute-player (sculptor, carpenter, shoemaker, lyre-player--to use his own examples) is to play the flute (sculpt, etc.) and the fact that a flute-player is a man that the function of man is to play the flute (sculpt, etc). Indeed Aristotle does not take these examples as even showing by themselves that man has a function; and therefore he first tries to prove that man has a function and then gives an argument to show that the function of man is a certain activity of the soul. And in this latter argument Aristotle does not infer from the supposed fact that the function of a class of animals is a form of sentient life and that man belongs in this class that the function of man is a form of sentient life.[32] And conversely, after he concludes that the function of man is a certain activity of the soul, he does not infer that the function of an animal is this psychic activity, although man is clearly an animal. Again the function of something, or class of things, is attached, or glued, to a description of that thing or class of things; and applies, or fails to apply, to it under some description.

It is not clear how the notion of function is to be analyzed, or represented, in order to capture its essential features. And the brief account Aristotle gives in the functional analysis is itself unclear and perhaps misleading. For in that discussion he starts from things which are paradigmatically functional (flute-player, builder, eye, etc.). There seems to be here a necessary connection between the thing and its function, perhaps even a connection of meaning. Although Aristotle does not call it a connection of meaning, but rather views it as a necessity resulting from the nature of things, it is important to point out this aspect of the examples he uses. But when he comes to the case of man he seems to be looking for an activity which is unique or peculiar to man by proceeding to eliminate as candidates for the function of man the activities that man shares with other animals. It is natural therefore to take the function of man as that which is unique to man or that for the performance of which man is a necessary and sufficient condition.[33] But it is obvious this is not all there is here. For let Φ be the unique function of man *qua* man and G a unique property belonging to man (e.g. his learning grammar--to use one of Aristotle's examples.) If we take the function of man to be what belongs uniquely to it--$(x)(Mx \longleftrightarrow \Phi x)$--from the fact that G belongs to man uniquely--$(x) (Mx \longleftrightarrow Gx)$--we can derive that Φ is the function correlated, or associated, with learning grammar.

But perhaps one can block the above inferences and capture Aristotle's notion of function by introducing the modalities, thus taking into account our intuition that the connection between being a builder and building (sculptor and sculpting, etc.) is a necessary one--at least in the case of paradigmatically functional terms. This however may not prove adequate either, given some well-known Aristotelian views about essentialism, necessary and unique properties, accidental properties, etc. For consider two necessary and unique properties of man, e.g. his learning grammar and his learning mathematics:

(1a) N [x is a man $\longleftrightarrow$ x learns grammar]
(1b) N [x is a man $\longleftrightarrow$ x learns mathematics].

And let the function correlated with the property (or capacity) of learning grammar be Φ (e.g. speaking a language) and the function correlated with learning mathematics be Ψ (e.g. solving mathematical problems):

(2a) N [x learns grammar $\longleftrightarrow$ Φ x]
(2b) N [x learns mathematics $\longleftrightarrow$ Ψ x].

But we can derive, as can be seen easily, from these propositions in any ordinary modal system

(3) N [x learns grammar $\longleftrightarrow$ x learns mathematics].

And from (1a, b), (2a, b) and (3) we can derive

(4a) N [x learns grammar $\longleftrightarrow$ Ψ x]
(4b) N (x learns mathematics $\longleftrightarrow$ Φ x].

So we might consider the possibility here that the necessity in (1a, b) is not the same in (2a, b). But the distinction between *de dicto* and *de re* necessity would not by itself alter anything here. What rather seems closer to our intuitions is that the necessity in (2a, b) is a necessity of meaning, whereas this is not so in the case of (1a, b). We may rewrite then the N in (2a, b) as Nm to indicate the different type of necessity here, the necessity connected via meaning, and this would block the inference of (4a, b), since it would be an inference across different types of necessity. But it is not at all obvious that Aristotle thought of the connection between the function of F and the characterization of something as F in just these terms, since considerations of meaning do not seem to play any role in this thought. What little he says in this connection seems to indicate that he thought of the connection between the property of being an F and the correlated function Φ to be necessary and causal in the strictest sense. So he speaks of the capacity, or faculty, of building as the (necessary) cause of the function of the builder.[34] And even though some other property may be necessarily and uniquely connected with being an F–e.g. learning grammar and learning mathematics in the above example–it may not be the cause of the function of F–e.g. learning grammar is not the cause (the capacity, faculty) of the function correlated with learning mathematics.[35] So we might distinguish the necessity in (2a, b) as being a causal necessity (Nc) in contrast to the necessity in (1a, b). And most probably the terms *oikeios* and *idios* that Aristotle often uses to characterize the function correlated with some particular property or capacity or faculty imply more than the relation of uniqueness or peculiarity; they imply also this necessary causality that he takes to hold between the property (faculty, capacity, etc.) and the function. And the clearest examples in this context are the functions of the various bodily organs (eyes, ears, etc.) and the activities (functions) that are correlated with them and their unique faculties (the power to see, to hear, etc.).[36] But it is perhaps obvious that to say all this is not to resolve all or even most of the difficulties, since the problems are indeed many and deep here. Causality, especially in the way Aristotle uses this term, is not easier than meaning and meaning is not easy at all. And unless one was able to give an account of this relationship of causality that presumably holds between a property F and its correlated function Φ but not between G and Φ, although G is necessarily and uniquely related to F, one would not have advanced very far. But these are problems which go beyond the scope of this paper.

Now, as we all know, Aristotle took man to have a

function.[37] But, as critics of Aristotle never fail to point out, this is not at all obvious. It is not obvious that there is a characteristic activity, or work, or product that pertains to humans. There seems to be no verb that comes to mind easily which is associated with "man"--at least not in the way we have verbs associated with "lyre-player", "builder", "eye", etc. and not even in the way the verb "to father" is associated with "father", a case where the existence of such a verb puts the noun clearly into the functional class, although the meaning of the verb, and hence the function, is unclear.[38] Aristotle however gives some arguments in the *N.E.* to show that man has a function. Whether these arguments are good or bad (and everyone takes them to be bad) is not our concern here, since they do not seem to be the real reasons even to Aristotle for taking man to have a function or assimilating "man" to functional nouns. Aristotle then proceeds to identify the function of man as the activity that is correlated with the essential feature of the human species, i.e. the possession of the reasoning faculty. And this would clearly be the function correlated to humans *qua* humans and be properly called *the* function of humans; or, as Aristotle puts it, without qualification (*haplōs*), in contrast to other functions that may be true of some, or even of all humans, by virtue of different properties or capacities--e.g. growing, seeing, building, learning grammar, etc. It is interesting to ask here whether Aristotle takes the function of man to be a single activity or takes the noun "man" to have a single verb correlated with it, in contrast to many activities or many correlated verbs. This is not an altogether clear question, for it is not obvious as to what is to count as a single activity. Is building one activity or many? But the linguistic counterpart of this question seems to be easier to understand, for it deals with the identity and individuation of linguistic items (verbs). So in the case of a builder we have a single verb associated with the term "builder" and we may say here that we have one activity as well. In the function argument Aristotle speaks in the process of identifying the function of man of the dual role of reason in the exercise of

the intellect in pure thinking and in action. This in itself is
not clear and is not developed in this section of the text, but
he also speaks of the activity of the soul (*psychēs energeia*)
and actions (*praxeis*) as the function of man. And again at
times he speaks in the plural of the activities of the soul
related to function as if they are many. But it is obvious that
even in the function argument itself Aristotle seems to think
primarily of a single activity, however we construe "single"
here. So at 1098a7 he takes it to have been established
(although it is given in hypothetical form here since it
functions as a premise) that "If then the function of man is
an activity of the soul (*psychēs energeia*)..." And the same is
true in the final definition of the good of man as an activity
of the soul (*psychēs energeia*, 1098a16). A careful
examination of the text shows, with a few exceptions where
he speaks of activities, that he mostly refers to the function
and the good and happiness of man in the singular, an
activity (*energeia*).[39] Admittedly this evidence is not
conclusive, since "activity of the soul" could very well be
taken to mean "the exercise of the faculties of the soul," as
some have taken it to mean[40] and not necessarily imply a
single activity. But what we also see in the development of
the *N.E.*, and especially in Book X, is the emergence and
dominating role of the verb "to contemplate" (*theōrein*) and
its cognates as the unique activity of the distinguishing
element of man. There is then this tendency in Aristotle to
assimilate man to the things that have a single activity as their
function, or "man" with the one-verb class of functional
nouns. The reasons for this assimilation are not too clear, but
we might consider two things that may have influenced him.
First, he usually takes as his examples things that have a
single activity associated with them as a function, or nouns
with a single verb correlated with them—builder, doctor,
lyre-player, eye, ear, etc. are the examples he uses in the
function argument. These are the paradigms with which he
usually deals and therefore he might have assimilated man to
these. Second, and more important, is his belief that to one
organ or faculty corresponds one function or use and that

this is a principle exemplified in all nature.[41] If one accepts such a principle–and there is no doubt that Aristotle and Plato accept it, for it underlies the whole theory of the *Republic*–and takes the rational element to be a distinct element and the organ of reasoning (contemplation or thought) one most likely would take the function of man to be a single activity. But the importance of this question goes beyond the interest in determining in which class of nouns (or things) Aristotle puts "man" (or man) in relation to function. It is important in relation to an interesting problem that has been discussed recently, namely whether Aristotle conceived of the human good as a single thing and identified it with the activity of contemplation, or thought of the good as consisting of the many activities, actions and goals that constitute human life.[42] This question cannot be resolved here, but I would like to point out that if indeed Aristotle assimilated "man" to the one-verb class of nouns as far as the function of man is concerned and if he identified the good and the function, then there is no room for choice: he had to accept the first alternative, the good of man being a single activity.

I would now like to suggest that Aristotle takes the expression "the good of F" to have the attributive character also and that it is this belief on his part that accounts for certain segments of the text and in part explains why he introduces the function argument in relation to the good. I believe that the whole of the discussion about the good in the *N.E.* and *E.E.* presupposes this character of the good, although it is not identified as clearly and explicitly as one would have liked. It is of course obvious that the account of the good he gives has this attributive feature since it is given in terms of two interrelated notions–virtue and function--that have the attributive character. But this cannot be used as evidence that he took the notion of the good to have the attributive feature independently of his own account of the good and that his account itself aims in part at explaining this feature. But Aristotle does speak of the good of a doctor as being health–and in general he speaks of the various goods of those who exercise the many arts or skills–but does not infer from this and the fact that a doctor is a man that the good of man is health. And the reason for this is not merely the fact that not all men are doctors. For even if this were so, it would not follow that the good of man is health as it does not follow that the good of man is the good of an animal with the faculty of nutrition, although all men possess such faculty. The good of some F is characterized by him as proper, *oikeion* or *idion*, terms which have a variety of meanings; but understood in one way he often uses them to describe other things which clearly have the attributive character (virtue or function). Liddell and Scott give "proper to its nature" as one of the meanings of *oikeion* and it is clearly taken in this sense when Aristotle characterizes the function of F as *oikeion*.[43] The function of x then *qua* F is proper to its being an F and the most important of the functions that may be true of something is the one that is proper to its essential nature, that corresponds to the essential characterization of x. The function of a man *qua* doctor is then proper to his being a doctor or to the nature of a doctor, whereas his function *qua* man is proper to his (essential) nature as man. But this is perhaps brought out more clearly in his use of *oikeios* in relation to virtue.[44] For as he points out in *Met.* 1021b21 something is complete if "...in respect of excellence (virtue-*aretē*) and goodness it can't be excelled in its kind; e.g. we have a complete doctor or a complete flute-player, when they lack nothing in respect of the form of their proper (*oikeias*) excellence (*aretēs*)." If indeed the role of *oikeios* is to mark the connection between the excellence, function, etc. of F and its being characterized as F, then the proper good (*oikeion agathon*) of F must have the same connection. And again it is the same connection that is marked by the use of *idios* in this context. For in its most characteristic use in Aristotle's works it is used to mark the connection between something and its function, or the function of something and a set of objects which are associated with the function.[45] To characterize then the good of F as *idion* of F is to mark this connection that holds between its being F and the good of F. So when Aristotle takes health to be the peculiar (*idion*) good of the body he rules out that health is the good of man as man, although a man has a body and the good of an animal *qua* possessing a living body is health. Similarly with the case of sight as the good of the eye and of an organism *qua* seeing organism.

If then I am correct in claiming that Aristotle takes the interrelated notions of good F, the virtue of F, the function of F and the good of F to be attributive, we can perhaps understand that curious passage of the *N.E.* in the opening lines of the function argument--that the good and the "well" of things that have a function may be found in their function--as well as understand partly the motivation for introducing the function argument. For one way of reading this line is to take the "well" as the virtue or the doing well of some F which has a function. And this would perhaps indicate that Aristotle was clear that the two notions of the good of F and the virtue of F (or the doing well of F) share the same logical feature and may therefore be given a similar analysis. An analysis of "the good of F" in terms of the function of F (the associated verb Φ) would capture and explain the attributive feature of the good and perhaps even tell us what the good of F is. And Aristotle's general conclusion is that the good of F, when F has a function, is the doing of that function in accordance with the excellence of F. In the case of man the good of man is the performance of man's function--the unique activity of his soul--in accordance with the excellence of man. Leaving aside questions about the truth or falsity of the above analysis of the good of F, it is evident that it accounts for the attributive character of the notion of the good of F, since it is in terms of two other interrelated notions that have the attributive character also.

I therefore take the functional argument as being important for Aristotle's account of the good, despite the fact that it appears to be out of context in the *N.E.* and unrelated to the long and rather elaborate discussion of the good of man in terms of the nature and structure of desires.

For the argument in part aims at giving an account of a logical feature of the notion of the good of something.[46] And to see the importance of the function argument it is worth considering whether Aristotle would have been able to account for the attributive character of the good in terms of the first line of argument alone, i.e. the "desire argument" that takes the good of man to be the ultimate object of desire, the end of all desire.

As was pointed out at the beginning of this paper, in the course of the desire argument Aristotle defines the concepts of highest (supreme), most final and self-sufficient good. These definitions do not by themselves show or imply that there is such a thing which is the highest good, etc., of man and Aristotle does not take them to do so. But as Professor Williams has pointed out, they do imply that there can be at most one supreme good and at most one most final good and at most one self-sufficient good. Moreover, if there is a supreme good (x) and if there is a most final good (y) and if there is a self-sufficient good (z), then these are one and the same thing (x=y=z). In any case Aristotle concludes that as a matter of fact there is such a thing that satisfies the definition, namely happiness.[47] So he could have used these definitions and the accepted opinions (*doxai*) about, or considered what he calls the "phenomena" in relation to, happiness or the highest good in order to identify what happiness and the good is.[48] Here he might have examined, for example, what humans claim to, or in fact, desire or pursue in order to determine what object as a matter of fact is the ultimate object (if any at all) of their desires or pursuits and whether it also satisfies the conditions of being most final and self-sufficient. Such a procedure would have ruled out wealth, honor, virtue, etc. as the highest good, as in fact Aristotle rules them out by applying such a procedure,[49] and may have led perhaps to the identification of the good and happiness.

Now such a procedure–like all procedures–may, of course, not be successful, for one may fail to hit upon the right thing and thus to identify the end of man. But this is not the problem here. For even if the procedure were to be successful, it would not account for the attributive nature of the good. Desire, in the ordinary sense of the term, is not attributive. The term "desire" does not seem to attach to the term that identifies a certain kind in expressions of the form "Some F desires O". For consider the simplest expressions involving "desire". "This man desires O" is analyzable into "A is a man and a desires O." Or a general statement "Man desires O" is analyzable into "If x is a man, x desires O." And the same would be true even if what was involved were unique desires. Suppose, for example, that desire for wealth were a unique desire to humans. This would give us that "x is a man if and only if x desires wealth." And this would allow inferences of the type that should be excluded if desire were attributive. But we might attempt here to connect desires to descriptions and therefore make expressions of desire attributive also. We might, for example, argue that certain desires for certain things belong to man not as man, but as being an animal, whereas some desires which are related to his being a man, or to man's essence, belong to him as being a man. Such a way of thinking would not be foreign to Aristotle,[50] but there is no evidence that in the desire argument he took desires in this sense. He rejects virtue, wealth, and honor as the good of man in that argument not because these things are not the objects of desires that belong to man *qua* man, but because they fail to satisfy the definitions of highest, most perfect and self-sufficient end. But it is important to realize that if the program of construing desires attributively were viable, one would be able to account for the attributive nature of the good by using the notions of desire together with the notions of the nature, or essence, of something in order to single out that desire which belongs to a class of things in virtue of their essential characteristics. It is also important that we keep the nature of desires clear when we attempt to construe them attributively, especially in the case of the desires that we take to apply to something as characterized by its essential features. For it is easy in this context, as it is obvious from the recent literature, to move from desires to interests or purposes, notions which lend themselves to the attributive analysis much easier than desire does, precisely because they seem to be connected more closely than desire is with the notion of what something is or the essence of something. Now Aristotle seems to be talking about desires (occurring or standing or dispositional) and not merely interest, where there may be no desire at all.

I have assumed then here that when Aristotle speaks of the end of man (builder, flute-player, doctor, etc.) in the desire argument he thinks of the object, or goal, of desire or pusuit: that he is thinking of a psychological state, or attitude, of an agent, or organism, and its associated object or goal. Traditional commentators have always understood Aristotle to be speaking of desires, or pursuits, and their ends in the ordinary sense of these terms. For he uses in this context terms like "wish" (*boulēsis*) which signifies a species of desire, what he calls *orexis*; at other times he uses *orexis* itself, leaving it open which kind of desire is involved.[51] And he often speaks of the good as what is pursued (*diōketai*),[52] and as the end of (all) action (*praxeōn*) or what can be done (*tōn praktōn*).[53] But it is Aristotle's view in his ethical and psychological works that one element of action is a species of desire (*orexis*), and the end of action is the end of desire in one form or another.[54] Let us call this conception of end "orectic end."

Although I do not want to question the traditional interpretation of Aristotle's views concerning the notion of end, nor to examine the evidence in any detail here, I would like nonetheless to consider briefly this other notion of end which appears to have the attributive character. For besides speaking of the ends of agents or organisms--that is, beings that can have desires, pursuits, or psychological states or attributes in general--he at times speaks of the ends of arts, sciences, artifacts, parts of living body, social and political organizations, etc.[55] In the opening chapter of the *N.E.*, for example, he attributes ends (*telos*) to medicine (health), art of shipbuilding (a vessel), art of strategy (victory), domestic economy (wealth), etc. In later chapters he attributes an end to the science of politics, mathematical knowledge, and science (knowledge) in general. Now Aristotle does not attribute desire to any of these things. He explicitly rules out in the discussion of desire in the *De Anima* the possibility that something has desire without possessing a soul. For desire is a faculty of the soul, although not of all souls--the most elementary living organisms (e.g. plants) have souls that have the nutritive faculty only. But even in the case of an organism that has a soul with the faculty of desire, the parts of the body of such an organism do not have desire.

In what sense then do these things have ends, if they cannot be said to have desires or pursuits? It is natural to suppose here that, since there are organisms or agents associated with such things, to speak of the ends of such things is really a way of speaking of the ends (i.e. the object of the desires or pursuits) of the organisms or agents associated with them. The case of the arts (crafts) is the clearest example in this connection. Aristotle takes the agent who practices a certain art and the art to have the same end: health is the end of the art of medicine and of the physician; a house is the end of the art of building and of the builder, etc. However this is not obvious in other cases. We are all too familiar with the problems philosphers and political theorists have had in trying to show that the ends, or goals, of the citizens (the agents associated with the political association) are identical with ends of the state or the political association. But even if more cases were like the case of the arts or crafts and the identity of the ends of the agents and of the associated arts (or any other entity) were transparent, it is not obvious which is the more primitive notion here: the end of the art or the end of the agent who exercises the art. I am myself inclined to believe that Aristotle (and Plato) took the end of the art to be the more primitive notion of the two[56] and the end of the agent who exercises the art to be determined in terms of it, although I cannot discuss it and examine the text in detail here. But whatever the answer to this particular issue is, I would like to point out here that the move to reduce every claim about the end of a non-agent to a claim about the end of an agent, or organism, associated with the non-agent will not do. For how are we to account for the claims that parts of a living body have ends? Or that plants have ends? Such claims need not and cannot be reduced to claims about the ends of an agent as objects, or goals, of his desires or pursuits. Now this non-orectic notion of end is attributive and Aristotle understands it in terms of the notion of function. All of the things that we mentioned above in relation to the non-orectic notion of end he takes as functional. As it was pointed out earlier, there are good reasons to believe that in the desire argument Aristotle speaks of the good as an end in the orectic sense of end. The line however between the orectic and non-orectic sense of the term is not always clear in Aristotle when he talks about the end and the good, although he is clear about the distinction.[57] But it is quite clear that if Aristotle was thinking of the good as an end in the non-orectic sense, he would have had an explanation for the attributive nature of the good ready-made and it would have been again in terms of the notion of function.

I take then the function argument in relation to the good and in general the functional analysis of terms related to "the good" as quite important for Aristotle's ethical views, since these arguments, or analyses, aim at accounting for an important logical feature that these related terms possess. But is the functional argument (or analysis) of the good of F necessary in order to account for the attributive nature of the good and is Aristotle's analysis sufficient by itself to show that the good of F is what Aristotle says it is? Aristotle gives this argument in the *N.E.* with no apparent reference to the desire argument, so it looks as if he took it to be sufficient by itself in order to give an account of the good without any reference to the desire argument. Indeed, the desire argument seems to be redundant. And it is not obvious that there may not be other ways of accounting for the attributive nature of the good. For example, one might argue that "good" is a comparative term and its attributive nature is to be accounted in the same way that the attributive nature of other comparative terms (real, large, etc.) is accounted for and not in terms of the notion of function. But even if one were successful in showing that the attributive character of the good of F can be explained only by connecting it to the function of F, this would not be enough in order to show that *identifying* the good of F with the function of F is the only way to account for the attributiveness of the good, for there may be other things (e.g. virtue) that are related to function (and therefore attributive) that could account for the attributiveness of the good.

There is no doubt that the function argument or analysis is problematic, as commentators of the Aristotelian texts have often pointed out. I will not however discuss the argument in detail here, but only make a few remarks about the general questions we raised above. To begin with, the conclusion and the general principle that underlies Aristotle's conclusion–the good of F is doing the function of F in accordance with the virtue(s) of F–seems to be by itself counter-intuitive. It seems indeed to diverge from ordinary conceptions of what the good of something is and seems in need of further argument that would make the claim that doing one's function is the good more acceptable. Aristotle seems to have been aware of this counter-intuitive aspect of his conclusions and most probably this is what motivates the rather elaborate discussion in Book I of the *N.E.* aiming at showing that his conclusions about the good and happiness of man are not inconsistent with and do not diverge from the ordinary conceptions about the good and happiness. But I do not really want to press this point about the intuitiveness or counter-intuitiveness of Aristotle's conclusions. For after all, how many of the most interesting things that philosophers have said are not counter-intuitive?

What rather is more important here is whether the functional analysis by itself forces us to identify the function of F with the good of F in order to account for the attributive nature of the good or whether there are indeed other possibilities here. For clearly there are other things that satisfy the attributive condition as well--why are not they taken to be the good? Why not, for example, the excellence (virtue) itself of F--i.e. the necessary and sufficient conditions for doing the function of F well. This would satisfy the attributive condition, or at least Aristotle takes it to do so. It would also be more intuitively correct to take as the good of the eye, for example, the excellence (virtue) of the eye--its power, or capacity, to see efficiently--rather than the activity of seeing (its function).[58] It is interesting to point out here that Aristotle himself in at least one place (*E.E.* 1218a32-33) takes the good of the eye to be its power or capacity to see (*opsis*), i.e. its excellence, and not the activity of seeing (*horasis*), i.e. the exercise of its power or capacity (its function). And he also takes in the passage referred to above the good of the body to be its health (its excellence) and not the activities that result from health (its function). Now Aristotle had reasons for not taking the virtue of F to be the good of F, although it is a good for F. He explicitly tells us in the *N.E.* that virtue is not the most final end, since it is not desired only for its own sake and can be desired for the sake of something else. In a similar argument in the *E.E.* he argues that although excellence is a good the function or work (*ergon*) that corresponds to an excellence is a greater good since it is the end.[59] It is clear, however, that the considerations Aristotle brings forth in order to eliminate the possibility that the virtue of F is the good of F and at the same time to support his claim that the doing of the function of F is the good F derive from the desire argument and his discussion of the good as the end.

Again, why not take what the function of F brings about, or produces, to be the good of F? These "products" are taken by Aristotle to have the attributive function also. And again this appears more intuitive as an account of the good of F, for the good is explained in terms of something which the performance of a function, the exercise of an activity, brings about--a certain good or object that is attained. Consider here some typical and uninteresting products, such as a house (building), a shoe (shoemaking), a vessel (ship-building)--to use some of Aristotle's examples; and some less typical and more interesting products such as wealth, power, and finally, pleasure which has often been taken to be the product for which all activities are done. But there is something quite interesting going on in the Aristotelian texts in relation to the possibility of taking the product of the function of F as the good of F that again underscores how strong the connection between function, end and good is in Aristotle's mind.

We normally take the function of something to be an activity or at least a process that something undergoes.[60] And Aristotle himself gives as the most paradigmatic examples of function characteristic activities of things. Consider, for example, the cases he gives in the functional argument itself: the various craftsmen or artisans and their functions–flute-player, sculptor, carpenter, shoemaker all having characteristic activities; the various parts of the body: eye, hand, foot and "each of the various parts of the body," some of which have clearly a characteristic activity (eye), while others not so clearly, but can be understood to have a variety of activities associated with them; lastly we are given nutrition, growth and sensation as the functions of the various faculties of souls and some of these are clearly more like processes than activities. But it would be a mistake to conclude from all these and our intuitive understanding of the notion of function that Aristotle takes the function of F to be necessarily an activity related in a certain way to F. For he draws a distinction between the use or exercise (*chrēsis*) of something (tool, part of body, art, etc.) and that which results from the use or exercise of it. Now the use or exercise of F is what we take normally to be the function of F--e.g. seeing is the use of the eye, building is the exercise of the art of being a builder, etc. But Aristotle says that where the use or exercise of F result into something which is distinct or different from the use or exercise of F the result (product) is the function of F (and not the use or exercise).[61] In contrast, in the cases where nothing distinct or different results from the use or exercise of F, the function of F is the use or exercise of F.

Consider, for example, the cases he gives to illustrate this point at *E.E.* 1219a13-24. I give them here in the form of a table. (The terms in brackets do not occur in this segment of the text, but most of them are given in many other places by Aristotle and can be easily supplied.)

	A Art, Faculty Capacity	B Agent, Organ	C Activity, use of the Art	D Function of A, B, C,
1.	Building *oikodomēsis*	Builder *oikodomos*	Activity of Building *oikodomēsis*	House *oikia*
2.	Medicine *iatrikē*	[Physician] [*iatros*]	Healing-curing *hugiansis-iatreusis*	Health *hygieia*
3.	Shoemaking *skutotomikē*	Shoemaker *skuteus*	Activity of Shoemaking *skuteusis*	Shoe *hypodēma*
4.	Sight *opsis*	[Eye] [*ophthalmos*]	Seeing *horasis*	Seeing
5.	Mathematical Science *mathematikē epistemē*	Mathematician *mathematikos*	Contemplation *theōria*	Contemplation

In the last two cases the function is the use or exercise of the art, science, faculty or organ, whereas in the others it is not. One may suggest here that even in the cases where the activity is not the function we can think of an activity that is very close to the thing that the art produces--e.g. we can think of *making* a house, *making* someone healthy, or *making* a shoe, and these will be the respective functions of the arts. But this will not do, for it is precisely this that Aristotle wants to deny here--the function is not the activity or process of making a house (the use or exercise of the art or capacity) but the house itself, which is not a use, or an activity, or process, or exercise of an art. (*Oikodomikēs oikia all'ouk oikodomēsis kai iatrikēs hygieia all' ouch hygiansis oud' iatreusis*--the function of the art of building is a house, not the process of building, that of medicine health, not the process of healing or curing.) Aristotle's text brings this out very clearly, since some of the terms that signify the use, or exercise, of an art, or faculty, mean just what one is tempted to substitute in order to convert the products into activities--e.g. *oikodomēsis* means making a house and *hygiansis* means making someone healthy--and the morphology of these terms makes this plain. So what he denies here is that the function of the art of building (medicine, etc.) is the making of a house--*oikodomēsis*--(making someone healthy--*hygiansis*--etc.)

Now there are a host of problems that arise in this context and most clearly the perennial problem of the individuation of actions and activities surfaces again in relation to the specifying of the function of something. There is however no room to discuss these issues here. The more interesting question in relation to our concerns is about Aristotle's criterion for determining that in some cases the function is the use or exercise of that thing while in others it is the product that results from the use or exercise and about the basis of this criterion. In some cases it is perhaps easy to see whether the use or exercise of an art or faculty has a result, or produces something, which is different and distinct from such use or exercises. And such are the cases that Aristotle gives. But undoubtedly there will be cases where it would be hard to say where the use or exercise ends and the product begins and there would be problems in deciding which is the function in such cases. And how can we tell that nothing results from even the clearest cases that Aristotle gives where the use of exercise of something is the function of that thing? What if something did result in such cases?[62] What if something resulted from seeing? What if something resulted from health--the activities of the body for example? And again how can we tell what *the* product is that results from the use or exercise of F? These are questions about the basis of Aristotle's distinction. The answer that first comes to mind here is that in some cases the *use* or *exercise* of F is the terminal point, whereas in other cases *what results* from the use or exercise of F is the terminal point. So in the case of the eye and sight the activity of seeing is the terminal point, whereas in the case of building the house is the terminal point. Although I cannot discuss this in detail here, it is obvious that this is not the whole answer here. Viewing the phenomena that Aristotle took to be functional phenomena simply as sequences which terminate in something (use or product) which we then take as the function would not account for the fact that he views these phenomena as essentially teleological. Without examining the texts in detail here, I would like to point out that the function of something is not merely the terminus of a sequence of events, processes, activities, or what have you, but rather the end of these in the sense that it is that for the sake of which the members of a sequence exist or are done.[63] The house then is the function of building and of the builder not only because it is the terminal point of the activity or process of building, but because it also (and primarily) is that for the sake of which building is undertaken and the art exists.

Let us now return to our original question. Why can't we take the good of F to be what results from, or is the product of, the doing of the function of F? I think we can now see that it is not possible and why it is not possible, given the above teleological conception of function. For in those cases where we clearly have something that is produced by the characteristic activity or use of F and in which we would normally take the product as the end and good of F, Aristotle takes the product to be the function. And this rules out the possibility of there being something brought about by the function of F and distinct from F that would qualify for being the good of F--for it would be the function of F according to Aristotle.[64] The most interesting case in this context is the case of pleasure, something that has often been taken to be the product of many activities and that for the sake of which most activities are pursued--doctrines that were familiar to Aristotle. It is interesting to point out that Aristotle took pleasure itself to be attributive. He speaks of the proper pleasure of a species and he connects this to the characteristic activity and function of the species and in general he takes pleasure to be inseparable from their activities.[65] Pleasure then would be a reasonable candidate to consider as the good. But, as we know, Aristotle did not want to embrace hedonism, in one form or another. It is important to see how problematic it was for him to turn down pleasure as the good given his views on function. For either some one type of pleasure is distinct and different from the characteristic activity of man or it is identical with it. But accepting either side leads into hedonism. Taking the latter alternative makes pleasure identical with the function of man, hence the good of man. But if one takes the former alternative, applying Aristotle's criterion stipulating that when something distinct and separate results from the characteristic activity, then it is the function, one is led back into hedonism. There seems very little room to move here, and Aristotle makes what seems like an impossible move: he denies each of the possibilities separately and therefore seems to assert both of them. According to the notorious doctrine of the *N.E.* pleasure is neither identical with nor different from the characteristic activity of man and therefore it seems to be both identical and different from it.[66] It is not clear or certain that Aristotle's account of pleasure took the form it took for just these reasons, but it is obvious the account he gives is the only move possible to someone who holds the views he held about function and wants at the same time to avoid hedonism.

I have been arguing here that in certain cases Aristotle clearly relies on certain principles that derive from the desire argument, or are at least based on certain teleological views of his, in order to eliminate certain things from being the good of man and strengthen his own position that the performing of the human function (the exercise of intellect, or contemplative activity) is the good of man. But Aristotle relies on many different principles and introduces a variety of considerations which seem to be unrelated to the desire argument or to his teleological views. At times this is misleading, for what lie behind some of these principles are precisely considerations that derive from the desire argument or his teleological views. Take, for example, the claim that having the dispositions to attain the good cannot be the good or happiness. It is clear that what lies behind this claim is the proposition repeated over and over again that the activity associated with the disposition is the end. But there may very well be also instances where the considerations introduced by Aristotle do not derive from the sources mentioned above. Such seem to be the cases where Aristotle brings in many of the ordinary beliefs about the good and happiness and tries to show that they are consistent with his claims that the good and happiness is contemplative activity. And there are bound to be cases where the considerations introduced are such that it is difficult to tell whether they derive from the desire argument or broader teleological views or views altogether unrelated to matters of teleology and desire. In this class we would probably want to include the famous discussion in Book X of the *N.E.* about human perfection and identity (the true self) in terms of the performance of the human function (contemplation) and the extent to which humans can partake in divine happiness and approach the divine realm by exercising their contemplative power, the element that is most divine in them. These considerations are clearly too complex to be reduced to the nature of desires or to the nature of teleology in general and it would be a mistake to suppose that they can be, as some commentators have supposed. They are clearly connected with his deepest metaphysical and theological beliefs and cannot be easily separated from them. But even if we were successful in analyzing these considerations it is not obvious that they prove or support the contention that the performance of the function of something is what confers perfection, identity and is the good of that thing. For Aristotle himself seems to have held different opinions. At times he speaks of virtue itself as conferring perfection on something and as making it realize its nature.[67] And this seems to correspond with our intuitions better. For what makes something a perfect, or true, F is the possession of the excellence of an F. A knife is a perfect knife and realizes the nature of a knife fully if it has the powers that we take to be the excellence of the knife and not only when it exercises these powers.

My intent in bringing up these considerations is not to discuss the many problems surrounding them, but rather to point out that Aristotle relies on such considerations to strengthen his claim that the good F is to be analyzed in terms of the function of F. For as we saw, it is not necessary without the use of these other considerations to connect the function of F and the good of F in the way Aristotle connects them—namely, to identify them—in order to account for the attributive nature of the good. Commentators were of course quick to point out that the function argument would not do by itself—it would not give us the conclusion Aristotle wants about the good of F—and they were quick to suggest explanations as to how Aristotle got the conclusion, namely by fallacious reasoning or gross equivocations on his part. I myself doubt that these are the problems with Aristotle's argument, although I do not mean to deny that he was perfectly capable of reasoning fallaciously or commiting gross equivocations. On the contrary I believe that the problems lie much deeper in his conception of the good as an end, its connection to desire and his broad teleological views that encompass almost all of his philosophical thought. There is no doubt that desire plays a central role in his conception of the good and almost all readers of Aristotle have recognized this. H. A. Prichard may have gone overboard, as Austin points out, in arguing that Aristotle took the relation between "being good (*agathon*)" and "being desired" to be one of identity of meaning. But Austin himself did not deny that there is a relation. He found only that "the relation between 'being *agathon*' and 'being desired' is one of the most baffling puzzles in Aristotle's, or for that matter Plato's, ethical theory."[68] But in addition to the puzzling relation between "being a good" and "being desired" there is the problem of how clearly Aristotle distinguished between the notion of end as the object of desire (orectic end) and the notion of end as applies to teleological systems without any reference to desires (non-orectic end) and whether he always kept them apart. I myself believe that what lies behind the function argument and what would make it valid is the notion of good as end, but it is not altogether clear in what sense the term "end" is used here, for Aristotle seems at least in this case not to have kept the notions of orectic and non-orectic end clearly apart. But this is the end of another project.[69]

Notes

1. For a discussion of the role of knowledge and its place in the philosophic conception of the good life see Werner Jaeger, *Aristotle* (Oxford University Press), pp. 426-461.

2. *Diog.* II 10.

3. *E.E.* 1215b6. I will use hereafter *E.E.* and *N.E.* for *Eudemian Ethics* and *Nicomachean Ethics* respectively.

4. *Theaetetus* 174a.

5. According to Aristoxenus, quoted from W. Jaeger, *op.cit.,* p. 434, "and it happened to most of those who heard Plato give his lecture on the good: everyone came expecting to learn something about those recognized human goods such as wealth, health, strength, and in general some wonderful happiness; but when it became plain that his discussion was about mathematics and numbers and geometry and astronomy and finally that good is One, I think it seemed an absolute paradox to them. Thereupon some of them despised the matter and others condemned it."

6. Bernard Williams has argued that Aristotle takes it as an intensional property of happiness that it cannot be desired for the sake of anything else. Whether this is so or not, does not affect what I am saying here. See Williams' paper for a discussion of the desire argument, "Aristotle on the Good: A Formal Sketch ," *The Philosophical Quarterly*, Vol. 12, No. 49, October 1962.

7. J. L. Austin, *"AGATHON and EUDAIMONIA* in the *Ethics* of Aristotle," in J.M.E. Moravcsik (Editor), *Aristotle* (Notre Dame: University of Notre Dame Press, 1968), p. 282; John M. Cooper, *Reason and Human Good in Aristotle* (Cambridge: Harvard University Press, 1975), p. 146. There is no reference made to the function argument in the paper by H.A. Prichard, "The Meaning of *Agathon* in the Ethics of Aristotle," in Moravcsik, *op. cit.;* the function argument is however briefly discussed in the important paper by W.F.R. Hardie, "The Final Good in Aristotle's Ethics," in Moravcsik, *op. cit.*

8. Actually Aristotle does not use the exact phrase "x is the (a) good of ——" in the case of man. The closest he comes is at *N.E.* 1097a27 (the good in the case of man–*to agathon...tō anthrōpō*) and *E.E.* 1218b26 (using the same phrase). He does use however "human good" (*To anthrōpinon agathon*) repeatedly: *N.E.* 1094b7, 1098a16, 1102a14 and *E.E.* 1217a23; also "human goods" (*Ta anthrōpina agatha*): *N.E.* 1140b21, 1141b8 and *E.E.* 1217a23.

9. The occurrences of *agathon* in its incomplete form are too numerous to list here. The claim that "x is a good" is always used in relation to someone, or some y (the relational view), is made by Geach and is one of his main criticisms against the Oxford moralists and the intuitionists who, according to him, failed to see this relational character of the good but instead searched for the good without any reference to anything. See P.T. Geach, "Good and Evil," *Analysis,* Vol. 17, No. 2, December 1956.

10. E.G. sight is the good of the eye and health is the good of the body (*E.E.* 1218a32); health is the good of medicine, victory of strategy, etc. (*N.E.* 1097a20).

11. Cf. B. Williams, *op. cit.,* pp. 292-295, where he discusses whether Aristotle's definitions of highest, most final and self-sufficient good (end) imply the existence of a single good (i.e. happiness) or whether he arrives at the conclusion that such a good (end) exists on the basis of *a posteriori* considerations; but it nonetheless follows from his definitions that there could only be one such good. To say that Aristotle took the good in the case of man to be a single thing appears to be touching upon a controversial matter. This controversy stems primarily from the work of W.F.R. Hardie, *op. cit.,* and his distinction between two conceptions of the good, i.e. as a dominant end and as an inclusive end; and his claim that in some instances at least Aristotle takes the good as an inclusive end. This issue has been discussed recently by J. Cooper, *op. cit.,* pp. 98ff, where he opts for the inclusive-end conception at least in the *E.E.* (an early work according to him) in contrast to the

tendency to view the good as a dominant end in the *N.E.* (a later work according to him). But see A. Kenny, *The Aristotelian Ethics* (Oxford: Oxford University Press, 1979) where he argues that the *N.E.* precedes the *E.E.* in date of composition, the latter being Aristotle's mature work. Kenny also takes Aristotle to have held the dominant-end view of the good in the *N.E.*: see A. Kenny, "Happiness," in J. Feinberg (Editor) *Moral Concepts* (Oxford: Oxford University Press, 1970), pp. 43-53. To say however here that Aristotle took the good in the case of man to be a single thing is not to take sides in the above controversy. For all I am saying here is that he took the good to be happiness, whatever that may turn out to be, in the same way he identified some one thing to be the good in various other cases (e.g. the body, eye, medicine, etc.)

12. This way of distinguishing between the good of a certain thing, or kind of thing, and the other things that are good for it is adopted by G. H. von Wright, *The Varieties of Goodness* (London: Routledge and Kegan Paul, 1968). Although Aristotle does not use exactly the same means for distinguishing the good of F from what is good for F he does make a similar distinction. See below.

13. See, for example, the use of *oikeion agathon* in *N.E.* 1173a5, 1178a6 and the use of *idion agathon* in *E.E.* 1218a30.

14. Cf. *N.E.* 1096b15 where he distinguishes between goods in themselves and goods as a means to these; *N.E.* 1097a19 and 1096a7 where wealth is argued to be good for man but useful (*chrēsimon*) and for the sake (*charin*) of the good of man; also *E.E.* 1218b20 where some of the good things for F are the causes of the good of F, e.g. wholesomeness is a cause of (contributes to) health, the good of the body.

15. P. Ziff has discussed the common tendency of taking "good" as an adjective and some of the problems that result from this common move. See his *Semantic Analysis* (Ithaca: Cornell University Press, 1967), Ch. VI. Ziff is of course correct in doubting that "good" functions as an adjective, for, as we shall see, in some cases at least it really plays the role of an adverb.

16. See P. Geach, *op. cit.* J.L. Austin discusses a number of other terms--especially "real", but also briefly "good"--which have the peculiar logical features of being "substantive hungry" and not detachable from the substantive. See his *Sense and Sensibilia* (New York: Oxford University Press, 1964), Ch. VIII. This feature was of course noticed by Aristotle and not only in the case of "good". See the discussion of "perfect"*(teleios)*in *Met.* 1021b12.

17. Geach takes this to show just by itself that G.E. Moore was fundamentally mistaken in treating the good to be like yellow, a simple quality. See Geach, *op. cit.* I shall use the distinction between attributive and predicative uses in the narrow and strict sense given above and not in the wider sense given by S. Hampshire, "Ethics: A Defense of Aristotle," *University of Colorado Studies,* Vol. 3, (1967), where he construes the distinction as being primarily between uses where reasons and arguments are given and cases where no such things are given. For I do not see why we could not give arguments or reasons that something is yellow and has four feet.

18. See, for example, Philippa Foot, "Goodness and Choice" and R.M. Hare, "Descriptivism," in W.D. Hudson (Editor), *The Is-Ought Question* (London: St. Martin's Press, 1969).

19. Zeno Vendler, "The Grammar of Goodness," *The Philosophical Review,* Vol. LXXII, No. 4, October 1963.

20. As Vendler points out, besides the class of functional nouns with a single verb associated with them, there are other functional nouns where this is not so, but instead more than one verb may be associated with them. Vendler considers "father", "dog", and possibly "man" to fall in this category. Aristotle takes "horse" to belong in the more-than-one-verb class and he takes other nouns to be functional which would have to be put in this class (e.g. "hand", "foot", etc.).

21. Some contemporary philosophers (Foot and Vendler, for example) have taken the connection between F and its functions to be a connection of meaning. Aristotle views such connection not in terms of meaning, but rather in terms of what he calls the "nature of things".

22. For the use of *haplōs* to express that something applies (or fails to apply), or is true of, something without qualification, or simply, see also *N.E.* 1148a11 and 1148b16.

23. This term is used repeatedly by Aristotle as a synonym for "good" (*N.E.* 1098a9, 1098a12, 1106a20, 1152a21, 1180a35, etc.; *E.E.* 1219a22, 1219a23) and applies it to persons (*N.E.* 1098a15, 1099a23) and things (*E.E.* 1219a21). It therefore has no moral connotation. Liddell and Scott, *A Greek English Lexicon,* give "excellent of its kind" as the translation relevant in this context and take it as a synonym for *agathos.*

24. See, for example, *Met.* 988a17, 992b26, 993b12. J. Burnet in his edition of the *N.E.* takes *to eu* as synonymous with *to agathon.* Also Bonitz, in *Index Aristotelicus,* takes the occurrence of *to eu* in the

function argument as a synonym for *to agathon*.

25. Ross in the Oxford translations of the works of Aristotle correctly preserves the difference between *to agathon* (the good) and *to eu* by rendering the latter as the "the well", thus preserving its adverbial form. The same translation is adopted by J. Warrington, *Aristotle's Ethics* (London: Everyman's Library, 1963) and J. Welldon, *The N.E. of Aristotle* (London: Macmillan & Co., 1908). The difference between *to agathon* and *to eu* is blurred by assimilating the one into the other by J.L. Creed and A.E. Wardman in R. Bambrough (Editor), *The Philosophy of Aristotle* (N.Y.: Mentor, 1963); H. Rackham, *Aristotle: The N.E.* (The Loeb Classical Library); and M. Ostwald, *Aristotle: The N.E.* (The Library of Liberal Arts).

26. Some of these, e.g. "hand" or "foot", do not belong in the class of nouns that have a single verb associated with them and it is not clear what the function of the hand or foot is. Nonetheless Aristotle, taking often as his main examples the eye and the ear, considers all bodily organs and parts to be paradigmatic cases of functional things.

27. He speaks of human virtue (*anthrōpinē aretē*) in contrast to the other excellences that a human being might have (*N.E.* 1102a14). See also *Met.* 1019b24 where he talks of the proper (*oikeia*) excellence belonging to each thing–e.g. to a thief or scandal-monger.

28. See *N.E.* 1106a 15-20. This conception of virtue is obviously the conception Plato puts forth at the end of Book I of the *Republic*.

29. Hence the dispute among scholars as to whether virtue is to be determined in terms of function or the other way around, seems to be clearly answered by Aristotle: the function of something is the primary notion. But it is another matter whether Aristotle follows his theoretical program when he discusses the virtues of man.

30. See the use of *aretē anthrōpou* (virtue of man) at *N.E.* 1106a22; *aretē anthrōpinē* (human virtue) at *N.E.* 1102a14, b3 and *E.E.* 1219b16. See also *E.E.* 1219b35 where he rules out the virtues (excellences) of nutrition and growth as the human virtue, since these characteristics are not the essential properties of man.

31. See *Physics* 191b5. And this of course goes back to Plato, *Republic I*.

32. See also *E.E.* 1219b40 where nutrition and growth are ruled out as the characteristic aspects of man, whereas, "if considered as a man"

(*ei hē anthrōpos*), he must possess a reasoning faculty.

33. Almost all the commentaries on Aristotle's text take the function of F to be a unique or peculiar activity of F—see the commentaries by Joachim, Burnet and Stewart to mention only a few; also A. Kenny, "Happiness," *op. cit.* and Hampshire, *op. cit.* See also a similar account of function in terms of uniqueness or necessary and sufficient conditions by E Nagel, "Teleological Explanations and Teleological Systems" in B.A. Brody (Editor), *Readings in the Philosophy of Science* (Prentice-Hall, Inc., 1970), pp. 106-120. Obviously there are problems here. As Hampshire points out, why not take the activity of imagining as the function of man. Moreover, if the function of F is to be represented as Fx $\longleftrightarrow$ Φx (Nagel), it is not clear that we can tell which is the function here-- Φ or F. One may think here that Φ is the function, since it is an activity. But contrary to the common belief, the function need not be an activity and it is not in many cases that Aristotle gives. See below.

34. See the discussion of causality in the *Physics,* in particular the causal relation between faculties or arts and their respective activities and products at 191b5, 195b22, 197a14; also the discussion of necessary and accidental causality in *Met.* 1026b and 1027a where he again discusses various arts and faculties and their functions.

35. So if the essential feature of a species S is F, then Φ would be the function of S if F is the cause of Φ, in addition to the conditions of necessity and uniqueness. The activity then of imagining, suggested by Hampshire, would be ruled out as the function of man if the faculty of reasoning is the essential feature and we assume that the faculty of reasoning is not the cause of imagining. But there might be problems with the case of a faculty causing two activities. Aristotle seems to have been aware of just such cases in his scientific works and the notion of *parergon* (secondary function) is an attempt to deal with such instances; see *Parva Naturalia* 444a27, 473b24.

36. See *De Anima* 418a10, 425a15, and 425a29 where he discusses the faculties of sense, their functions and their objects.

37. It is important when discussing Aristotle's (and Plato's) views on function to avoid the common misconception of thinking it is necessary that F be used by someone in order for F to have a function. So Hampshire, *op. cit.,* insists that man is not used. And Joachim, *op. cit.,* seeing that there is a problem here, tries to argue that in some cases what F does while it is used coincides with what F does in virtue of its own nature. In some cases we could speak of the use of functional

things (e.g., shoe, coat, medicine, etc.--to use some of Aristotle's examples). But why is it necessary, and is it possible anyway, to speak of the use of the flute-player, the soul, the bodily organs, plants, etc.--to use Aristotle's examples again? In any case, what is wrong with putting man in the class of functional things that have a use? Those who object to doing so often insist that the function of man is not to be used. But clearly it is unlikely that the function of anything is just to be used; rather it is to be used for (doing) something--e.g. a knife is used for cutting, medicine for curing, etc. So why can't we say that every man is used by someone for (doing) something--e.g. reasoning, playing music, etc. If what the critics want to deny is that reasoning, playing music, etc., is like cutting in the case of the knife, i.e., that it rests *wholly* with the use, it would not be in disagreement with anything that Aristotle says.

38. And therefore it is not surprising that the transformation, or equivalence, "x is a good F $\longleftrightarrow$ x Φ *'s* well," which is characteristic of functional nouns (*a* is a good lyre-player $\longleftrightarrow$ *a* plays the lyre well), is not readily available in the case of "man". I know of no place (other than the function argument itself) where Aristotle asserts such an equivalence in the case of "man". He does assert however what derives from the commonsense conception of the happy man, namely the equivalence "*a* is a happy (*eudaimōn*) man $\longleftrightarrow$ *a* lives well (*eu dzēn*) and does well (*eu prattein*). But, as the commentators point out, these phrases are too vague and too ambiguous, implying at best a connection between "happiness" and "fortune" or "faring". So they do not really provide us with a verb (or verbs) to be associated with "man". But as soon as Aristotle "proves" to his satisfaction that man has a function (1098a4) he promptly gives an analysis of "good man" in terms of the transformation "x is a good F $\longleftrightarrow$ x Φ *'s* well". (1098a14)

39. In several places Aristotle uses the plural--*energeiai*: *N.E.* 1098b19, 1100b10, 1100b14, 1117a11; at other places he uses the singular--*energeia*: *N.E.* 1099b25, 1102a5, 1102a18, 1176b1, 1177a18, 1177a20, 1177b30; and in one place (1099a30) he writes: "And it is the best activities, or one activity which is the best of all (*mian toutōn tēn aristēn*) in which according to our definition happiness consists."

40. Rackham renders *psychēs energeia* as "the active exercise of the soul's faculties."

41. See *Parva Naturalia* 476a10 for a statement of the principle that one organ is for one use or purpose. But see *Parts of Animals* 659a23, 659b, 659b34, 660a and 660a19 for the claim that some things have more than one function.

42. See note 11 above.

43. Cf. *N.E.* 1139a17, 1167b34, 1175a36, 1176a5.

44. Cf. *N.E.* 1098a15, 1177a17.

45. See *idion agathon* at *E.E.* 1218a35 and 1218a35; and the use of *idios* to characterize the function and object of the various faculties of the soul in *De Anima* and *Parva Naturalia*.

46. Accounting for the attributive character of the good is only a part of what Aristotle is trying to do. For he is also, and primarily, trying to explain what the good is and this is also done by using the notion of function.

47. See footnote 11 above.

48. For a discussion of the importance and role of this approach in Aristotle's thought, see G.E.L. Owen, "*Tithenai Ta Phainomena,*" in J.M.E. Moravcsik, *op. cit.*

49. *N.E.* 1095b15–1096a10.

50. See *N.E.* 1118b5 where he says in reference to the sense to which profligacy is related that "it belongs to us not as human beings but as animals...it is bestial to revel in such pleasures and like them better than any others." And I have in mind also his tendency of correlating desires with the various faculties of the soul.

51. E.G. *boulometha* at *N.E.* 1094a20, *oregetai* at *N.E.* 1095a15, *E.E.* 1218a33; and *ephienai*, which is taken as a synonym of *oregesthai*, at 1094a2, 1097a5.

52. See the use of *diōketai* (pursued) *N.E.* 1094a15, 1096b19, 1097a31.

53. *N.E.* 1095a17, 1097a19, 1097a23, 1997a24, 1097b20; and *E.E.* 1218a34, 1218b21.

54. See *De Anima*, Book III, Ch. 9, 10, 11. Aristotle's views have been discussed by G. Santas, "Aristotle on Practical Inference, the Explanation of Action, and *Akrasia*," *Phronesis* 14, 1969, and R. Milo, *Aristotle on Practical knowledge and Weakness of Will* (The Hague: Mouton and Co., 1966).

55. See the opening sections of the *N.E.* where he talks about the ends of the various arts and sciences. And *E.E.* 1219 where he talks about the end of a coat, a ship and a house. In the psychological and biological treatises he repeatedly talks of the ends of the bodily organs and parts.

56. We might call this the autonomy of the arts and sciences. See, for example, his distinction at *E.E.* 1216b13 between the end of the sciences and the various uses which they may have.

57. So in *Physics* 199b26 he clearly distinguishes cases where we speak of "for the sake of" and there is no deliberation from cases where there is deliberation. See also 197b5, 199a20.

58. He usually takes the activity of seeing as the function, end and good of the eye.

59. See *E.E.* 1219a9 where he says that "...it is plain that the function is a greater good than the disposition, for the End is the best as being End..." Also 1219a33, "since an activity is a better thing than a disposition..."

60. This is true of almost all the commentators of the Aristotelian texts and seems to reflect the intuitive conception we have of the function of F as something that F does or performs, etc. We think primarily of the function as being expressed by a verb.

61. See *E.E.* 1219a13. See also the opening lines of the *N.E.* The Greek term which translators render as "function" or "characteristic activity" is *ergon*, a term that signifies both the result and use (exercise). The best English term, therefore, for rendering *ergon* is "work", for it signifies the product as well as the activity or exercise. The conflation of use and product was discussed in relation to Plato by J. Hintikka, "Knowledge and its Objects in Plato" in J. Moravcsik, *Patterns in Plato's Thought* (Boston: D. Reidel, 1973). Although I think Plato does not identify the function with the product as Hintikka claims (see the criticism of Hintikka's view by G. Santas, "Hintikka on Knowledge and its Objects in Plato," in *Patterns in Plato's Thought, op. cit.*) Aristotle clearly does so and he is fully aware of it.

62. Aristotle may, of course, term such things incidental, but it is not obvious how these cases can be handled without begging any questions.

63. The teleological nature of function is a theme that runs through most of the works of Aristotle--*Physics,* psychological and biological

treatises--and is one of the things that he considers as one of the advances he made over his predecessors in the understanding of change, causality and necessity.

64. Contemplation, of course, has according to Aristotle no by-product and the activity itself is the function. See *N.E.* 1178a20, *E.E.* 1216b12 and *Met.* 1050a34.

65. See 1176a4 where he claims that pleasure, like function, is peculiar to each animal and 1175a28 where pleasure is viewed as what perfects an activity and therefore is attached to the activity.

66. For some recent discussions of Aristotle's views on pleasure, see J.O. Urmson, "Aristotle on Pleasure," in J.M.E. Moravcsik, *op. cit.;* G.E.L. Owen, "Aristotelian Pleasures," *Proceedings of the Aristotelian Society,* 1971-1972, pp. 135-152; and Amelie O. Rorty, "The Place of Pleasure in Aristotle's Ethics," *Mind,* Vol. LXXXIII, No. 332, Oct. 1974.

67. See *Physics* 246a 10-20.

68. J.L. Austin, *"AGATHON and EUDAIMONIA* in the *Ethics* of Aristotle" in Moravcsik, *op. cit.,* p. 296.

69. I am indebted to Professor Avrum Stroll, William McKnight, Ezio Vailati and especially Professor Mark Wilson for a number of helpful discussions on the topics of this paper.

VIRTUE AND FLOURISHING

IN ARISTOTLE'S ETHICS

CHARLES M. YOUNG

I

Introduction. On the Greek concept of *eudaimonia,* one lives a happy, healthy, or flourishing[1] human life to the extent that one is engaged in the successful development and (especially) the active exercise of one's mature, characteristically human capacities across time. Different conceptions of human flourishing would flow from this concept, given a specification of the capacities characteristic of persons. Aristotle, for example, attempts in *NE* I.7[2] to make plausible the idea that what is characteristically human is the realization of rationality in thought and action,[3] and from this he argues that a flourishing life is one in which rationality is realized in accordance with the excellences[4] appropriate to it. It is not always appreciated, though, that the conception of human flourishing articulated in *NE* I.7 is itself formal in character. By this I mean that Aristotle's definition tells us only that humans are said to flourish in respect of their realization of the excellences, whatever they may be, involved in the exercise of rationality, but it does not tell us what those excellences *are.* And while Aristotle

138

certainly believes that courage, temperance, justice, and the other virtues of character (which he analyzes both generally and specifically in Books II through V of the *NE*) are among these excellences, this is something we do not learn from the definition in *NE* I.7.[5] The connection between virtues of character and human flourishing must come from somewhere else.

Aristotle seems to have recognized this, for in *NE* VI he assigns to practical wisdom *(phronēsis)* the task of specifying the components of human flourishing. In *NE* VI.5, for example, he writes:

> It is the mark of the practically wise man to be able to deliberate well about the things that are good and advantageous, not in one area–like about what sorts of things are good in relation to health or strength--but about what sorts of things are good in relation to living well *(to eu dzēn*[6]) generally.[7] (1140a25-28)

Aristotle elsewhere hints at what will be the results of such deliberation. Thus at *NE* VI.12, 1143b19-23, he says that not wisdom *(sophia)* but practical wisdom *(phronēsis)* "investigates that from which a person will flourish," and that it is concerned with "just things, and noble things, and things that are good for a person."[8] So it is Aristotle's belief, at least, that deliberation about "what sorts of things are good in relation to living well generally" will issue in the determination that courage, temperance, and the other virtues of character are indeed components of human flourishing.[9]

The problem with this is that Aristotle nowhere *argues* for this result.[10] That is, he never presents us with deliberative arguments which show why it is that a flourishing person will display virtues of character in the circumstances that call for their display, arguments which would allow us to see virtues of character as components of human flourishing. My task in this paper is to show how Aristotle might have closed this gap in his theory, at least in the case of courage: I hope to present a deliberative argument from premises Aristotle accepts to the conclusion that courage is part of what constitutes human flourishing, as Aristotle understands courage and flourishing.[11]

I restrict myself here to the case of courage for two reasons. The first is that the argument I present linking courage with flourishing appeals to special features of Aristotle's conception of courage. That this seems unavoidable suggests that a *general* solution to the problem of connecting virtue and flourishing in Aristotle is not possible. What one must *do* instead, I think, is to work through Aristotle's accounts of the various virtues of character in turn, and to use these accounts to construct links between the virtues and human flourishing. A project of this size would, of course, be quite beyond the scope of this paper; I shall, however, make some remarks about the implications of this project for the interpretation of Aristotle's conception of virtue of character.

My second reason for concentrating on the case of courage is that courage is, in a sense, a critical case. Courage may well result in loss of life, and according to Aristotle, this is a major loss, at least for a flourishing person (cf. *NE* III.9, 1117b9-15). It is not obvious how actions which might well terminate one's life, and therewith one's flourishing, could nonetheless count as manifestations of flourishing. So successful treatment of this case in particular will tend to confirm the idea that the project sketched above is a fruitful approach to the problem of connecting virtue and flourishing in Aristotle's ethics.

II

Aristotelian Courage. On Aristotle's analyses, virtues of character typically emerge as mean states of character between two extreme states.[12] Thus temperance is a mean state between licentiousness and insensibility; wittiness, between boorishness and buffoonery; and so on. Courage, though, has a more complex structure. Aristotle says that it is "concerned with fears and cheers" (*peri phobous kai tharrē*, III.6, 1115a5-6; cf. III.9, 1117a29), but he does not view courage as hitting a mean somehow intermediate between the emotions of fear and cheer. Rather, he allows for excess and deficiency with respect to *each* emotion:

> Of those who exceed, he who exceeds in fearlessness has no name...but someone would be mad or insensitive to pain if he fears nothing...He who exceeds in cheer is rash...He who exceeds in fear is a coward, for he fears the wrong things, in the wrong way, and so on. And he is also deficient in cheer, though his excess in the face of pains is more apparent. (III.7, 1115b24-1116a2)

Aristotle here tends to conflate excess in fear and deficiency in cheer (or at least to view them as typically conjoined vices), but it nonetheless seems clear that he understands courage to differ from other virtues in involving *two* means, one relative to fear--call it *fortitude*--and one relative to cheer--call it *confidence*: he allows for excess in fear, excess in cheer, deficiency in fear, and deficiency in cheer. One problem in understanding Aristotle's conception of courage is to lay out its structure in such a way that both fortitude (medial fear) and confidence (medial cheer) may be seen as integral parts.

I believe that Aristotelian courage has the complex structure it does as a consequence of the complex nature of the circumstances in which, as Aristotle sees it, courage is called for. In *NE* III.9, he writes:

> Perhaps it is not courageous persons, but persons who are less courageous, who make the best professional soldiers. Less courageous persons have nothing good except life to lose; they face danger readily and trade their lives for small gains. (1117a17-20)

Here Aristotle clearly implies that the willingness to face death in battle does not, by itself, suffice for courage: both courageous persons and the "less courageous" persons mentioned here have this willingness. The less courageous risk their lives for trifles; what marks off genuinely courageous persons, apparently, is that they risk their lives only in the attempt to obtain something relatively worthwhile--victory in a battle on the outcome of which, say, the fate of their city depends.

So courageous action, for Aristotle, involves not only an evil the courageous agent wants to avoid (notably, loss of life) but also a good the agent wants to attain (notably, victory in battle). This allows us to see why, on Aristotle's analysis, courage has a complex structure: the circumstances which call for courage are circumstances in which one must face an evil to attain a good. Since the prospective evil will give rise to the emotion of fear and the prospective good will give rise to the emotion of cheer,[13] mediality with respect to each emotion will be crucial. It will be important that agents avoid too much fear, lest they take flight, and also that they avoid too little fear, lest they welcome too much risk. And it will likewise be important for them to avoid too much cheer, lest they risk their lives needlessly,[14] and that they avoid too little cheer, lest they fail to press to their goal. Courage, on this reading, is found exactly where Aristotle wants it, in a middle position relative to each set of extremes. Courageous agents will exhibit medial fear (what I have called fortitude): they will not run, but they will attempt to preserve their lives. And they will exhibit medial cheer (confidence): they will press to their goal, but not by exposing themselves to too much risk. So on this view of Aristotelian courage, both fortitude and confidence are essential to its display.

III

The Rationality of Courage. Let us see how this account works in a particular case. Late in the sixth century B.C., according to Livy,[15] Lars Porsena, the king of Clusium, launched an attack on Rome in an attempt to restore the Tarquins to the Roman throne. To attack the city Porsena's army had to cross the Sublican bridge, which in those days provided the only access to the city from the west. In Macauley's melodramatic poem on this theme,[16] the Romans realized that the city could be saved if the bridge were destroyed, but the attack came with such swiftness that it was–apparently–too late. As the Consul on the scene observed:

> Their van will be upon us
> Before the bridge goes down;
> And if they once may win the bridge,
> What hope to save the town?
>   "Horatius," XXVI

But one Horatius Cocles saw a way to buy the needed time, and said:

> Hew down the bridge, Sir Consul,
> With all the speed ye may;
> I with two more to help me,
> Will hold the foe in play.
> In yon strait path a thousand
> May well be stopped by three.
> Now who will stand on either hand
> And keep the bridge with me?
>   "Horatius,"XXIX

The rest is history, or at least legend. Two men, Spurius Larcius and Titus Herminius, volunteered to stand with Horatius, and the three of them defended the far side of the bridge until its destruction was imminent. Horatius then sent his colleagues back to safety and faced the enemy alone until the bridge came down. After a prayer to the Tiber, he leapt into the river and swam across to safety,[17] winning, in Livy's words, "more fame than credence from posterity."

Whatever the historical accuracy of this story, Horatius' action approximates a case of Aristotelian courage. Horatius risks his life, but his doing so is prompted by the prospect of saving his city. As the Consul's remarks make clear, Rome falls if Porsena's army takes the bridge. Moreover, the prospect of saving Rome is, in Horatius' estimation, a realistic one. The delay of the opposing army is all that is necessary, and their delay can be secured by his fighting at the bridge. And interestingly, he is not willing to fight alone; he insists upon the assistance of two others.[18] Horatius thus seems to exemplify all the features of Aristotelian courage. He feels medial fear--he is prepared to risk his life, but he takes appropriate precautions. And he feels medial cheer--his city can be saved only if he fights, and there is a real prospect of saving his city if he does.[19]

Aristotle's analysis thus seems to work quite well. But notice also that Horatius' decision to stand and fight may be re-described without significant distortion as the outcome of a rational decision-making process. Horatius obviously attached considerable value both to the preservation of his city and to his own life. Moreover he seems committed to judgments about the respective likelihoods of saving his city and saving his life, given his prowess and the circumstances in which he finds himself. We may say that he judged, in light of these values and likelihoods, that it was better to stand and fight than not, and so chose to defend the bridge. His decision may thus be seen as entirely rational, as a strict consequence of the principles of rational choice,[20] given his values and his assessment of the likelihood of their attainment in his circumstances.

This view of courageous action as the product of rational choice is confirmed as a partial[21] interpretation of Aristotle's conception of courage in that it provides us with natural readings of the Aristotelian vices correlative to courage. As we have seen, Aristotle distinguishes between rash persons and insensitive persons, who fight when they should not, on the basis of the different explanations for their not fighting: the former feel "too much cheer"; the latter, "too little fear." Similarly, cowards fail to fight when they should, because they feel "too much fear"; cheerless persons, because they feel "too little cheer." A parallel taxonomy of vice emerges from a decision-theoretic reading of courageous action. The cowardly fail to fight when they should, because they exaggerate the expected loss from fighting; the cheerless, because they underrate the expected gain. The insensitive fight when they should not, because they underrate the expected loss; the rash, because they exaggerate the expected gain. Courageous agents fight when, and only when, rationality dictates that they fight. In Aristotle's words:

> The rash man (endures painful and destructive things), even if reason (*logos*) does not bid; the coward does not, even if reason does bid; the courageous man faces them only if reason bids. (*EE* III.1, 1229a9-11)[22]

IV

Courage and Flourishing. According to Aristotle, adequately to explain a human action is to connect that action to a conception its agent has of human flourishing, or as we might nowadays prefer to put it, to show its part in a rational plan of life.[23] Thus if I am in a bookstore and purchase a new book on Aristotle's ethics, the Aristotelian explanation of my doing so might run something like this:

(1) Flourishing requires having a rewarding vocation.
(2) Doing this requires (for me) being a competent student of classical philosophy.
(3) Doing this requires keeping up with new books in the field.
(4) Doing this requires keeping up with new books on Aristotle's ethics.
(5) The best way of doing this is to purchase such books when they appear.
(6) So, purchase new books on Aristotle's ethics when they appear.
(7) Here's a new book on Aristotle's ethics.
(8) So, purchase it.

In this illustration the judgments recorded by (1) through (5) are reached by a process Aristotle calls deliberation (*bouleusis*); deliberation results in what he calls a choice (*prohairēsis*), expressed in (6), which is a desire, formed after deliberation, of sufficient specificity[24] that, in the appropriate (perceptual) circumstances (7), it results in action (8). Deliberation reaches not only judgments, like (5), about instrumental means to ends, but also judgments, like (1) through (4), about the components of ends. Only if judgments of the latter sort are included within the scope of deliberation as Aristotle understands it can deliberation assume the importance it does in Aristotle's theory. For, as our example suggests, means-ends judgments, while they may on occasion be difficult, will involve at most technical complexities. Judgments about components, in contrast, strike to the very heart of human life, even in this relatively insignificant example. Thus (1) implies or presupposes a conception of what in life is worth pursuing; (2), a view as to how that conception is best realized in my own case, given my interests and talents; (3), an account of what constitutes being a competent student of classical philosphy; and (4), a conception of that field. These are large questions, not easily answered.[25]

I am interested here, though, in connecting courage with human flourishing, and for this purpose the importance of the distinction between judgments about means and judgments about components is that it places limits on what counts as an adequate connection. For a deliberative argument connecting courage with flourishing will show courage to be a component of flourishing only if each of its steps record judgments about components. Failing this, the argument would at most show courage to be a necessary concomitant of flourishing (cf. *NE* I.9, 1099b26-28), and not one of its components. Our decision-theoretic reading of Aristotelian courage makes it possible to present a deliberative argument meeting this condition:

(1) Flourishing requires the realization of rationality in action.

(2) This requires accepting relatively small risks in the attempt to attain relatively small gains.

(3) To act courageously in the circumstances which call for courage is to accept exactly such a risk.[26]

(4) So, flourishing requires courageous action in the circumstances which call for its display.

Here (1) expresses one of the components of what Aristotle argues in *NE* I.7 to be the correct conception of human flourishing, and (3) comes from our account of Aristotle's conception of courage. The bridge between them, (2), makes the idea of rationality in action in (1) determinate by appealing to the principle of rational choice[27] apparently operative in courage, as Aristotle conceives courage.

Horatius' deliberations might have continued in some such fashion as this:

(5) My present circumstances are the circumstances that call for courage: my city's preservation can be secured, but only if I risk my life.

(6) The best way of saving my city is to attempt to hold off the enemy on the far side of the bridge while others attempt to destroy it.

(7) So, when the enemy approaches, stand at the bridge and fight.

(8) Here is the enemy.

(9) So, stand and fight.[28]

I do not claim that (1) through (9) represent stages in some calculation through which Horatius reached his decision to stand at the bridge and fight. Indeed, in Macauley's account at most steps (6) and (7) seem to have been conscious. But I do claim that this is a deliberative argument through which Horatius could (on the assumption that he is both courageous and flourishing, as Aristotle understands those notions) see his standing at the bridge as expressive of flourishing: it is an argument which shows his courageous action to be a display of rationality in action.

V

The Need for Courage. The natural objection to this account of courage and flourishing in Aristotle is: if rationality dictates courageous action in the appropriate circumstances, what is the point of courage? Why is courage necessary if rationality would, by itself, produce courageous action, given the appropriate circumstances, values, and assessments of likelihoods?

But for Aristotle rationality is not, by itself, sufficient to produce action at all, much less courageous action; for him, thought produces action only in the presence of desire (cf. *De Anima* III.10, 433a13-20 and probably *NE* VI.2, 1139a35-b4). He holds that the practically wise have the correct conception of flourishing and through deliberative excellence correctly determine what contributes to flourishing thus conceived (VI.9, 1142b32-33), but choice, the starting point of action, involves both desire and thought (VI.2, 1139a30-33), and so correct choice requires correct desire. Now in ordinary circumstances we may presume that what agents want to do and what they ought to do will coincide, but what is special about courage, it seems, is that its circumstances of their nature introduce threats to this coincidence.[29] Courage, in the paradigm case, bids one to risk one's life to save one's city, and in such a case the risk will be relatively small in comparison to what is to be gained by courageous action. But in absolute terms the risk will be quite great: life, for Aristotle, is itself a good thing (cf., e.g., IX.9, 1170a19-20). The circumstances of courage, then, are circumstances in which there are natural temptations to do other than what rationality dictates. The courageous person is precisely the person who would not be moved by these temptations;[30] his achievement is that, even in a hard case, what he wants to do and what he ought to do are the same. In this sense, courage may be seen as an excellence corresponding to the realization of rationality in action. It ensures rational action in circumstances in which, humans being what they are, rational action might not be forthcoming.[31]

VI

Conclusion. The argument of section IV connects Aristotelian courage with Aristotelian flourishing *via* a principle of rational choice. Seeing courageous action as also dictated by a principle of rational choice allows us to see courage as a component of human flourishing understood as the realization of rationality in thought and action. Since the appeal to the details of Aristotle's conception of courage in that argument seems crucial, to forge links between flourishing and other virtues of character will probably require a similar strategy. One must work through Aristotle's analyses of other virtues of character with a view to discovering what is rational about the forms of conduct they require; one will then be able to argue in analogous manner for connections between them and human flourishing.

This general approach to the topic of Aristotelian virtue is, I believe, strongly suggested by what Aristotle actually says. He defines virtue (*aretē*) generically by saying that it is "a disposition to choose, consisting in a mean state--one relative to us--which is determined by a *logos*, namely, that *logos* by which the practically wise person would determine it" (II.6, 1106b36-1107a2). But in discussing specific virtues of character Aristotle does not proceed as his generic definition would lead us to expect. He does try to defend the idea that the virtues are mean states, but he does this through a discussion of the extreme states relative to which the virtues count as mean states. He does not, in the *NE* at least,[32] specify for each virtue the *logos* which, according to his generic definition, determines the mean state that virtue consists in. This is what I have attempted to do for him in the case of courage; my general suggestion is that the *logoi* implicated in Aristotle's generic definition of virtue are principles of rational choice.

Let me end by correcting a possible misunderstanding of what I have been saying. I do not mean to attribute to Aristotle the view that all those whose actions conform to the principles of rational choice are virtuous persons and have flourishing lives. Quite the contrary: these principles will no doubt play a prominent role in the lives of most persons, virtuous and non-virtuous alike.[33]

If the difference between the virtuous and non-virtuous cannot be found in a set of principles which the former accept and the latter reject, where is it to be found? For Aristotle, the world of the virtuous person is different from that of the non-virtuous. The non-virtuous make incorrect choices in the belief that they are correct (cf., e.g., VII.8, 1150b29-30). They incorrectly apprehend goods in themselves (cf., e.g., III.4, 1113a29-34). And they lack the correct conception of happiness or human flourishing (VI.12, 1144a31-36; cf. III.5, 1114b4-5), that sketched by Aristotle in *NE* I.7. It is this last difference which should be regarded as fundamental, for there is no good reason to suppose that the non-virtuous fail to flesh out accurately the (incorrect) conception they have of flourishing, or that they err in determining what contributes to flourishing as they conceive it. They make the wrong choices and pursue the wrong things because they correctly believe that these conduce to their understanding of human flourishing; their choices and pursuits are wrong, because their conception of flourishing is wrong. As Aristotle says, a non-virtuous person "does bad things through ignorance of the end, thinking that through them the greatest good will be his" (*NE* III.5, 1114b4-5).

This difference between the virtuous and the non-virtuous implies a difference in the *attitude* persons of each sort will adopt towards the principles of rational choice. Both sorts will make use of these principles in determining what to do.[34] For the non-virtuous, though, the principles of rational choice will play a merely regulative role; they will accept and act on these principles because the principles are, in fact, the best means for attaining their objectives in life. The virtuous will take a different view. Having the correct conception of human flourishing, that of *NE* I.7, they will see themselves as beings whose essense is the capacity for the realization of rationality in thought and action. Since acting on the principles of rational choice constitutes rationality in action, the virtuous will see their acting on these principles as constituitive of who they are.[35] This is a perspective which is not available to the non-virtuous. They cannot see what they do as the expression of who they are, for they lack the correct conception of who they are.[36]

Notes

1. "Human flourishing" as a translation of *eudaimonia* is implicitly suggested by G.E.M. Anscombe in "Modern Moral Philosophy," *Philosophy*, 33 (1958), pp. 18-19, and defended by J.M. Cooper in *Reason and Human Good in Aristotle* (Cambridge, Massachusetts, and London: Harvard University Press, 1975), p. 89n; the more traditional "happiness" is defended with reservations by J.L. Austin in "*Agathon* and *Eudaimonia* in the *Ethics* of Aristotle," in J.M.E. Moravcsik, ed., *Aristotle: A Collection of Critical Essays* (Garden City, New York: Doubleday, 1967), pp. 279-283, and with enthusiasm by R. Kraut in "Two Conceptions of Happiness," *Philosophical Review*, 88 (1979), pp. 167-197. To Cooper's reasons in favor of "human flourishing" should be added the fact that "flourishing" tends to preserve, while "happiness" tends to sever, the organic connection a Greek would see between having *aretē*, human excellence, and being *eudaimōn*. (Consider, for example, *Gorgias* 492A-494A. There--to oversimplify drastically--Callicles conceives of *eudaimonia* as getting what one wants and of *aretē* as luxury, licentiousness, and liberty, backed by force" (492C), while Socrates views the former as liking what one has and the latter as temperance. Despite their differences, Socrates and Callicles share a conceptual link between *aretē* and *eudaimonia:* each conceives of *aretē* as that which gives rise to *eudaimonia*, as he conceives *eudaimonia*.)

2. I refer to the *Nicomachean Ethics* as *NE* and to the *Eudemian Ethics* as *EE*; to books with Roman numerals, and to chapters with Arabic ones. Unindicated references are to the *NE*.

3. The *ergon* of a thing is its defining characteristic activity (on this point, see my "Plato's Theory of Crafts," unpublished, pp. 12-15), so Aristotle, in inquiring after the *ergon* of a person, is seeking to specify

what is characteristically human. His answer is that the human *ergon* is "activity of soul according to *logos*" (*NE* I.7, 1098a7-8; cf. 1098a 12-13); in light of (a) his distinction between practical and theoretical reasoning (cf., e.g., *NE* VI.1, 1139a6-15), (b) his specific inclusion of *actions* in the human *ergon* at 1098a12, and (c) his emphasis on the active exercise, in contrast to the mere possession, of these faculties (1098a5-7), I take him to be saying that the human *ergon* consists in the realization of rationality in thought and action.

4. I translate *aretē* as it occurs in *NE* I.7 as "excellence;" when it describes courage, temperance, etc., I use "virtue" or "virtue of character." I take this slight liberty to emphasize that it must be argued that the *aretai* referred to in I.7 include these traditional *aretai*.

5. Cooper (*op. cit.,* pp. 146-47) is one who does recognize the formal nature of Aristotle's definition, but he regards the definition as more formal than in fact it is. Aristotle does not leave us with "the bald and unanalyzed fact that excellence means goodness of work"; he has, in this argument, offered the non-trivial analysis of the "work" (*ergon*) of persons as the realization of rationality in thought and action. And while it is true to say that "we cannot derive from this argument any significant information as to how it is that (justice, temperance, etc.) contribute to a flourishing life," it is a mistake to regard this as a criticism of Aristotle's argument. For, as I go on to argue, Aristotle could not have provided such information in I.7: such questions, for him, fall within the scope of practical wisdom, *phronēsis*, a faculty not under discussion in *NE* I.7.

6. "Living well" is equivalent to "flourishing," according to *NE* I.4, 1095a19-20.

7. Cf. also *NE* VI.7, 1141b12-14; VI.9, 1142b31-33; VI.12, 1144a28-b1; as well as *Rhetoric* I.9, 1399b20-22.

8. Cf. also *Rhetoric* I.9, 1366b20-22 together with I.6, 1362b9-14.

9. This by no means exhausts the scope of practical wisdom: the practically wise have the correct conception of human flourishing (VI.9, 1142b32-33), determine accurately what conduces to ends set by virtues of character (VI.10, 1144a6-9; VI.13, 1145a4-6), and have an accurate perception of particular matters of fact (VI.7, 1141b14-15; VI.8, 1142a14-15). See also section IV and the discussions in the references in n.23 below.

10. The contrast with Plato could not be more striking. Plato

nowhere attempts, in the manner of *NE* I.7, to articulate his conception of human flourishing, but he takes great pains in the *Republic* to argue for a connection between justice, as he conceives it there, and human flourishing. Aristotle does elucidate his notion of flourishing, but he nowhere attempts to explain why virtues of character are components of flourishing.

11. It may be that virtues of character are not a part of what Aristotle argues in *NE* X.7 to be the most flourishing life (a recent defender of this view is Cooper, *op. cit.*, pp. 155-68), but this issue is irrelevant to the concerns of this paper. For whatever his view of the components of the most flourishing life, Aristotle does in Book X (1178a9-13) regard the life devoted to the cultivation and exercise of virtues of character--the life of the *politikos* (X.8, 1178a26-27; cf. 1178b6-15)--as *a* flourishing life, if only in a secondary sense. And the question remains as to how it is that virtues of character are components of this diminished flourishing.

12. This account of the structure of Aristotelian courage follows closely that in section II of my paper, "Aristotle on Courage," in Q. Howe, ed., *Humanitas: Essays in Honor of Ralph Ross* (Claremont, California: Scripps College Press, 1977), pp. 194-203. I am grateful to the editor and to the publisher for permission to use this material here.

13. Aristotle specifies the object of fear in courage (III.6, 1115a24-35, esp. 32-35) but not that of cheer, so that the claim that (e.g.) victory in battle is its object is interpretation on my part. In holding fear to spring from the anticipation of a painful or destructive evil (*Rhetoric* II.5, 1382a21-22) and cheer to be its opposite (*Rhetoric* II.5, 1383a15-17), Aristotle seems to agree with Plato (cf., e.g., *Laches* 199B) that the object of cheer is a future good. But courage involves two future goods, preservation of life and victory, either of which might serve as the object of cheer, and since these are connected it will often be difficult to distinguish between them in particular cases. (Thus at *Iliad* XV. 254-261, Apollo urges cheer on Hector with promises both of protection and of success.) Aristotle, because he regards excessive cheer and deficient fear as distinct vices, seems committed to holding that victory in battle rather than preservation is the object of cheer. For if fear is felt in relation to prospective loss of life and cheer in relation to prospective preservation, excess in cheer and deficiency in fear would be two sides of the same emotional coin.

14. This is a slight change from what I said in "Aristotle on Courage," *op. cit.*, p. 201.

15. Accounts of the Horatius story are found in Polybius (*Histories,* V.55.1), Livy (II.9.10), and Dionysius of Halicarnassus (*Roman Antiquities,* V.23-25). Virgil has a brief allusion at *Aeneid* VIII. 646-651.

16. Lord Macauley, "Horatius," in *The Lays of Ancient Rome and Miscellaneous Essays and Poems* (London: J.M. Dent and Sons, 1910), pp. 418-34. Macauley largely follows Livy's version, though see n. 18 below.

17. Horatius drowns in Polybius' version. Polybius tells the story only *inter alia,* as an example of the sort of noble death the narration of which in funeral orations would inspire young men to seek the same; he may have needed a dead Horatius for this purpose.

18. This is unique to Macauley's version. Polybius has Horatius fight alone, while in Livy and Dionysius, Herminius and Larcius fight with him at their own initiative.

19. Notice also how each of Aristotle's vices points to a distinct error Horatius, had he not been courageous, might have committed in the circumstances as Macauley relates them. To have fought without the belief that his city could be saved would have been rash, and it would have been cowardly to preserve his life by refusing to fight. Not to have been moved to fight by the prospect of saving his city would have been to display deficiency in cheer; not to have insisted on assistance would have shown deficiency in fear. Note too the importance of Aristotle's inclusion of medial fear in the structure of courage: those agents who strive to preserve their lives through the course of their engagements in courageous actions are more likely than others to attain their objectives in fighting. On a point related to this, see "Aristotle on Courage," *op. cit.,* pp. 197-99, and n. 30 below.

20. See n.27 below.

21. See also section V below.

22. The *Eudemian* account of courage, in recognizing only the two vices of rashness and cowardice, is less sophisticated than the *Nicomachean.*

23. In my remarks on deliberation in this section and on the interpenetration of reason and desire in the next, I am indebted to Cooper, *op. cit.,* as well as to G.E.M. Anscombe, "Thought and Action

in Aristotle," in R. Bambrough, ed., *New Essays on Plato and Aristotle* (London: Routledge and Kegan Paul, 1965), pp. 143-58; R. Sorabji, "Aristotle on the Role of Intellect in Virtue," *Proceedings of the Aristotelian Society*, n.s. 74 (1973-74), pp. 107-29; D. Wiggins, "Deliberation and Practical Reason," *Proceedings of the Aristotelian Society*, n.s. 76 (1975-76), pp. 29-51; and T. H. Irwin, "Aristotle on Reason, Desire, and Virtue," *Journal of Philosophy*, 72 (1975, pp. 567-78.)

24. In this I follow Cooper, *op. cit.*, pp. 30-33.

25. Notice that none of these problems are what we would call *moral* problems: thus judgments about components are not restricted to Aristotle's theory of moral reasoning, if he has one. (Aristotle has a theory of practical reasoning, but not a theory of moral reasoning as such. Comparison of the two suggested specimens of Aristotelian deliberation in this section suggests that he was not wrong in this: structually they are the same.)

26. For, according to Aristotle, "the good of a state is clearly greater and more complete (than that of one person), both to secure and to preserve" *NE* I.2, 1094b7-9.

27. What little I know about the principles of rational choice I have learned from J. Rawls, *A Theory of Justice* (Cambridge, Massachusetts: Harvard University Press, 1971), pp. 411-13; D.A.J. Richards, *A Theory of Reasons for Action* (Oxford: Clarendon Press, 1971), ch. 3; and the classic R.D. Luce and H. Raiffa, *Games and Decisions* (New York: John Wiley and Sons, 1957). It should be observed that the principles these writers discuss are all instrumental principles. Aristotle, as we have seen, would not regard the scope of practical reasoning as exhausted by such principles. The articulation of the principles which stand behind judgments about components, though, is a task which is comparatively neglected, and it does seem to be an instrumental principle which is at work in the case of courage. But in speaking of "the principles of rational choice" in the remainder of this paper, I mean to refer not merely to instrumental principles but also to the principles, whatever they are, involved in judgments about components.

28. See Cooper (*op. cit.*, p. 85) for a different suggestion as to the nature of the Aristotelian deliberations leading to a choice to act courageously.

29. Here I treat only the most obvious threat to coincidence; the others flow naturally from the account of the vices correlative to courage in section III above.

30. Indeed, as I argue in "Aristotle on Courage," (*op.cit.*, pp. 194-99) a courageous person would not even *feel* these temptations. To be sure, a courageous person will feel (medial) fear, and this will involve a desire to preserve one's life. But the desire to save one's life will be a temptation to act in other than a courageous way only if it takes the form of a desire to *flee*; if it takes instead the form of a desire to preserve one's life through the course of one's courageous actions, it will not be a temptation.

31. On this view of Aristotelian virtue of character it should not be surprising that Aristotle includes in his catalogue of virtues qualities, like magnificence (which consists in suitable expenditure in great things: cf. *NE* IV.2, 1122a23), which we might not include in ours. Different societies may present different threats to the realization of rationality in action, and so require different virtues.

32. In the *EE,* more so than in the *NE* (though cf. VI.1, 1138b33-34), Aristotle seems aware of the need to specify the *logos* or *logoi* involved in virtue (cf. *EE* II.5, 1222b7-8 and VIII.3, 1249a21-b6), but the answer he gives there (*EE* VIII.3, 1249b16-23), that the right *logos* is what best produces the contemplation of god, is not especially helpful.

33. Cf. Aristotle's remarks on cleverness at *NE* VI.12, 1144a23-27.

34. In view of the fundamental differences Aristotle sees between the virtuous and the non-virtuous, he might take the fact that one of the few things they have in common is acceptance of the principles of rational choice as evidence for the correctness of his analysis of the human *ergon* as rationality in thought and action in *NE* I.7.

35. It is along these lines that I am inclined to interpret Aristotle's quite interesting remarks on self-love in *NE* IX.8. (I learned much about this topic from reading Marcia Homiak's "Virtue and Self-Love in Aristotle's Ethics," unpublished.)

36. An ancestor of this paper was read at the University of Redlands. I did some research for it in 1975-76, when I held an Andrew Mellon Post-doctoral Fellowship at the University of Pittsburgh.

ARISTOTLE ON

VIRTUE AND PLEASURE

EUGENE GARVER

I

The principal theme of Aristotle's *Ethics* is announced in the first few lines. All actions aim at some good, and the relation between actions and the goods which are their ends is the subject of the *Ethics*. There are two basic relations an action can have to an end–an action can either lead to an end as an external product, or an action can be an end. Moreover, just as some ends are subordinate to others, so actions are ordered to each other.

However, as soon as one tries to apply these distinctions and relations, complications come in. Actions which are their own end are the special subject of the *Ethics*: happiness is an activity which is always desired for its own sake, and virtuous action is similarly valued as its own end. But actions which are their own end, *energeiai* or *praxeis,* do not exist in a world distinct from the actions which lead to some external end, which are by contrast called *kinēsis* and *poiesis.* [1] Many actions can be viewed both as done for their own sakes and as having an external end. One can be fishing because one enjoys fishing, and one can still catch fish. [2] As we shall see,

Aristotle would make a similar point about courageous action—we can act courageously because it is the noble thing to do, and can still rescue our friend. And so Rorty asks "if the apparently sharp distinction between *kinēsis* and *energeia* [is] compatible with what appear to be instances of cross-classification."[3]

The subordination of actions to each other is similarly problematic. Gauthier and Jolif see subordination as so problematic that it becomes an impossibility. "We cannot see how moral actions, whose nature it is to be themselves their own end, could also be ordered to something else to form a hierarchy."[4] Aristotle uses *energeia* to characterize two separate, but central, ideas in the *Ethics*, virtuous action and happiness, and Ackrill thus rightly points out that "the idea that some things are done for their own sake and may yet be done for the sake of something else is precisely the idea Aristotle will need and use in talking of good actions and *eudaimonia*."[5]

Aristotle's *Ethics* must thus deal with the relations between actions and ends, and at the center of Aristotle's concern is one relation between action and ends, namely the idea of action which is its own end. Since the idea of an action which is its own end is not self-evident, two other terms, in addition to "end", are continually related to action to make ethical phenomena intelligible. It is by exploring the different connections action can have, respectively, with ends, with pleasure, and with knowledge, that Aristotle is able to make virtue a fully understood idea. Pleasures are activities, not motions, but it is a sign of the complexity of that assertion that Aristotle tells us both that pleasure is to be identified with virtuous activities, and that making such an identification would be absurd. The virtues are not reducible to reason controlling the passions, but all the virtues involve a rule of reason that is often hard to distinguish from self-control. Ends, pleasure, and knowledge form different dimensions through which we can understand action, and virtuous action in particular.

Activities which are their own end, and their relation to

actions done for the sake of something else, form the subject of the *Ethics,* and to unravel completely the relation between *energeia* and *kinēsis, praxis* and *poiesis,* in the *Ethics* would be equivalent to giving a full commentary on the text. Instead, I propose to take some of the problems from the *Ethics* in general and to focus them on a single virtue, a single kind of action for its own sake, namely courage, and then to focus still further, to a single line in the text. Proper analysis of that line will illuminate the sense in which one can call courageous action its own end, and that, in turn, will have consequences for our understanding of ethics in general.

II

Courage is a good place to explore the complications in Aristotle's use of the distinction between *kinēsis* and *energeia* because courage presents in an extreme form three of the central problems of ethics–what it means for an action to be its own end, what the relation is between activity and pleasure, and what the difference is between virtue and self-control.

While Aristotle tells us that good action is its own end,[6] praised on its own account and thought good even if it brought no other benefits, he also tells us, in what seems either a severe qualification or even a contradiction, that practical virtuous action is inferior to contemplation because "the activity of contemplation may be held to be the only activity that is loved for its own sake: it produces no result beyond the actual act of contemplation, whereas from practical pursuits we look to secure some advantage, greater or smaller, beyond the action itself."[7] Nowhere is the connection of the moral virtues to external ends more immediately apparent than in the case of courage. Pears, in fact, singles courage out, inadvertently restricting Aristotle's claim about moral virtue, saying that "courage is essentially an executive virtue, always practiced in the service of further goals, but temperance is not essentially an executive virtue."[8] Whether or not Pears is justified in exempting temperance and perhaps the other moral virtues from Aristotle's claim, courage does present the general problem in an extreme form. No one would expose himself to risks without some external goal, and it would seem to follow that the value, the praiseworthy quality, of putting one's life in danger comes not from that description of the act but from the external goal for the sake of which one exposes oneself. Without a comrade to save, or something similar, no one can act courageously, or want to, so how courageous action can be valuable in its own right is obscure.

Because it is hard to see how courageous action can be done for its own sake, the relation between courage and the pleasure that is supposed to accompany all virtuous action is similarly obscure, and its clarification should illuminate the relation between pleasure and virtuous action generally. Aristotle tells us that "courage itself is painful," that "the end which courage sets before itself is really pleasant, only its pleasantness is obscured by the attendant circumstances," and finally that "it is not therefore true of every virtue that its active exercise (*energeia*) is essentially pleasant, save in so far as it attains its end."[9] Virtuous activity should always attain its end, because it is the nature of *energeia* to be complete, be successful, attain its end, at every moment, and not to need time to achieve its end. Moreover, since pleasure is defined as unimpeded activity, courage, with its attendant pains, must be an example of impeded activity. An obscured pleasure is no pleasure at all, and the idea of an impeded activity seems to be a similar contradiction.[10]

Finally, because of the problematic character of courage as its own end, and the puzzling relation of pleasure to courageous activity, courage offers in an extreme form the problem of distinguishing virtue from self-control.[11] The other virtues are harder to confuse with self-control, because the passions with which the other virtues are concerned evidently are matter actualized, by the appropriate virtue, into a right desire.[12] The temperate passion for wine can lead to the right desire for a single bottle, and the right passion for pride can lead to the willingness to accept appropriate

honors. But the fear felt by the courageous man--fear of the
right object, at the right time and with all the other
qualifications--that right fear is still an aversion to death, and
it does not, at least in any obvious way, become the matter
for the desire to stand firm.[13] It may be possible, when
speaking abstractly of virtue in general, to distinguish virtue
from self-control, but courage presents specific difficulties
for our understanding of the relation of passion, habit, and
activity.

III

Consideration of courage has raised problems about three
central themes in Aristotle's *Ethics,* virtuous activity as its
own end, the relation of pleasure to virtuous activity, and the
distinction of virtue and self-control. I propose to take a
single sentence--in fact, a single word--from the section on
courage, a sentence and word which concentrate all the
difficulties encountered so far. An understanding of this
small piece of text should lead to some more general
understanding, first of courage, and finally of the relation
between passion, habit, and activity in the *Ethics* as a whole.
The line that will be the subject of this crucial experiment
is: "It is not therefore true of every virtue that its active
exercise is essentially pleasant, save in so far as it attains its
end."[14] The line allows us to focus all our difficulties on a
single question: what is the meaning of the word end *(telos)*
here? There are two possible answers: (1) the end is
something achieved *by* the courageous act, e.g., "having
rescued the children" (Kelly),[15] the "external end"
(Keyt);[16] (2) the end is something achieved *in* the act itself,
e.g., "doing what is fine." (Ackrill).[17] Either reading has its
problems.[18]
Kelly does not note that second possible meaning of end,
but tries to defend the external sense of end. Since he relies
on the distinction between *kinēsis* and *energeia,* his argument
is worth some attention. Since courageous action involves
motions, as does any instance of moral virtue, Kelly suggests
that we look at the performance (his, following Kenny's,

translation of *kinēsis*) to find the pleasure of courage: "For what would it be like to enjoy acting generously or courageously and not take pleasure in doing such things as benefiting those in need or saving people's lives?" (405) Now since performances "unlike activities, can be the source of pleasure in two different respects" (*ibid.*), one can either enjoy the process or be satisfied at the accomplishment, and since, at least in the case of pleasure, the process itself is not pleasant but painful, it must follow that the pleasure of virtue is the feeling of successful accomplishment.

Although Kelly's argument is attractive in its simplicity and clarity, it is clearly wrong. If it were true that the pleasure of virtuous activity was the pleasure of successful accomplishment, then the pleasure would come *after* the virtuous action. Note Kelly's inadvertent shift in tenses of the verbs in the following sentence: "A man who *enjoys acting* generously is one who takes pleasure in *having benefited* those who are in need even though he may not *have enjoyed* making the sacrifices which were necessary to bring about that end." (406) And again: A "person performing such an act could *take pleasure in having rescued* the children despite the fact that the experience of rescuing them was harrowing." (405 Ital. mine)

It is impossible for the pleasure of virtue to come after the action. The first time Aristotle introduces virtuous pleasures he makes it clear that they occur simultaneously with the action itself: "A man is temperate if he abstains from bodily pleasures and finds this abstinence itself enjoyable, profligate if he finds it irksome; he is brave if he faces danger with pleasure or at all events without pain, cowardly if he does so with pain."[19] Since taking pleasure in the act is a sign that an act is not merely a virtuous act but is done virtuously,[20] Aristotle defines pleasure as unimpeded activity, and the pleasure of virtue must be virtuous activity *qua* unimpeded.[21] It is impossible for this pleasure, the pleasure of virtue, to come after the act.

The first possible meaning of "end", a state brought about by the action, has led to identifying the pleasure of virtue with a feeling temporally distinct from the activity of virtue. The second meaning that "end" can take in our critical passage is the end of courage *qua energeia,* acting courageously, withstanding the fear of death because it is the noble thing to do.[22] Success in attaining this end is quite different from succeeding in rescuing one's comrades, and this meaning of "end" immediately creates a whole new set of difficulties.

Aristotle tells us in general that good action is its own end,[23] and as such it is complete at every moment;[24] it does not take time to attain its end, but attains its end at every moment of the practice of the activity. The pleasure of virtue, then, should accompany virtuous activity throughout its duration. But that simple relation of activity, end, and pleasure is what is explicitly denied for the case of courage. On our present reading of end, the condition "only in so far as it reaches its end" *(plēn eph' oson)* seems redundant. The activity of courage must always attain its end; that is what it means to be activity and not motion.

IV

We can begin to do justice to the complications in the relation of activity, end, and pleasure by attributing to Aristotle the following claim: sometimes courage is pleasant and sometimes it is painful; nevertheless, when the courageous man is pleased and when he is pained, neither the pleasure nor the pain is accidental to the act of courage. (In the language of the *Topics,* pleasure and pain are properties, not accidents, of individual courageous acts.) The distinction between painful courage and pleasant courage is a distinction between a painful, impeded activity of courage and a pleasant, unimpeded activity. Courage is the despising and withstanding of fears *(kataphronein, hypomenein)* and sometimes withstanding fears requires feeling them and despising them means actively rejecting them, while sometimes, perhaps more rarely, withstanding fears consists in temporarily being able to ignore them.[25]

Courage is sometimes painful and sometimes pleasant; the simplest picture of the relation between painful courage and pleasant courage is a motion of becoming courageous followed by a state of being courageous, the picture of the courageous man screwing up his courage, conquering fears, with a growing feeling of confidence, until finally coming to the point at which courageous action is no longer "against the grain" and therefore is no longer painful. This picture is a useful one, but it is an oversimplification, because the fear of death is never conquered permanently, and the courageous man is always liable to back-sliding--when he must concentrate on avoiding being ruled by fear, courage is painful; when he can, for a time, ignore the conquered fear, courage is pleasant.[26]

There is a good reason why courage should consist in being able, each time necessary, to despise and stand up to one's fear of death and wounds, rather than conquer it permanently, as one conquers, say, lust and greed. The fear of death, even the fear of dying in noble circumstances, is not a passion that one could wish to be without, since one should value one's life highly, and a courage founded on habituating oneself by constantly placing a low value on one's own life would not be a virtue. Courage consists in recognizing that the evil one fears is indeed an evil, but not the greatest of evils: dishonor is the greatest evil. (Rashness is the error of feeling, because life is not the greatest good, it is not good at all.) Courage consists not in placing a low value on one's life but in placing a higher value on action for the sake of the noble.[27]

To see what is demanded of the courageous man, such that the phrase "impeded activity" should begin to look less oxymoronic, contrast the valuations involved in his choice, choosing the good life over life itself, with the valuations involved in justice. The unjust man thinks that because something is good in the abstract, it is good for him here and now. Justice consists in recognizing that one should choose what is good for oneself, and should wish that what is good in the abstract be good for oneself. It is characteristic of the unjust man to infer, e.g., that because money is good, I should try to get some, and get as much as I can. Hence to an unjust man, or to an apparently neutral moral observer, justice looks like self-sacrifice, resisting the desire to take more than one's share of goods.[28] But in the just man's eyes, the goods he does not take are not good; the sacrifice is only apparent, and apparent to everyone except the good man. The courageous man, by contrast, really is sacrificing something good, not only good in the abstract but good to him: "Life is desirable and especially so for good men, because existence is good for them, and so pleasant (because they are pleased by the perception of what is intrinsically good)."[29]

The difference between the apparent sacrifices of the other virtues and the real sacrifice of courage can be expressed in the following way. What is true for courage, as *hexis* and *energeia,* is true for all of the other virtues done by someone on the way to becoming virtuous; such a man may perform temperate, liberal, or just actions thinking of himself as sacrificing one good for a greater one. Virtuous actions done by the non-virtuous are done against the grain and so may be painful, although the elation of success can override the pain of doing something difficult. But in the case of courage, to act from a *hexis* of courage can still be to act against impediments; the courageous man is not impeded by his own *hexis* as is someone acting against the grain, but he is impeded by the passions which form the matter of courage. This relation between passion and *hexis* is unique to courage among the virtues, and it produces the unique relation between *hexis* and *energeia.* Only courage pursues the good life at the possible cost of life.

Courageous *hexis* is to courageous *energeia* as acquiring other virtuous *hexeis* is to having those *hexeis.* This proportion accounts for the apparent contradiction in the phrase, "impeded activity." An impeded activity is not a perfect activity, while pleasure follows necessarily from an activity being perfect, i.e., from both "object and agent being the best of their kinds."[30] The peculiar relation of *hexis* and *energeia* for courage explains how painful courage can be imperfect, while still being virtuous activity.

An activity, Aristotle tells us, can be imperfect either because of an imperfection in the object or in the agent. The imperfection of painful courage cannot be in the object, as breathing bad air makes for imperfect activity. Aristotle builds the perfection of the object into the definition of courage, excluding courage in the face of financial loss and disease as only courage by metaphor, and saying that courage is concerned only with the greatest evils in the noblest circumstances.[31]   Therefore,   the   imperfection,   the impediment to pleasure, must lie not in the object but in the agent.

What could be imperfect about the courageous man? The imperfection here cannot be that of someone who is not quite courageous in character, because Aristotle is here talking about the truly courageous man, not simply someone who acts courageously--such are called tropes of courage in III.8. The only imperfection possible is that the man of courageous character is courageous only potentially and not in act. In the case of courage, and only in the case of courage, possession of the *hexis* does not make the *energeia* smooth and pleasant.[33] Only in the case of courage is continuing in activity painful. Courage, that is, is the virtue least capable of continuous exercise; each courageous act calls for a continual conquering of fear. In the other virtues, the moral training, the habituation of acquiring a fixed character, consists in removing the impediments to the dependable operation of virtue. While in the other virtues, *acquiring* the *hexis* involves overcoming impediments, it is the *energeia*, not the *hexis,* of courage which consists in overcoming impediments. The fear of death is never permanently overcome as is greed or lust; the courageous man must face and conquer it each time he acts, and throughout each action.

Because the fear of death is not removed by habituation, it is easy to see why courage looks like self-control, like reason ruling recalcitrant passions, while the other virtues, having no impediments to their activities, are clearly distinct from self-control. But a more precise specification of the relation of passion, habit, and act will show the difference between courage and self-control.

Hexeis in general are defined as those things by which we stand well or badly with respect to the passions (II.5.1105b26). For the virtuous *hexeis* other than courage, it is easy to see what standing well means. The temperate man feels pleasures as he ought, and those pleasures are the matter actualized into a temperate desire. In courageous action, the fear of death is apparently an impediment to action, a competing desire, and not material actualized into the desire to act nobly despite the fears. But in fact the fear of death is matter actualized in desire, as well as an impediment to action. Courageous desire is desire for the noble in spite of the risks, and not simply desire for the noble. Full specification of the object of desire as standing firm in spite of the risks shows the fear of death to be part of the matter for courageous desire; hence, courageous action is generally *impeded* activity.[33]

Precise specification of the habit and act is crucial here. In the courageous man, fear of death is despised and endured, not lost.[34] The accurate description of the choice and act of the courageous man is not merely that he stands in battle but that he stands while fearing; to be true courage, both elements must be present in the act. Hence the fear of death does become actualized, as a part, in the desire to stand and fight in spite of the risk. The confusion with self-control comes from inaccurately describing the desire of the courageous man as the desire to stand instead of the desire to stand despite the risk.

Once we have correctly specified the desire, choice, and act, we can clarify the relation of passion, habit and act. The virtues are not only *hexeis* but *hexeis proairetikē,* habits of choosing. In the act of courage, deliberation and choice consist in evaluating the good life against one's life. "Life" is not simply an alternative discarded during the process of deliberation; it is incorporated into the choice as a rejected value. Usually, after deliberating between A and B, I can say that I choose A; when the courageous man deliberates between life and the good life, he does not simply choose the good life; he chooses the good life over life itself.

An analogy with theoretical reasoning should help here. One can have a theoretical inference from the two premises, "A or B," and "not-B," and one can state the conclusion either as "A," or as "A and not-B". From two practical premises, "These goods are incompatible" and "This good is preferable to that," the virtuous man can conclude "I will do this" or "I will do this rather than that." Whether or not one wants to say that the two theoretical conclusions are distinct, the two practical ones are, and the courageous man's choice is captured by the full formulation: "I choose the noble over life."

Because the rejected alternative is part of the conclusion, and the act of rejection is thus part of the act of choice, the object of fear is part of the object of choice. Hence, courage is usually painful, because fear, although only a part of the choice, can obscure the whole, and when it does, the pain of fearing harm will obscure the pleasure of acting virtuously. If courage were self-control, the desire to stand firm and the desire to flee would be in conflict; instead, the two objects of desire, safety and doing what is honorable, are combined in a single, complex, object of choice and desire.[35]

We can now give a simple formulation of the difference between courage and self-control. The difference is a difference in which faculty is being actualized. Self-control is the actualization of the faculty of reason, acting on a passive irrational soul.[36] In courage, the actualization is of a habit of both the rational and the non-rational soul since choice is deliberate desire or desiring deliberation, and since the fear of death is incorporated, as something despised, into the act of choice. The pleasure that may attach to self-control is a satisfaction at successfully controlling one's unwanted desire; the pleasure attached to courage is the unimpeded activity of the whole soul, of the rational and non-rational parts acting in accord, even though the accord involves tension.[37]

V

Courage is a virtue whose consideration has presented in extreme form some of the central problems of ethics. This paper began by showing the difficulties of moving from Aristotle's general account of virtue to his account of courage in particular. I should close by saying something about the implications for virtue in general of what is true for courage.

Clarifying the distinction between self-control and courage has shown some of the complications of showing how choice works. I have made the radical claim that sometimes the alternatives rejected in deliberation become incorporated as part of the object of choice, and that the following two propositions are not equivalent, when regarded as objects of choice: "I will do this" and "I will do this rather than that." Since the choice is the cause of the action, a careful description of the object of choice is crucial to understanding complex actions.

Precisely specifying the object of choice has made it possible to locate the pleasure of virtue in general. The pleasures intrinsic to activities, the pleasures of unimpeded activity, turn out to be the pleasures connected to the passions which are actualized in the actual desire which causes the activity. When a deliberation concludes with "I prefer this good to that good," the passion for this good is actualized in the desire and choice, and pleasure accompanies the actualization. The pains that obscure the pleasure of courage come from rejecting the other good. Only thus can one say that courage may be pleasant and may be painful, but that both the pleasure and the pain are intrinsically related to the activity of virtue.

Our discussions of choice and pleasure should lead to a fuller understanding of the idea of actions which are their own end. If an *energeia* is the *energeia* of some *dynamis* and only fully understandable as such, and if the *dynamis* of moral virtue is *hexis proairetikē,* then a richer understanding of choice is essential for understanding good action as its own end. If pleasure is unimpeded activity, then our examination of courage, as generally impeded activity, shows what it means to call pleasure an *energeia*, and hence something *done* for its own sake. In addition to enriching our understanding of choice and pleasure, and how they contribute to the idea of an action which is its own end, this examination of courage should lead to a better understanding of the interrelation of *kinēsis* and *energeia,* action done to produce something and action which is its own end. The fact that all moral activities involve *kinēsis* is not only a problem for moral philosophy, but is a problem for moral action. Not only does any morally virtuous activity admit of two distinct true descriptions, but the agent can perform any such action either as *kinēsis* or *energeia*.[38] As Aristotle says, "It is not the inherent nature of actions but the end for which they are done, which makes one action differ from another in the way of honor or dishonor,"[39] and so in the way of *kinēsis* and *energeia.* This is what makes the relation between *kinēsis* and *energeia* a problem of genuinely moral interest.

All morally virtuous activities have external ends and involve *kinēsis.* As Rorty points out:

> Some *energeia* are not only complex, but structured wholes, self-controlled but having a beginning, a middle, and end. The end falls within the *energeia* description; it is intrinsic, not extrinsic. But when intrinsic ends are temporally sequential, they can be interrupted.[40]

And she could have added, they are liable to all the contingencies open to the *kinēseis* that are their parts. Insofar as the complications of *kinēsis* and external ends affect problems of choice, those complications become moral problems, for the agent and the philosopher. The case of courage is in this sense an example of Aristotle's treatment of moral problems.

If *energeia* and *kinēsis* were mutually exclusive classes of acts, then *theoria,* as the only kind of activity which excludes *kinēsis,* would be the only activity valuable in its own right. The other virtues, as they range from virtues about the irrational part of the soul, about things and actions, and even through the intellectual virtues, show shifting relations between their structure as *energeiai* and the *kinēseis* involved. The example of courage indicates some of the considerations needed in constructing an adequate account of virtuous activity, and thus of happiness, as its own end.

Notes

1. The literature on the distinction between *kinēsis* and *energeia,* and the related distinction between *poiesis* and *praxis* is enormous. Here I follow Aristotle in initially identifying *kinēsis* and *poiesis, energeia* and *praxis;* such identification is provisional and subject to complication. See, e.g., Taylor, who, after noting Aristotle's identification of *kinēsis* with *poiesis* and *energeia* with *praxis*, tries to make his own separation. There is, he says, a distinction between the state the attainment of which terminates the activity and the end for the sake of which the activity is undertaken. The *kinēsis/energeia* distinction is elucidated by reference to the former, the *poiesis/praxis* distinction by reference to the latter. C. C. W. Taylor, "States, Activities and Performances," *Proceedings of the Aristotelian Society* (1965), Suppl. 39, p. 99.

2. The example, and much else, is Wick's. Warner Wick, Review of Hardie's *Aristotle's Ethical Theory* and Monan's *Moral Knowledge and Its Methodology in Aristotle, Ethics* (1969), 80:76-81; "The Rat and the Squirrel, or the Rewards of Virtue," *Ethics* (1971), 82:21-32.

3. Amelie Oksenberg Rorty, "The Place of Pleasure in Aristotle's Ethics," *Mind* (1974), 58:485.

4. In attempting to escape from the difficulty of subordinating one *energeia* to another, Gauthier and Jolif are by no means alone. But to escape from that difficulty is to escape from morality altogether. Hence they find *theōria*, since it is the only *energeia* which excludes external ends, to be the only *energeia* and the only form of happiness. But *theōria* is not a good for man as such, and hence is presented by Aristotle as a non-moral solution to moral problems. The rest of the *Ethics* is taken up with moral solutions to the same problem of good for man, and those moral solutions all involve inter-relations among *kinēsis* and *energeia*. Gauthier and Jolif, *L'Ethique a Nicomaque* (Paris, 1958-9).

5. J.L. Ackrill, "Aristotle on *Eudaimonia,*" *Proceedings of the British Academy* (1974), p. 343.

6. *Nicomachean Ethics*, VI.5.1140b7.

7. *N.E.* X.7.1177b1.

8. D.F. Pears, "Aristotle's Analysis of Courage," *Midwest Studies in Philosophy* (1978), 3:273.

9. *N.E.* III.9.1117a34-b17.

10. I should note here that the discussion of courage is not the only place where Aristotle gives to *energeia* predicates that seem to be incompatible with it. Elsewhere he talks about incomplete activity, and claims (X.6-8) that *theoria* is superior to other activities because it more fully possesses the properties of activity as such. If we can understand, in the case of courage, how activity can be impeded and still be activity, we should be in a better position to understand how some activity can have the properties of activity more fully than others. See also Ackrill, *op. cit.,* who points out that Aristotle calls happiness a most final end, as though there were degrees of finality.

11. W.D. Ross, *Aristotle* (London, 1949); Pears, *op. cit.*

12. For the relation of virtue to passion as one of form to matter, see *N.E.* II.6 & 7.

13. Hence Pears' (*op. cit.,* p. 274) talk about counter-goals as well as goals in the case of courage.

14. *Ou de en apasis tais aretais to hēdeōs energein hyparchei, plēn eph'oson tou telous aphaptetai. N.E.* III.9.1117b14.

15. Jack Kelly, "Virtue and Pleasure," *Mind* (1973), 82:405.

16. David Keyt, "Intellectualism in Aristotle," *Paideia* (1978), p. 151.

17. Ackrill, *op. cit.,* p. 252; see also, Ross, *op. cit,* pp. 204-5.

18. I have found only two writers who are explicitly aware of the two alternatives. Keyt sees them both and without argument opts for the external end (*op. cit.,* p. 151, n. 40), while Ackrill, also without argument, says: "The 'end' in question is not, e.g., defeating the enemy, but doing what is fine. The soldier does not in the least *enjoy* his weariness and wounds, but he does undergo them *gladly*–because, and only because, he knows that what he is doing is fine and honorable." (*op. cit.,* p. 252).

19. *N.E.* II.3.1104b5 Cf. Kelly, *op. cit.,* p. 408: "In general, the virtuous man will enjoy acting virtuously since he will be doing what he wants to do whereas when the vicious man acts virtuously, he will be acting across the grain."

20. *Hēdonē ē lupēn tois ergois.*

21. *N.E.* II.3.1104b4ff; VII.12.1153a13-16; VII.13.1153b10-13.

22. The end of all the virtues is attaining a standard in acting. Thus a virtuous act is done for its own sake, or "because it is noble to do so and base not to." *N.E.* III.7.1116a10-12; III.9.1117b7-9; this motive is "common to all virtues." IV.2.1122b6-8.

23. *N.E.* VI.2.1139b3; VI.5.1140b7.

24. *Metaphysics* IX. The literature on these marks of *energeia*, in metaphysics and in their application to ethics, is enormous. See e.g. Penner, Ackrill, Kenny, Owen, Rorty.

25. Because courage is more often painful than pleasant, i.e., more often consists in conquering fears than in ignoring them, Aristotle says that courage is about both fear and confidence, but not equally, but more about the fearful. *N.E.* III.1.1117a30. Evidence for this reading is that the claim just cited is the first sentence of III.9, and the rest of the chapter is taken up with the issue that concerns us, the pains and pleasures of courage. (*Pace,* Ross, Pears, *et al*).

26. Rorty, "Pleasure," p. 495: "When someone is playing a flute sonata, his attention must be carefully balanced between concentrating on exercising his *hexeis* and concentrating on the flute sonata. If he errs on the skin-side, focusing on the *hexis,* his pleasure in the *sonata* is diminished; if his concentrating is wholly on the sonata, what he is doing is more accurately described as attending to the sonata." See also, J. A. Stewart, *Notes on the Nicomachean Ethics* (Oxford, 1892), 2:303: "Of course *ta kata tēn andreian* stand in a somewhat exceptional position, as compared with *ta kata tas allas aretas.* They are painful in a sense in which the other virtuous actions are not. Other virtuous actions indeed imply a restraint put upon inclinations; but when once the moral character has been formed, they are no longer painful."

27. Feeling the pain of death or wounds is no less courageous courage than somehow not feeling them; what is courageous is not being determined in action by avoiding the pains. Whether the pains are such

to fully obscure the pleasure of virtuous action or not does not affect the virtuous quality of either act or person. *N.E.* III.9.1117b8f: "The death or wounds that courage may bring will be painful to the courageous man, and he will suffer them unwillingly; but he will endure them because it is noble to do so, or because it is base not to do so." And the more complete his virtue, the more pain will death cause him...But he is nonetheless courageous on that account, perhaps indeed he is more so, because he prefers glory in war to the greatest prizes in life."

28. E.g., Kelly, p. 401: "It seems unreasonable to expect the courageous man to enjoy risking his life on the field of battle or the just man to be pleased about having to pay his debts." See also, *N.E.* V.1.1129b1ff.

29. *N.E.* IX.9.1170a20. For an account of the relation of virtue, self-sacrifice and self-love, see IX.8.1169a25ff.

30. *N.E.* VII.13.1153b15: "No activity is perfect when it is impeded." X.9.1174b18: "When both the object and the agent are the best of their kind, then the activity will be the most complete and pleasant." See also J. Gosling, "More Aristotelian Pleasures," *Proceedings of the Aristotelian Society* (1973-4), 74:28: "The efficient cause [of perfect activity] is the perfect condition of subject and object, which produce it as the doctor produces health. But that, Aristotle says, is not the way pleasure produces it [i.e., perfect activity]. It, like health, is a formal cause of perfection."

31. *N.E.* III.6., *pace* Pears. Pears' entire treatment of courage is distorted by his initial failure to see the interdependence of the external and internal ends of courage. For him, the internal end is successfully withstanding fears, while the external end varies over situations. Thus he says (*op. cit.,* p.278): "If a brave man simply reflects on the risk of death, there is no reason for him to expose himself to it. It is true that on the field of battle he will decide in the end, all things considered, to expose himself to it. But that is because the things that he considers include the external goal, victory. He may also consider the internal goal, courageous action for its own sake, but that cannot be his only reason for exposing himself to the risk of death." Aristotle, by contrast, builds the external goal, victory in battle, into the definition of the internal goal, withstanding fears of death in the noblest circumstances.

32. At the beginning of Book V, Aristotle distinguishes *hexeis* from rational *dynameis* by saying that the same *dynamis* deals with opposite things as medicine studies both health and disease, but "a *hexis* which

produces a certain result does not also produce the opposite result."
N.E. V.1.1129a14. It follows that one can reliably infer back and forth
between *hexis* and *energeia*, but not between *dynamis* and *energeia*.
Usually the practical equivalent of a reliable inference is the smooth
transition from *hexis* to *energeia*; only in courage is the inference
reliable but the transition not smooth. Hence the activity is impeded.
See also, H. H. Joachim, *Aristotle: The Nicomachean Ethics* (Oxford:
Clarendon Press, 1951), p. 127.

33. That something can both be an impediment to action and the
matter acted upon should sound odd, especially when courage is
compared to the other moral virtues. A non-moral, non-Aristotelian
example might, therefore help. Kant uses the example of birds flying to
make an analogous point: the air feels like an impediment to flight, and
it is in fact resistance constantly needing to be overcome. But the air is
also the matter acted on by the bird's wings. Flight in a vacuum is
impossible, and so is flight in a medium whose resistance is too great.

34. *Kataphrōnein, hypomenein;* see also, *N.E.* III5b1, the brave man
disliking the thought of death.

35. Pears, *op. cit.,* p. 382.

36. *Politics* I.2.1254b3f, "It is in a living creature, that it is first
possible to discern the rule both of master (*despotikē*) and of statesman
(*politikē*): the soul rules the body with the sway of a master, the
intelligence the appetite with constitutional or royal rule." Recall that
citizens are parts of a state ruled by another part, while slaves are not
parts of the state but material conditions of it. The one place where
Aristotle thinks self-control an adequate description of moral
phenomenon is when it has for its object the same things as
temperance, pleasures of the body.

37. Pears cites Aristotle's distinction (*N.E.* VII.9.) between
temperance and self-control; the temperate man does not feel pleasures
which are contrary to reason, while the self-controlled man feels such
pleasures but is not led by them. Pears draws the implication (*op. cit.,*
p. 276) that the feeling of pleasure is what distinguishes temperance
from self-control. But whether or not one feels pleasure or pain is not
sufficient to discriminate virtue from self-control; the pleasures and the
pains involved in temperance and self-control are different because they
are pleasures and pains produced by the smooth working and the failure
to work of two different potencies. Corresponding to the difference
between virtuous and non-virtuous actualization is a difference in
meaning of self and of self-love, and hence self-sacrifice too. For the
virtuous man, self-love is love of the noble, while for the non-virtuous it

is love of the expedient. Hence, for the virtuous man, except in the case of courage, his sacrifices are not sacrifices of self, while for the non-virtuous man, self-love and self-sacrifice are constantly in conflict. For further elaborations, see IX.8.

38. Hence solutions such as Penner's two entity theory seem to me to miss the mark. They represent an approach to the theory of action remote from the practical problems of deliberation and choice. Terry Penner, "Verbs and the Identity of Actions—A Philosophical Exercise in the Interpretation of Aristotle," *Ryle,* ed., Oscar Wood and George Pitcher, pp. 393-460.

39. *Politics,* VII.14.1333a10.

40. Rorty, "Pleasure," p. 490.

EPICURUS AND

THE PLEASURE PRINCIPLE

DAVID K. GLIDDEN

I

We can distinguish the strategy one develops for living one's life from the measure of its success. Formulating a strategy requires the selection of goals as well as finding the means to achieve them. In the course of selecting a strategy or in evaluating a possible way of life as choiceworthy, we can question both the purported goals and the likelihood which the means enjoy of effecting them. Even so, determining how one ought to live one's life is distinct from evaluating one's success at living. On the one hand, various factors might well interfere with fully implementing the plan of life one adopts. Here we can measure an individual's success in carrying out his intentions. But there is as well a second measure of success which stands in a different relation to any particular life plan. Even if one could fulfill whatever the strategy of conduct might be, the question still remains whether one could, so to speak, be fulfilled in living that sort of life. Here we can measure the psychological impact of a given moral strategy, what its effects will be upon human nature or particular humans. And it is at this point that psychological considerations distinguish themselves from moral values.

This is not to suggest that psychology reigns supreme over ethics. Nor is it to claim that the question of personal happiness is paramount in weighing the value of different moral strategies. Indeed, circumstances might well require an individual to sacrifice his life out of moral considerations. In general, it might not be morally desirable to be psychologically well-adjusted in an unjust world. Moral values often run at cross-purposes with psychological ones. Furthermore, the failure of a particular moral strategy to safeguard one's mental health might not in itself condemn the plan, although psychological considerations are no doubt relevant in formulating one's plan of action. Presumably moral reasoning would have to be very compelling before one were to adopt a moral strategy which was psychologically destructive. Nevertheless, it is a separate question to ascertain the psychological effects of the moral strategy one adopts. Plato's philosopher, the ideal good man, sees himself as imprisoned in a body from which he yearns to escape. He struggles to free himself from the torment of his body's lust and the distractions as well of the perceptual faculties. He is sexually repressed and generally uncomfortable with human relations of all varieties. His distorted self-image and his fear of passions suggest a failure to cope with the elements of his personality, a failure tolerated, encouraged, and perhaps even required by his moral strategy. From any of a number of contemporary psychological theories the conduct of our lives which Plato's moral theory urges upon us seems at best neurotic, if not perverse. The path Plato invites us to take is paved with guilt, repression, anxiety. But this need not prevent us from taking it.

At the same time, Plato's psychological views differ from ours. He sees the personality as tainted by the body, so that the soul requires the purification of what we take to be sublimation and repression. In this way, measuring the success of a moral strategy is open to competing psychological interpretations, just as the choice of a particular strategy is open to competing ethical theories. Consequently it is easy to see that the psychological assessment of moral theories is an empirical determination of considerable complexity, due in part to the lack of a unified psychological theory. In the same way the role which psychological considerations assume in the formulation of moral theories is no less complex, as understanding the facts of human nature grades off against valuing certain moral traits above others. Nevertheless, there is a fundamental difference between deciding how to live one's life and evaluating in psychological terms the kind of life such a choice might bring, a difference no more or less important than the difference between 'ought' and 'is'. It is also the difference between purpose and function. The moral theorist provides content to human *purpose* by setting out goals for man to pursue. The clinical psychologist is interested in the *function* such moral intentions and attitudes play in the life of the person--from the structure of his mind and the condition of his body to the behavior he engages in.

Unfortunately, it is all too easy to confuse psychological considerations with ethical ones. This is especially the case with hedonism, where the goal which characterizes the moral theory--namely, pleasure--is itself supposed to be a psychological state. But, as we have seen, the pursuit of pleasure--as a characterization of moral intentions--cannot be identified, at least in any simple way, with the psychological state of mind achieved by those pursuits. Indeed, it is proverbial that many an avowed hedonist takes his pleasure and suffers accordingly. Such is said to be the case of the masochist. And in such cases the intentional description which the hedonist gives to his mental attitude (i.e. feeling pleasure, taking pleasure) is at variance with his actual psychological condition. This difference is symptomatic of the differing truth conditions between moral claims and psychological statements, where the way in which we represent our moral strategy to ourselves may be an accurate description of the intended strategy (e.g. hedonism) but a false description of our state of mind (e.g. self-hatred).

If it proves difficult to sort out ethical from psychological considerations in the case of hedonism or, for that matter, in the case of other moral theories, it is all the more difficult when it comes to Greek ethics, where the end-in-view of moral conduct is typically represented to be the psychological well-being, or *eudaimonia*, of the individual moral agent. From Plato to Chrysippus, from Aristotle to Epicurus, proper conduct and human nature are said to go together, so that a good human being is good at being human. Being good, as Plato says, is good for you. It is not surprising, then, that as moral strategies differ among the ancients, so do their psychological theories. This is true of the Stoics, whose peculiar moral views are well suited to their particular understanding of human nature. It is also true of Epicurus, who is the subject of this essay. Here we cannot explore the complete range of Epicurean ethics. Instead, we shall only interest ourselves in the psychological fit of Epicurus' moral strategy. But first we must continue this discussion of the contrast between ethics and psychology, as applied to hedonism.

II

We can categorize pleasure in any of a number of ways: as a feeling or as an emotion, as a propositional attitude akin to enjoyment or as the generic object of all desire. However we refer to it, we must bear in mind that reference to pleasure is contextually defined. In some cases we are referring to an intentional object which need not exist to be real. In other cases we are referring to an actual psychological state, which the subject himself may or may not fully apprehend. On the one hand, pleasure can be a goal which is not attained, as in the case of the frustrated hedonist. Furthermore, the sadist can take pleasure in hurting his victims without really deriving any pleasure from it. And we all do occasionally deceive ourselves into thinking that we are having a good time, when we are not. Only a very few philosophers would question the truth of a sincere, properly expressed report of a

pain. Yet most of us grow sceptical of a similar report of
pleasure, preferring joyful outbursts to reports of joy. When
confronted with 'I am happy' we become suspicious and
want proof, not wanting to take the person at his word
without at least a smile or some other behavioral
corroboration as well. This suggests that there are established
ways of finding pleasures out without having to take a person
at his word. Indeed, the very intentional inexistence of
phantom pleasures suggests other cases where our reference
to pleasure must succeed in denoting the appropriate
psychological state, however we define it and however we
detect it. Unlike the case of pain reports and phantom
pleasures, real pleasures are then publicly detectable,
susceptible to observation in the way in which other
psychological states are, like anger, fear, being in love.
Admittedly the relation between phantom pleasures and
actual ones is a complex matter. We need to decide, for
instance, whether the foot fetishist is deriving real pleasure
from the object of his affection. But the controversy
concerning false pleasures is at the same time inevitable, once
intentional avowals and the psychological assessment of
pleasure can come in conflict. Although we might or might
not be deceiving ourselves about our intentional pleasures,
whether we are feeling happy for example, it is a separate
question whether we are in that psychological state, whether
we are really happy.

Ethicist and psychologist alike interest themselves in both
phantom pleasures and actual ones. But the psychologist has
a special interest in being able to detect the actual
psychological state, especially in clinical situations. Whatever
the intentional life plan of the patient may be, whatever his
moral strategy, the therapist needs to measure both the
patient's intentional perspective as well as his behavior
against the background of the patient's psychological
condition, which is often determined by examining his
psychohistory. There are, of course, nonverbal ways for
determining the patient's psychological condition, such as
those used in biofeedback therapy which stress physiological

indicators: pulse rate, blood pressure, nervous twitches, and the like. But the Freudian therapist tries to map out his patient's conscious attitudes as structures which articulate the terrain of the unconscious and whose function (ideally) is to satisfy the patient's primordial, inchoate longings. The therapist can thereby examine, say, the various functions served by his patient's moral attitudes (whatever they might be) in giving satisfaction to these primitive desires. In this way the patient's attitudes and behavior are regulated by what Freud called the Pleasure Principle:

> In the theory of psychoanalysis we have no hesitation in assuming that the course taken by mental events is automatically regulated by the pleasure principle. We believe, that is to say, that the course of those events is invariably set in motion by an unpleasurable tension, and that it takes a direction such that its final outcome coincides with a lowering of that tension--that is, with an avoidance of unpleasure or a production of pleasure.[1]

The therapy works to adjust (when necessary) the patient's conscious attitudes and behavior to perform their function more efficiently in providing satisfaction to the patient within the circumstances in which he finds himself. And Freud described the weight of the patient's actual situation as invoking the Reality Principle:

> Under the influence of the ego's instincts of self-preservation, the pleasure principle is replaced by the *reality principle*. This latter principle does not abandon the intention of ultimately obtaining pleasure but it nevertheless demands and carries into effect the postponement of satisfaction, the abandonment of a number of possibilities of gaining satisfaction and the temporary toleration of unpleasure as a step on the long indirect road to pleasure.[2]

Now the therapist is interested in discovering how the

demand for immediate satisfaction and the postponement of pleasure in the course of rational planning are able to resolve themselves in a specific patient. For example, the therapist might question a particular patient's constellation of sexual attitudes, including the belief that sexual intercourse distracts the mind and pollutes the soul--questioning the functional value of such attitudes in providing libidinal satisfaction. In this way the therapist measures the success of his patient's strategies against his success at living, at finding genuine satisfaction in the real world. The psychoanalyst, then, always keeps his eye on what he takes to be his patient's real pleasures, his actual satisfaction.

Concerned as he is with the development and criticism of moral strategies, the traditional ethicist does not typically share the therapist's concern for the application of a particular life plan in individual cases. Of course, the ethicist hopes that the moral strategy which he favors will be psychologically plausible, but typically he does not attempt to demonstrate this fact nor does he construct his moral strategy in the first place with an eye to the details of human psychology. At best the traditional ethicist remains somewhat indifferent to the functional role played by moral attitudes in the specific life of the individual. Rather, he is more interested in comparing an individual's pattern of intentions against the blueprint of a specific moral strategy. Until recently, ethicists have preferred to concern themselves with the foundations of morals, the universal prerequisites to moral conduct, devoid of references to the specific circumstances individuals find themselves in. Furthermore, ethicists have preferred to concentrate on the moral reasoning which explains and defends a given moral strategy, and in this way they have proved adverse to the explanation of moral attitudes as vehicles of primal satisfaction. Consequently, ethicists have proved hostile to the Freudian Pleasure Principle. Generally, ethics has been content to do its work from within the intentional framework of the moral agent, without attempting to step outside to compare the moral strategy with the psychology of individuals. In the case of hedonism, then, pleasures tend to be discussed from within the Cartesian first-person perspective. From this perspective the hedonistic calculus compiles what the unreflecting moral agent would count as his pleasures, however they are subsequently categorized and weighted. This undoes the difference between phantom pleasures and genuine pleasures, as the psychoanalyst would count them. And self-deception becomes an embarrasing paradox for this Cartesian approach, just as visual illusions become problematic for those theorists committed to the veil of perception.

By comparison, the moral theorists of ancient Greece were psychologists as well, convinced as they were that the proper understanding of human nature determines the propriety of human conduct. In Plato's *Republic*, for example, we are only in a position to fathom the moral virtues once we have understood the psychological divisions in the soul and their hierarchy. Failure to understand the psychological foundations of Platonic ethics has caused considerable confusion among scholars. Such is also the case with Epicurean ethics, whose hedonism must be understood in psychological terms to be properly appreciated. For Epicurus it is the corporeality of the human soul which provides the measure of our success at living and points toward prudential self-interest as the natural human strategy. This is possible only because the intentional pleasures we conceive for ourselves are weighed against the real pleasure, as Epicurus defines it, which they give our material soul. Here Epicurus is much closer to Freud than he is to Descartes. Like Aristotle and Plato before him, Epicurus is well aware of the empty pleasures with which we can deceive ourselves. And his confidence in our ability to detect the feelings, or *pathē*, of pleasure and pain does not rest on the certainty of a Cartesian self-consciousness, but rather on the material identity of these *pathē* with atomic motions in our bodies, understanding these psychophysical experiences, with Freud, in mechanical terms.

III

We are blessed with an abundance of ancient sources on Epicurean ethics–from Epicurus' own writings to Lucretius, Cicero, Diogenes of Oenoanda, Diogenes Laertius, and Plutarch, to name some of the chief sources. Now there are some precious insights to be found in the literature, but I shall not discuss them. Instead I shall continue building on the foundations I have just laid. I shall begin with an arresting contradiction in the *Letter to Menoeceus*, one of three Epicurean letters preserved along with other primary sources in Book X of Diogenes Laertius. On the one hand, Epicurus makes the famous statement that pleasure is the primary good, the *proton agathon* (D.L. X 129). But then Epicurus turns around and awards the prize to *phronēsis*, which I shall understand here to mean prudential reasoning: Epicurus says that *phronēsis* is the greatest good, the *megiston agathon* (D.L. X 132). And if we compare the two passages we find other apparent contradictions. Both pleasure and prudence are said to be the *archē*, or point of departure, for choice and avoidance. Furthermore, if we turn to Cicero's summary of Epicurean ethics in Book I of his *De Finibus*, there too we find that both pleasure and moral reasoning, or *sapientia*, capture the highest honors (*De Fin.* I 12.42 & 13.43). Now if we were to understand these and similar passages in terms of ethical theory alone, it would seem that Epicurus had not made up his mind between ethical hedonism or ethical egoism, between taking pleasure as the basis for how we ought to live or appealing in an Aristotelian manner to self-interest as the foundation of morals. My own suggestion to resolve this dilemma should by now be obvious. The Epicurean measure of our success at living is whether we are living a pleasant life. At the same time the moral basis for ethical decision making is prudential reasoning, or *phronēsis*. In other words, for Epicurus first prize in psychology goes to the Pleasure Principle; first prize in moral theory is awarded to the Reality Principle. It is in this way that we should appreciate a statement by Epicurus which was prominent in the ancient discussions of his views:

> It is not possible to live pleasantly without living
> prudently (*phronimōs*), and virtuously (*kalōs*), and justly
> (*dikaiōs*), nor is it possible to live prudently and
> virtuously and justly without living pleasantly. This is
> because the virtues (*aretai*) are a natural, integral part of
> the pleasant life and the pleasant life is inseparable from
> them. (D.L. X 132)

But let us now, for the sake of analysis, separate the
unseparable to see how the psychological and moral elements
fit together, the pleasant life and the virtuous one.

Returning to the passage where Epicurus claims that
pleasure is the primary human good, the full statement reads
as follows:

> And thereby we say that pleasure is the beginning and
> the end (*archē* and *telos*) of living happily, for it is this
> which we have recognized to be the good, primary and
> congenital, and it is from this that we make our
> departure for all choice and avoidance, and it is to this
> that we go back again insofar as we judge every good by
> the standard of feeling (*pathos*). (D.L. X 129)

Rather than interpret Epicurus' statement as answering two
central questions in ethics (what has moral value? how should
we live?), we should understand it as a claim about human
nature. Epicurus has two points to make here: that pleasure
is the point of departure, or *archē*, for forming intentions and
that it is also the *telos* of the good life. Let us first consider
this second point.

The Greek '*telos*' encompasses two rather different sorts of
'end': the intended end-in-view, as in 'I am running to
Athens,' and the natural end or function, as in 'Man's *telos* is
the rational life' or 'The function of the heart is to pump
blood.' In contemporary philosophy the central case has
seemed to be the intended goal, with the notion of a natural

end or function as somewhat derivative, in the way in which an artifact derives its function from its inventor. This was not the case with the Greeks. Nature's ends, like nature's cycles, were recognized in the earliest cosmologies where each element in nature had its own proper function, its own *telos*. And this recognition of natural functions came long before Greek psychology had developed the notion of conscious intentional goals, as we would understand them. Now in the passage which concerns us, Epicurus questions man's natural function, what the good life is good for. Epicurus' answer is pleasure--that is to say, just as the eye's *telos* is to see, what living is supposed to do is to bring pleasure. And, as we have seen, this point is logically distinct from the determination of goals we should set for ourselves in any moral strategy. Epicurus describes pleasure as a *telos* in the following terms: "It is to this that we go back again insofar as we judge every good by the standard of feeling (*pathos*)." Consequently, we should be able to understand how pleasure serves as man's natural function, once we appreciate how it is that feeling (*pathos*) is the measure (*kanōn*) of all that is good for us (taking *agathon* in its usual meaning in such contexts).

Judging from all the Epicurean sources currently available, it is evident that Epicurean *pathos* was strictly delimited to the sensations of pleasure and pain. I have argued the point elsewhere.[2] Here I can only review some of my conclusions. Unlike other ancient theories where pleasure could serve to evaluate one's sense experience and in this way presuppose it (such as taking pleasure in the smell of a rose or enjoying the sight of the Parthenon), for Epicurus, pleasure, like pain, was itself an experience, rather than an aesthetic perspective on one's experience. The Epicureans identified both pleasure and pain with atomic events in the body, more specifically as categories of noticeable atomic collisions among the soul-and non-soul atoms which compose the bodies of all animals, including man. Cutting one's finger causes pain, because of the severe disruption of the finger's atomic structure. A pleasant odor is pleasant, because the impact of atoms bringing the odor to the nose actually enhances the atomic structures within the nose--the odor enters the nose smoothly and agreeably. Not only is this true of bodily pleasures and pains (sore feet and sexual experiences, painful sights and pleasant sounds); it is also true of mental delights and anxieties (the joy of having friends, the fear of death). Here too such states are identified as atomic episodes, but in this case limited to the motions of the soul atoms alone.

Once one appreciates the corporeal nature of pleasure and pain, the purely atomic identity of the *pathē*, one can then see through a number of philosophic problems which have long bedecked Epicureanism. For example, philosophers find it hard to make sense of these Epicurean *pathē* since most pleasures do not seem to be feelings so much as emotions or attitudes, which is to say that the intentional frameworks in which we refer to pleasures and pains are fundamentally different. Yet it turns out that Epicurus identifies both kinds of *pathos* not by the role they play in intentional discourse at all, but rather by their material identity as atomic episodes. Tickles and joys, toothaches and distrust, all come to be classified together as bodily states which can be referred to as such, thereby obviating the need for intentional descriptions by which to designate these states of mind. Of course the identification of pleasures and pains as bodily states will not affect the diversity and disparity of pleasures and pains within intentional contexts. After all, how we come to characterize a particular pleasure (as an emotion rather than a feeling, for instance) has to do with its intentional setting (taking pleasure in one's work, for example) rather than the quantity of excitation. Nor will reference to such atomic states in itself resolve our intentions or determine the goals we should pursue, because our resolve largely depends on how we characterize the significance of the intended plan, what we take to be the meaning of the proposed course of action. Now according to Epicurus, the full variety of intellectual and corporeal pleasures and pains can be roughly divided into two kinds of atomic events, those limited to clusters of soul atoms alone and those encompassing the activities of non-soul atoms as well (cf. D.L. X 136).

Nevertheless, in weighing the significance of such experiences within an intentional framework and especially in the context of deciding what to do, other (prudential) considerations are required, such as weighing the value of intellectual delights over sexual ones. The Epicureans are quite clear on the point, especially in their discussions of decision making (cf. D.L. X 129-132), the nature of justice (cf. D.L. X 150-154), and the importance of friendship (cf. D.L. X 148; *De Fin.* I 20).

Similarly, the much discussed distinction which the Epicureans draw between two generic categories of pleasure (katastematic pleasures and active pleasures, cf. D.L. X 136) does not distinguish two kinds of intentional states, as some have understood it, but rather two types of pleasureable atomic episodes. Active pleasures, such as the pleasures of bodily movement and sensory pleasures, involve the effects of external stimulation upon the atomic structures within one's body, so that the body responds agreeably to the external environment. So the ballerina enjoys performing as the black swan in "Swan Lake," moving across the stage in complicated patterns co-ordinated with the other dancers. And we enjoy watching her performance. The katastematic pleasures, on the other hand, are the pleasures we derive from ourselves alone, from the smooth functioning of the clusters of atoms which compose us. This mellow condition is what the Epicureans called *ataraksia*, a condition free from all pain and anxiety and not dependent on the outside world for its creation and maintenance, a condition where, as Epicurus says, the soul has escaped the tempest (cf. D.L. X 128). To be in this condition is to fulfill man's *telos*, to be in the best condition our corporeal nature can allow. We can imagine what *ataraksia* is like by subtracting away from our present state all the pains and anxieties which confront us. We can imagine the relief which comes upon the end of a splitting headache; we can think of a final release from an intense, prolonged anxiety. In this way katastematic pleasures are purely our own doing, depending entirely upon ourselves and the atomic harmony within us. At the same time, although active pleasures are dependent upon interaction with the external environment, both varieties of pleasureable atomic episodes share the same nature–namely, freedom from any atomic disruption affecting the smooth functioning of our bodies. Consequently, the Epicureans define the nature of pleasure as the absence of pain in the body or anxiety in the soul (D.L. X 131). But if one were to attain the harmony of *ataraksia*, one's active pleasures could at best be regarded as variations on the same theme (cf. D.L. X 121, 144).

Although I have silently passed over numerous scholarly debates and textual disputes, we are at least in a position to see in broad outline how it is that man's *telos* is measured by his *pathē*. Our success at living is measured over against the quantity of disruption within the atomic structures which compose us. The less atomic disruption there is, the greater our success at living. Although the exact quantity of disruption can of course only be measured indirectly, Epicurus made some guidelines for our calculations (cf. D.L. X 145; Diog. Oen. Frg. 38). But without trying to put too fine a point on it, the measure of our success is strictly biophysical. In this way, man shares his *telos* as a successful organism along with the other animals, a point which the Epicureans stress (cf. D.L. X 137; *De Fin* I 9.30). This is not to suggest that dogs and peacocks share man's moral dilemmas; it is only to claim that we are all made of the same stuff. Consequently, the measurement of whether a particular man is fulfilling his human nature is in the last resort a question in atomic mechanics. But the Epicurean must look for the presence, say, of anxiety and nervousness in order to detect disturbances among the soul atoms, just as he regards illnesses and injuries as signs for the condition of the body within (cf. Diog. Oen. frg. 37). Lacking better measurements and detection devices, this is the best he can do. Yet this is not doing moral theory badly but doing psychology rather well, all things considered.

If a limited technology inhibited the Epicureans from pursuing what has turned out to be psychophysics and biofeedback therapy, the Epicureans fell back upon the analysis of fears, anxieties, and other mental attitudes to gather evidence for the material condition of the soul. In this respect Epicurus' strategy coincides with Freud's *Project*, although of course they had different views on the physical composition of the soul (Freud preferring Fechner to Democritus). When it comes to the Pleasure Principle as the arbiter of mental health, this coincidence is striking, especially if we consider Freud's account of pleasure and pain (unpleasure):

> We have decided to relate pleasure and unpleasure to the quantity of excitation that is present in the mind...and to relate them in such a manner that unpleasure corresponds to an *increase* in the quantity of excitation and pleasure to a *diminution*."[4]

Epicurus' claim that *ataraksia* is the highwater mark of pleasure finds expression in Freud too:

> The mental apparatus endeavors to keep the quantity of excitition present in it as low as possible or at least to keep it constant. This latter hypothesis is only another way of stating the pleasure principle; for if the work of the mental apparatus is directed towards keeping the quantity of excitation low, then anything that is calculated to increase that quantity is bound to be felt as adverse to the functioning of the apparatus, that is as unpleasureable. The pleasure principle follows from the principle of constancy.[5]

The release of tension, or cathexis, which Freud sees as the mechanism of the mental life (the Pleasure Principle) finds its apotheosis in *ataraksia*. Both Epicurus and Freud see man's nature as striving to return to its own natural condition in the face of life's disturbances. And both Epicurus and Freud agree that "the feelings of pleasure and unpleasure...are an index to what is happening in the interior of the apparatus."[6] Pleasure is the measuring stick, or *kanōn*, of what is good for us, and so the pursuit of pleasure is the pursuit of man's *telos*. But even discounting their differences on mechanics, there are still important disagreements between the two accounts. For Freud it is the rate of change of the quantity of excitation, not the absolute amount, which measures human satisfaction. Furthermore, Freud understood man's inherent urge to achieve a constant level of excitation as "the instinct to return to the inanimate state," an instinct symbolized by postcoital depression—namely, a yearning for death.[7] In this way, man's *telos* is death. What Freud held to be the final entropy, Epicurus praised as the mellow state of *ataraksia*. Of course, the notion of entropy is foreign to Epicurean physics.

Once we understand how pleasure is man's natural *telos* (cf. D.L. X 146-148), we are in a better position to comprehend the companion thesis that pleasure is an *archē*: "It is from this that we make our departure for all choice and avoidance." Here too it is helpful to compare Epicurus with Freud. Paralleling the distinction between katastematic pleasures and active pleasures, Freud notes that the psychic mechanism attempts to minimize excitation by attempting, on the one hand, to shield itself from external stimuli and, on the other, by managing the reception of external stimuli in a controlled fashion.[8] This of course requires choice and avoidance, particularly as external circumstances make the individual adopt a strategy of survival, so that he postpones or abandons some sources of satisfaction in order to obtain others, often accepting unpleasure in the bargain (the Reality Principle). The economies of choice are made necessary by man's insatiable demands for satisfaction in a world with limited resources, or as Epicurus puts it, pleasure is the point of departure for all choosing. The need to choose, whatever the rationale of the particular choice might be, presupposes the need to act, and what explains the latter is pleasure--that is, the yearning for satisfaction. So it is not surprising that Epicurus connects this theory of pleasure with his account of natural and necessary desires (cf. D.L. X 127). Pleasure, or more strictly the physical disposition of the atomic structures within us to return to their natural harmony without interference from outside, is what manufactures the desires we have. Obviously, the propensities of the atomic structures which compose us to bond together in the way they do cannot characterize our desires in any way, except to explain their presence. The economies we choose and the decisions we make require an intentional criterion, not a psychophysical one. It is at this point, and not before, that Epicurean moral theory emerges out of Epicurean psychology. And it is here that Epicurus and Freud part company.

When he abandoned the *Project* and turned to the *Interpretation of Dreams*, Freud gave up the hope of explaining the details of our desires in mechanistic terms. Instead, he sought to map out the intentional terrain of our conscious attitudes (what Freud called the secondary process) against the intentional substructure of our unconscious thoughts (what Freud called the primary psychical process).[9] In this way, psychology could go on to explain the objects of our desires by their symbolic importance in our unconscious. As a consequence, each and every desire carries two intentions, one given to it by the secondary process and the other deriving from the primary process. A desire to teach, then, can have Oedipal origins. A desire to run long distances can be a form of narcissism. The moral philosopher concerns himself with the secondary process, while the psychoanalyst delves into the primary process, although certain philosophic problems such as *akrasia* and self-deception might encourage the philosopher to broaden his horizons. Moreover, the psychiatric patient learns to adjust his conscious attitudes as a result of discovering his unconscious ones. And so both moral theory and psychoanalysis can become involved in the formation of moral strategies. Epicurus, on the other hand, continued with the Project.

Without the invention of an intentional substructure with which to interpret our conscious attitudes, the Epicurean can only grade the success of those attitudes in creating a life free from pain and anxiety. But such retrospective measurement obviously cannot itself guide the individual toward the smooth functioning of his atomic body. Consequently a moral theory is required. Yet to call such a moral strategy "hedonism" is quite misleading. Hedonism suggests a rather subjective strategy subject to the idiosyncracies of our tastes and interests, what we happen to delight in (like running marathons, for instance). But as I have already pointed out, taking up the strategy of hedonism, as it is usually conceived, is to stand within the framework of conscious intentions and to lose sight of the difference between phantom pleasures and real ones (as the therapist would define them). This certainly is not Epicurus' point of view, which carefully distinguishes between what we want to take pleasure in and what in fact gives us pleasure, reserving moral value for the latter alone.

Within the intentional perspective all one's conscious attitudes and opinions have an equal standing, in that they all designate one's state of mind (how one feels about something) without necessarily referring to the way things are. We all have fears and fancies which do not correspond to reality. These are what Epicurus calls empty anxieties (cf. D.L. X 125) and empty desires (cf. D.L. X 127,130). Some of these fancies may prove obdurate, not because they are part of our nature (i.e. somehow necessary for our atomic microstructure), but merely because of the high opinion we place on them, although the opinion in question is an empty one (*kenodoksia*), not corresponding to reality (cf. D.L. X 144, 149). Consequently our moral strategy needs to sort out valid desires from empty ones. This requires in the first place an understanding of our atomic nature. But since our access to our atomic constitutions is limited to our *pathē* of pleasure and pain, it also requires the accumulated knowledge of human experience, the case histories of profligates and ascetics—in a word, *phronēsis*.

The Freudian analyst can employ the intentional substructure of the unconscious to explain idle fancies and phantom pleasures as cases of self-deception. The way the patient regards his mental attitude ('I am happy.') can be discounted in light of his unconscious attitude ('He is suicidal.'). The Epicurean handles the problem of self-deception differently. On the one hand, there are groundless fears and false expectations which cannot measure up to reality. These are, as it were, false beliefs concerning the coming state of our atomic constitutions, causing needless anxiety or leading us on to future pains and disappointments. We can recall the fate of LaMettrie whose expectations of the pleasures of pheasant pâté in the court of Frederick the Great led to a painful death from indigestion. But whether we can deceive ourselves about our present *pathē* (that is, our present atomic state) is a difficult question, simply because no surviving Epicurean texts address the point. Theoretically, such self-deception is of course possible since pain and pleasure are defined in terms of the atomic microstructure. And there is no reason to believe that even our estimates of our own physical condition would be infallible, no matter how reliable they might be. There is, after all, a difference between crying out in pain and describing that condition (cf. Diog. Oen. frg. 45, D.L. X 118). It is also worth noting that in the surviving texts the Epicureans do emphasize the truth of perceptual appearances, while making no such claims about the *pathē*. Whatever the details on self-deception might be, it is at least clear that pleasures and pains (both mental and corporeal) need to be weighed and evaluated by an outside examiner–*phronēsis*. And so it is that prudential reasoning bears the burden of Epicurean moral theory.

Epicurus says that pleasure is the primary good, the *archē* and *telos* of choice and avoidance. Epicurus also says that *phronēsis* is the greatest good and the *archē* as well. In this way the pleasurable life and the virtuous life are inseparable. This is a coherent thesis, once we understand its blend of psychology and moral theory. The theory of pleasure is part of a general theory of human nature. Prudential reasoning makes use of that theory to flesh out our intentions, to determine the sorts of things we should seek or avoid. For example, we are to prefer mental pleasures to sensual ones, catering to our soul atoms (cf. D.L. X 144-145). In his *Letter to Menoeceus*, Epicurus gives us an adequate sketch of how prudential reasoning is supposed to work. And Diogenes Laertius lists some of the things Epicureans are supposed to engage in (such as law suits and patriotism) and some which they are supposed to shun (such as drink and marriage), although fortunately this list may be dubious (cf. D.L. X 117-121). Here I cannot pursue the details of Epicurean ethics any further. Like Plato and Aristotle before him, Epicurus is convinced that the virtuous life is in our self-interest. Nevertheless, this leaves the specific moral strategy which *phronēsis* contemplates somewhat open-ended. Any of a number of moral positions will do, just as laws differ in different countries (cf. D.L. X 151). Consequently, it is misleading to speak of a well-defined Epicurean moral theory at all. Furthermore, the alliance which Epicurus negotiates between psychology and self-interest is a fragile one. As long as we lack an adequate technology which can observe and predict our atomic harmonies, the measure of genuine satisfaction may well be hard to figure. *Phronēsis* notwithstanding, we can always deceive ourselves about what we fancy. And so Epicurus, like Freud, is in the embarrassing predicament of knowing that when it comes to our intentions all men are liars; yet in the end our word is all there is to go on.

Notes

1. Freud, S., *Beyond the Pleasure Principle*, trans. by James Strachey (New York: Norton, 1961), p. 1.

2. *Ibid.*, p. 2.

3. Cf. "Epicurus on Self-Perception," *APQ* 16 (1979) 297-307; and "*Sensus* and Sense-Perception in the *De Rerum Natura*," *California Studies in Classical Antiquity* 12 (1980).

4. Freud, *op. cit.*, pp. 1-2.

5. *Ibid.*, p. 3.

6. *Ibid.*, p. 23.

7. *Ibid.*, cf. pp. 32-37.

8. *Ibid.*, cf. pp. 18-27.

9. *Ibid.*, cf. pp. 28-31.

10. This essay is a revision of a lecture designed for a general audience. For this reason I have not here attempted to defend my thesis by discussing the textual details with which it can be defended against the standard interpretations in the scholarly literature. Accordingly, the references I do give are general and incomplete. In revising the lecture I am particularly indebted to many pleasant conversations with Gisela Striker over Epicurus and espresso. And I am deeply grateful to the Alexander von Humboldt Stiftung for making those conversations possible in Göttingen.

ON WHAT WE AIM AT

AND HOW WE LIVE

JULIUS M. E. MORAVCSIK

The perils of a human life can be divided into two kinds. On the one hand, we can be harmed by actions and circumstances that work against realizing what is in our interest and what would help fulfill our potentialities. On the other hand, our actions and attitudes can harm or diminish our contributions to the benefit of others. The dominant ethical theories of modern philosophy separate these kinds of perils into matters of what we want to do with our lives and how we find means to carry out such plans on the one hand, and matters of morality, to be specified in terms of an autonomous set of rules, on the other.

In this paper this conception will be challenged. First a case will be presented to illustrate certain salient facts about our choices and related attitudes. These facts show that moral choices are partly a matter of the exercise of sensitivities that are not rule-governed. The development of these sensitivites is inextricably linked to questions about the over-all aims, or "meaning" in our lives. Adequate consideration of "meaning-of-life" questions turn out to be based on conceptions of human nature. Hence the claim of the autonomy of morality is ill-founded. There is no sharp line between the moral and the non-moral in terms of choices, relevant considerations, and desirable character traits. The structure of this alternative pattern for construing our moral lives will be laid bare, and in the last section it will be shown that the ethics of Plato and Aristotle fit this alternative, and more adequate, pattern rather than the pattern into which the modern theories of utilitarianism and Kantian ethics fall. The point of this illustration is not merely historical; it is meant as a spur towards a reconsideration and revitalization of thought along the alternative pattern in contemporary philosophy.

I

A Case. On my way to San Francisco I turn on the car-radio. On a "talk-show" a woman is phoning in. She is poor, sick, and without friends or relatives. She cannot pay for her medicine, and at times goes ten to fourteen days without talking to anyone. This radio-show is one of her few links with the outside world.

Having parked my car in Union Square, I pass by Magnin's. They have a fur sale. I see people rushing in and out. They spend thousands of dollars on expensive furs--to be worn to parties or the theater. They are preoccupied with their pleasure in acquiring luxury items and thus possession of goods that will gain them prestige in the community.

I find the situation incongruous. In a .world in which we have so many lonely shut-ins, people ought not to be preoccupied so much with luxury and with prestige. A society in which people exhibit that degree of indifference towards the lonely cannot be a morally sound society.

There are, however, many people who, though they regret the predicament of the lonely, disagree with me. They claim that there is nothing incongruous about the scene I described, and that the people rushing to Magnin's are not doing anything unethical. They are not harming anybody, and they are not doing anything that worsens the condition of the lonely woman who phoned in to the radio station. On the contrary, they might go on, acquiring wealth and luxury often leads to expanded charitable activity; hence in a society in which scenes like the one at Magnin's are allowed, the lonely might get more relief in the long run than they would in a society in which such preoccupation with prestige and luxury is not permitted.

Since the disagreement between me and the hypothetical opponent is about ethical matters, the dominant modern ethical theories would attempt to construe it as one concerning rules or principles.

Can we construe it as a disagreement about the application of the principle of maximizing happiness for the greatest number of people? The difficulty with such a construal is that nothing in the case presented so far indicates that this principle is violated. Furthermore, even if someone should show that everything is being done in our society with regard to the shut-ins that maximizes happiness for the greatest number, this would not assuage my feeling of disapproval and sense of incongruity with respect to the situation. What bothers me is the indifference on the part of the people, and not what is done or not done to the shut-ins.

One might try to construe the disagreement as being about the application of the categorical imperative. But the universalization principle leaves the situation unscathed. If everyone were concerned with luxury, etc. we would not have necessarily a society in which people harm each other or take advantage of each other. It would be a society of self-indulgent people; how does one show on Kantian grounds that this would be a morally reprehensible society?

It is important to see that the problem concerns features of the situation of the lonely that could not be alleviated by more rigorous application of a fair principle of distributing goods. It is not the poverty of the woman but her loneliness that is in the focus of the predicament.

One might think that the disagreement is about some "local" moral rule, rather than about the application of the most general ethical rules. Plausible candidates might be: "Do not neglect lonely people!" or "Do not buy luxury items as long as you could use your time and energy to help those who are shut-ins!"

Are these really rules, or are these exhortations? We all agree in general that one ought not to neglect the lonely; but there are serious disagreements about what constitutes, in any given context, neglect of the lonely. Again, nobody would accept the second candidate as a rule of ethics without qualifications. As it stands, it would be difficult to derive it from any of the acknowledged higher moral principles.

The claim of this paper is that even if two people agree on all of the relevant moral rules, they could still disagree on how the predicament of the lonely woman described above should be handled. Two arguments will be advanced to support this claim.

The first argument rests on the fact of "historical moral blindness." People in different historical periods may accept the same set of moral principles and yet one period may have customs that are morally abhorrent to the people of the other period. For example, in earlier periods of history people in the Western world professed the same moral principles as we do today, and yet they thought nothing of impaling their foes on stakes in case of war. In fact, one cannot help but wonder which of our own current practices will be singled out by future generations as abhorrent. It would be easy to find examples of historical periods in which people professed the same principles as I do, and yet found indifference towards the shut-in not morally repugnant. Apparently, we need moral sensitivity in addition to moral rules, and some of these sensitivities are historically conditioned.

The second argument rests on a premise--to be defended in detail later--that rules apply primarily to actions. We can have rules governing how we act, but it makes no sense to talk of rules governing how we should feel. But in the case under consideration a crucial element is feeling. I complain about indifference, and urge more care and kindness exhibited towards the shut-in. Care and kindness are matters of feeling and attitude; not only matters of what we do. Hence what is at issue is the desirability of the development and manifestation of certain feelings and attitudes. But such matters must be regarded as something additional to the formulation of moral rules.

Once we reach the stage at which we discuss the desirability of certain feeling and attitudes, we reach the point at which—in order to justify our preferences—we must appeal to some over-all aim and choice of pattern in human life. Such choices involve "meaning-of-life" questions; i.e., questions as to what gives value to certain patterns of human life, and questions concerning worthwhile over-all aims in our lives. An adequate defense of options in this sphere requires as its foundation some conception of human nature. We cannot have an adequate view as to what are human potentialities that are worth developing unless we have some general conception as to what the class of human potentialities is. Why should I be the kind of person who tries to be kind to others and cares for their feelings? On the one hand, this is a matter for choosing as my over-all aim a certain kind of life-pattern and the development of a certain kind of personality. On the other hand, this is also a matter of moral interest, since my developing or not developing certain attitudes such as kindness and care affects the well-being of other humans.

Thus the case presented illustrates the following two facts. First, it shows that in addition to moral rules the possession of certain attitudes and feelings is also relevant to the assessment of the moral congruousness or incongruity of a given situation. Secondly, it shows that through the consideration of personality traits whose possession is not a matter of rules, ethical considerations are inextricably linked to questions of over-all aims in life and "meaning-of-life" issues, and that these, in turn, are linked to questions about human nature. Hence ethical theories, construed as made up of rules governing actions, are not autonomous; their justificatory basis must reach matters of meaning in human life, and questions about human nature.

II

"Meaning of Life" Questions. Reflections on the case presented in the previous section led us to see that we must answer questions of the form: "Why incorporate such-and-such a capacity or disposition into one's life?" As a first attempt, one might try to answer this question by saying that it is (or is not) in my interest to incorporate the capacity in question. But this just pushes matters one step further back. For we cannot characterize the notion of interest without some conception of the human agent, and hence some conceptions of what the over-all aims of such an agent should be.

Another possible approach would be to say that such-and-such a capacity should be incorporated into one's life because it is ethically desirable. That is to say, having that capacity will enable the agent to have certain attitudes towards others, and these attitudes enrich the lives of those towards whom it is directed. But this approach too pushes things one step further. For we still need some conception of one's over-all aims in life according to which the incorporation of attitudes that enrich the lives of those who are in contact with the agent is of intrinsic merit.

Thus the question: "Why be kind?" leads us to "meaning-of-life" questions, i.e., questions about what our over-all aims in life should be. There are a number of ways of formulating such aims.[1] Certain formulations yield for the agent self-esteem and self-respect. If I can mould my life into a pattern whose instantiation I can regard as having intrinsic value, then I can have respect for myself as the partial embodiment of something worth while. Some people try to find such aims and fail. This is the predicament of the nihilist, portrayed so perceptively by Turgenev in *Fathers and Sons*.

There are people who never bother to formulate over-all aims in their lives. They live by a vague principle of minimal coherence. One cannot say that such persons could not live in a morally acceptable way, or that they could not be leading happy lives. But there are three features of a well-lived life that are more likely to be realized by someone with over-all aims than by someone lacking such. One of these is the retaining of *interest* in things. For instance, we talk of people having retained interest or losing interest; "having the will to live," or having lost that will. If one's interest fits into a general pattern, the interest is less likely to be lost.[2] Another such feature is *hope*. If one has over-all aims in life, and thinks that one's life leads up to something, then one can entertain hope even under adverse circumstances in which the prospects of doing well appear dim. Without over-all aims such hope is more difficult to sustain. Finally, an over-all conception of what is worth while in a human life enables us to find *acceptance* of conditions beyond our control (e.g. aging, death) without lapsing into phlegmatic inactivity that prevents us from working towards changing what is not inevitable.

One can specify one's over-all aims in life in three ways. Our purpose may involve basically either what one can have or *possess* (wealth, pleasure, etc.) or what one can do or *accomplish* (contributing to economic welfare, gaining prestige, etc.) or what one can *be* (an intelligent, kind, cooperative human being, etc.). The link we saw between ethics and "meaning-of-life" issues assumes that the third of these is the most adequate way of specifying one's over-all aims. In the last section we will see how, e.g., Plato and Aristotle argue for this position.

Someone might object at this point by saying that one could form the view according to which any over-all scheme in life is acceptable as long as it leads to enjoyment. This is, however, to put the cart before the horse. For human nature is very plastic with regards to the possible sources of enjoyment. If we enjoy a certain life-pattern, and we decide that another life-pattern would be intrinsically more valuable, then in most cases we can reorient our lives so that the new pattern becomes enjoyable. For example, some persons lead happy and self-centered lives. At some point they might become convinced that a life devoted more to contributing to communal goods would be more valuable. Such a person can easily change his life in such a way as to become the sort of individual who enjoys doing things for others.

Someone might wonder why one should change one's pattern of life if one is happy and contented. But the decision *not* to change is in itself a choice between values and norms. It reaffirms, tacitly, the claims that the life led at present is as valuable as the options to be turned down. In the words of William James, one can say that having some view about over-all desirability of human lives is a "forced and unavoidable" option for humans. Or in the more recent terminology of the existentialists, humans are "condemned" to be value-seeking and norm-setting creatures.

Thus in some form or another we all have views on the desirability of forming over-all aims for one's life, and on the relative merit of different patterns. There is another aspect of the notion of "meaning-of-life". If one adopts a pattern that gives one self-esteem, then this yields a conception according to which the pattern chosen, the kind of personality exemplified, has intrinsic merit; that is to say, it is a valuable contribution to nature from an objective point of view.

The case to be made out is that an adequate conception of moral judgment leads eventually to the consideration of these types of questions and choices, thus negating what has been called in modern times the autonomy of ethics. As we shall see this is not so much a claim that ethics has to be based on something else, rather than a claim that the distinction between moral and non-moral considerations shaping our commitments in life is tenuous, and can be made out only within specific contexts.

III

Utilitarianism and Kantian Ethics. The two most dominant modern ethical theories are utilitarianism and Kantian ethics. How would these theories deal with the case presented earlier? This brief sketch of the dominant modern ethical theories in the Anglo-American tradition is based on the excellent introduction of William Frankena.[3]

At the base of these theories concerning what we ought to do lies the distinction between morality and prudence.[4] Morality tells us what our duties and obligations are, regardless of our individual interests, while prudence tells us what we should do if we are to serve our interests.

Theories of duty and obligation are either teleological theories, specifying duty in terms of the maximization of pleasure, utility, happiness, etc. for the greatest number, or they are deontological theories specifying duty in terms of some intrinsic character of the right actions.[5] Kant's theory, basing duty on the universalizability of one's maxims, is a unitarian deontological theory. Those opting for more than one such basic principle are pluralistic deontological theories.

Orthagonal to these distinctions is the one separating ethical theories depending on whether they regard rules or character traits as central and the other element derivative. Frankena regards the ethics of Plato and Aristotle as theories dealing with duty that construe traits as primary.[6]

Most versions of utilitarianism and Kantian ethics are rule-oriented, and embrace either some version of the maximization principle or some formulation of the principle of universalizability.

Since utilitarian principles construe morality as leading to the increase of some form of non-moral value, a general theory of value has to say something about this topic as well. In the later chapters of his book Frankena surveys various suggestions concerning non-moral value, and includes Plato and Aristotle among the philosophers who contributed to this topic. Frankena suggests that perhaps no one pattern of life would do for all humans.[7] It appears, however, that the modern literature does not have much to say about how one justifies proposals for non-moral value.[8]

Let us consider first the heavy stress that these modern theories lay on "big rules," be they those of maximization or of universalizability. When applied to concrete situations, these rules seem singularly uninformative. My judgment that the scene described in a previous section is morally incongruous is not based either on a maximization rule, or on a rule of universalizability. Even if someone were to demonstrate that the situation involving the lonely woman represents the maximization of pleasure for the greatest number as much as the realization of such a rule is possible for us, I would still be dissatisfied with the situation from a moral point of view. The same holds for deontic principles. After all, the situation described is neither logically inconsistent, when generalized, nor one that could not be regarded as satisfactory by a completely rational being. But assurances of this sort will not assuage my sense of moral dissatisfaction.

Perhaps the criticism of our indifference towards the shut-ins can be based on the claim that some less general rule–possibly derivable from the "big rules"–is violated. We saw, however, that at the heart of my criticism of the status of the shut-in is not simply what people do, but what they feel. And, as we will see in the next section, there can be no rules about what attitudes we should have and how we should feel.

The situation can be summed in the following way. The ethical is concerned with how we affect other humans. Ethical rules, however, can only regulate actions. We do, however, affect others not only through what we do, but also through what we feel and what attitudes we adopt towards them. But feelings and attitudes cannot be regulated exclusively by rules. Hence there are ethically relevant matters that cannot be settled simply by invoking the rule-systems of either utilitarianism and that of Kantian ethics.

Thus these dominant modern theories do not do justice to the role that certain sensitivities play in moral contexts. This shortcoming leads to the central weakness in the claim that ethics is autonomous. Apparently it is ethically relevant what feelings and attitudes I have. But this, in turn, is tied to questions about over-all aims and purpose in life. It is a question of what *to be* and not simply a question of what *to do*. Neither the utilitarian principles nor Kant's principles tell us what sort of a person we should be.[9]

Finally, neither utilitarian nor Kantian ethics can explain what was called above the phenomenon of "historical moral blindness." For this phenomenon does not involve changes in the rules of ethics. Rather, it involves shifts in the sensitivities that affect how we construe certain situations involving interpersonal relations. The conflict between those who see nothing wrong in impaling a foe on a stake and the rest of us cannot be a matter of our being able to deduce an injunction against such a practice from one of the "big rules", while the others fail to see this consequence. The conflict is one of differences in sensitivity and not one of differences in logical acumen.

In this preliminary critique of utilitarianism and Kantian ethics we assumed that there are non-rule-governed sensitivities, that rules can govern only actions, and that the question of which of the normal human capacities for sensitivity we should develop leads to "meaning-of-life" questions. It is time to defend these assumptions in detail.

IV

Rules and Sensitivity. Though the notion of a rule rarely receives independent treatment in philosophy, it plays a vital role in explanations offered in philosophy of mind, language, and in moral philosophy. Though we may not be able to offer a complete definition of what a rule is, as a first pass, it should be pointed out that rules are things that one can follow, choose, adopt, reject, or formulate. This much, however, holds also for principles. What is it, then, that distinguishes rules from principles? Let us consider the sequences of events and processes that make up human digestion or blood-circulation. One can describe the principles governing these processes. But though one could express these principles within rule-systems, it makes no sense to talk about *rules* for humans to follow or act in accordance with when digesting or having their blood circulate. The reason for this is that rules govern what we do and have control over, while principles govern also that which is a part of our given natural make-up. The violation of a rule raises questions of responsibility. The break-down of a process governed by principles might raise only questions about the likely causes.

We can choose, decide on, reject, or deliberate upon plans of action. Hence these plans can be formulated with reference to rules. But can we decide or deliberate upon how and what we should feel? Can we decide what personality traits we are to have? We can, of course, decide to adopt a rule according to which we should do everything in our power so that we will become such-and-such a person, e.g., a courageous individual. Or we can try to do everything in our power so that we will develop into kind persons. But one cannot decide to be kind, or to become kind; and one cannot decide to be courageous or to become courageous. What we feel and what we are is not a matter of decisions, or mere actions; and if rules govern solely actions, then there can be no rule governing feelings or character traits. There can be rules of the kind: "Do everything you can in order to become a kind person!" But a statement like: "Be kind!" is not a rule; it is an exhortation.[10]

Similar considerations hold for states of character or bodily states. We can have rules telling us everything that we can do to restore or maintain health. But we cannot have a rule saying: "Be healthy!"; for to be healthy is a state. It makes no sense to say that someone is (in a state) in accordance with a rule, or that someone is (in a state) by following a rule, though it does make sense to say that someone got himself to be in a state by following a rule. What can one say to someone who is not healthy? If you say: "Do not be unhealthy!", this is not a command or the formulation of a rule; this is an exhortation.

Thus rules do not cover states and feelings; yet—as we saw—some of our states and feelings affect the welfare of other human beings; hence they are within the sphere of the ethical. It is not surprising that Aristotle does not say much about rules when he describes the *phronimos*, or person of practical wisdom. For the state of a person of practical wisdom cannot be defined in terms of rules. There may be causal links between following certain rules and becoming a person possessing wisdom, but no set of rules can define practical wisdom.

What the rules do not cover has been described so far as feelings and sensitivities. It is time to look at the notion of sensitivity in more detail.

A certain kind of sensitivity is needed in applying rules of conduct or laws. A good judge, whether he ranks individuals on a scale, or delivers judgments in accordance with the law, must be sensitive. He or she must be aware of special circumstances that might surround a case, special interpretations placed on certain kinds of conduct by people from certain socio-economic groups, etc. Though this kind of sensitivity too is not a matter of following rules, it is not a matter of feelings either.

The sensitivities relevant to our topic are exemplified by capacities such as kindness, forgiveness, or care. Each of these has feelings as well as actions as components of their manifestations. What is ethically relevant is not the mere possession of these capacities, but the creating of contexts which facilitate the manifestations of these capacities, or dispositions.

Still, one might reply that this cannot be all that we want. One can "kill" with too much kindness, and forgiving too easily and too often can harm rather that help a child or partner. Do we not need moral rules to tell us what the proper objects of kindness and forgiveness are, and what the appropriate ways and modes of expressing these feelings are?

Certainly, merely being kind or forgiving is not sufficient for leading a successful life. One needs good sense and judgment in developing the appropriate dispositions for the expressing of the relevant feelings. But this "good sense" is not a matter of rules either. The "rule" telling us how to manifest kindness is at best saying that kindness should be manifested in the appropriate way, in the appropriate circumstances, towards the appropriate person; which is to say that it is not a rule at all, moral or otherwise. Rather, it involves skill in interpreting concrete situations, in perceiving correctly the needs of others, etc. As we saw above, this is--as Aristotle would emphasize--a matter of practice and habit, and not a matter of rules.

Suppose that one formulates the following "rule": "Express kindness only when this is in the interest of the person who is the object of the feeling!" Can we regard this as a moral rule? Since kindness involves as a component feeling, this "rule" cannot apply to it. Thus, rephrased, it would say to the person who is overly kind that she/he should repress these feelings unless it helps others. Thus, it is now a rule about what we should do, or try to do. But even in this phrasing, it will not do as a moral rule. For we cannot separate what we mean by the "interest" of the person affected from our conception of what it is for people to live in a healthy state. We have no notion of someone's welfare independent of such considerations as to whether it is good or not good for humans to live in a community within which feelings and affection are shared. Thus the desirability of kindness as a capacity in humans and the concept of human welfare are intertwined. The claim that we can first decide what is or is not in the interest of humans, and then formulate "rules" like the one mentioned above, will be taken up--critically--in the next section.

V

The Moral and the Non-moral. In this section we shall consider critically the alleged autonomy of morals. Let us treat first teleological theories. At their heart lies some form of maximization principle. For our purposes it is irrelevant whether it is pleasure, happiness, or utility that is maximized. For with regards to each of these we can distinguish the subjective from the objective employment of these concepts. What I feel to be useful to me is often not what is in fact useful to me. Teleological theories are in trouble on either alternative. If we take what is to be maximized in the subjective sense, from the point of view of the people affected, we run into the difficulty that the agent would be forced into doing things for others that he believes or even knows to be harmful to them. Can we be morally obligated to do what we know to be harmful to others? If, on the other hand, we take the objective sense, then teleological theories are incomplete. For they have to presuppose and rest on theories of human nature that describe what is in fact useful, leads to happiness, etc. In reply modern ethical philosophers would say that the incompleteness is not harmful, for teleological theories of the right can be supplemented by theories of non-moral good.

An analogous incompleteness affects deontological theories. Underlying the universalizability principle is the notion of respect for human beings. This respect leads to the construal of every human as a member of the kingdom of ends. Is this respect justifiable? If it is simply an ultimate principle, then it is arbitrary. Respect for a person p is always respect for p on account of some characteristic F. For example, we respect people for their intelligence, fairness, altruism, etc. Why should this not hold for moral respect? If we do try to justify this respect, then we fall back on a theory of human nature. For example, Kantians might suggest that it is on account of their rationality that we should respect all humans. Alternatively, one could argue that it is on account of their capacity for kindness and altruism that one should respect humans. In either case, the deontological theories need to be grounded in some theory of human nature that allows us to see which prominent human potentialities should command the kind of respect on which a Kantian will base the notion of moral obligation.

Thus both utilitarian and Kantian ethical theories are incomplete. But if one can draw, in a relevant way, a distinction between moral and non-moral goods, then the incompleteness is harmless. A theory of non-moral goods should tell us that we should feel morally obligated to maximize, or--alternatively--what we should take as the ground for universal respect of humans.

There are many ways in which one can draw distinctions

between the moral and the non-moral. For example, one can say that a certain system of distributing grain is good from the moral point of view but not good from the farmer's point of view. Again, we can say that a law ensuring equal treatment in court is a moral good, i.e. helps morality to flourish. Grain, on the other hand, is a non-moral good. It feeds our stomachs rather than our moral consciousness. We can also draw a distinction between character traits for which we admire others and those which are also viewed as desirable but not grounds for admiration. For example, we admire people for their courage or cooperativeness, and we do not admire them for their capacity to enjoy physical exercise, even though the latter too is a useful trait to have.

Within the context of the main argument of this paper, however, none of these distinctions is relevant. Our problem is that in discussing the morally desirable we are forced to include in our discussions treatments of certain character traits. Since rules govern actions, these character traits, having to do with feelings as well as actions, cannot be defined by a set of rules. It seems, furthermore, that the assessment of the desirability of some of these character traits cannot be analyzed into moral and non-moral components. If we can show that these character traits figure prominently in moral characterizations, then the incompleteness of Kantian and utilitarian theories is no longer harmless; their relationship to theories of human nature becomes essential, and one that exhibits mutual dependency.

To some extent we can draw the distinction between morally and non-morally desirable characteristics. For example, shrewdness is a non-morally desirable characteristic. Can we find any "purely morally desirable" characteristics? The answer to this question depends on one's construal of human well-being. If well-being includes one's relations with others, then any of the morally desirable characteristics can be also regarded—under some conception of the self—as being non-morally desirable.

In any case, there are character traits whose consideration

casts doubt on the tenability of a strict moral vs. non-moral character assessment dichotomy.

Friendliness is deemed generally to be a desirable characteristic. Having friendly relations with others enhances–on some accounts–our lives. At the same time, whether a person is friendly or not is not irrelevant to a moral assessment of his conduct. So, is friendliness a moral or a non-moral good? The problem could not be resolved by saying that it is both. Such overlaps would be harmless. But our difficulty is that the grounds for both what would be called "moral" and what would be called "non-moral" assessment is the same; i.e., our conception of what are healthy or desirable relationships between humans. The notion of a healthy relationship--in one of the uses of 'healthy'–spans the gap between the moral and the non-moral. Similar considerations apply to kindness, cooperativeness, and other character traits that play crucial roles in determining our relationships with others. How would one go about determining whether lack of kindness or lack of cooperativeness are moral or non-moral flaws of character?

There are conceptions of the self--e.g., hedonistic egocentric conceptions--that would not include kindness and friendliness among the desirable character traits. But there are many other conceptions of the self that include these. The choice between these is a mixture of empirical prudential and moral considerations.

The relationship of kindness to the moral and non-moral is analogous to the relationship of the notion of health to the prescriptive and the descriptive. As we shall see later, one cannot define health in terms of maximizing pleasure and minimizing pain. Health is a normative concept, since it tells us how the body should function. But this role of the concept is grounded in its other role of describing what the normal bodily functionings are. So the descriptive element contains an ineliminably normative notion, that of normality, and the prescriptive element contains an ineliminably descriptive element, namely that of bodily functioning.

Health is not simply both prescriptive and descriptive. The point is that the dichotomy breaks down in the analysis of such a term. I claim the same with respect to terms like kindness and cooperativeness in relation to the moral non-moral dichotomy.

On the basis of these reflections we can conclude the following. The incompleteness of utilitarian theories is not harmless, since the specification of happiness (and other maximizable qualities) is not independent of the issue of whether certain character traits are to be included in the realization of a happy life pattern. The assessment of these character traits does not admit of a break-down into moral and non-moral components. Similarly, the incompleteness of the Kantian theory cannot be defended by invoking a moral vs. non-moral distinction. For among the candidates for grounds of respect for humans we find some of those character traits whose assessment does not admit of the breakdown into moral and non-moral ingredients.

There is no morally value neutral concept of the self, or the "healthy" self. Consequently, there is no morally value neutral concept of interest or benefit. Assessing what kind of a person one should be, and what kinds of things we should do, from the so-called moral point of view are inextricably interwoven.

VI

An Alternative Account. In this section an account will be sketched that offers a radical alternative to utilitarianism and Kantian ethics. According to this account we start by forming a conception of human nature. We saw above that this is necessitated already by what was called the "plasticity" of human nature with regards to possible objects and sources of enjoyment. This "plasticity" has its limits. Hence a conception of human nature should reveal the basic human potentialities, the limits of what humans can do and can expect of themselves, and the sources of what can keep humans going as purposeful creatures. Such a conception will be no more "value-free" than the analogous conception of physical health.

In the light of such a conception of human nature we formulate a conception of the type of person we should want to be. In this paper such a conception will be called an *ideal*. Adequate ideals cannot be deduced from conceptions of human nature; but they must be consistent with and grounded in such conceptions. Thus the general form of the arguments spelling out adequate ideals will be the following: "Given that humans have the following (unique?) potentialities G, H, K, etc., our ideal should be to become a person with characteristics C_1, C_2...C_n."

If the ideal is adequate, then a part of it must be concerned with our relationships with others. At this point, considerations of the ideal and ethical considerations become inextricably intertwined. Thus ethics is construed by this pattern as having essential relationships to the over-all aims that we set for ourselves, and thus to "meaning-of-life" questions.[11]

For example, the development of intellectual capacities, our sense of beauty, and our ability to cooperate and to feel kindness and sympathy towards others might fit into the specification of an adequate ideal. Given the "plasticity" of human nature with regards to enjoyment, we are forced to form an ideal for ourselves, tacitly or consciously.

If the ideal we form includes the characteristics listed above, then it also goes a long way to determine our relationships with others. Hence there is no need for a system of independent rules spelling out what our conduct towards others should be. There are, however, other types of ideals that require supplementary ethical principles. Suppose that the ideal-specification emphasizes meditation and self-searching. If it says nothing about our relations and attitudes towards others, then there is a need for additional independent principles to govern one's relations to others. Again, to take another case, if the ideal specifies a tough warrior as the desirable character to be emulated–as in Homer–then there will be a need for additional principles governing one's relations to others, in order to curb the egocentricity and competitiveness of the warrior-type.

Ideal-formation and ethics-formation are most intimately related in those cases in which the ideal involves being kind, cooperative, etc. The notions of "interest," "benefit," etc. can be defined only once we have formed an ideal. The situation is analogous to that of bodily well-being. We can talk of what is beneficial to the body only after we have formed a conception of what a healthy body is.

Thus if we have the right kind of ideal, we will want to do what the ethical rules tell us. These rules, then, function at best as a means to help us to achieve our end. Depending on the ideal formed, much or little of what we call "ethical" falls out of the conception of the ideal.[12] This alternative pattern does not deny, however, that for certain areas of inter-personal relations we might need rules not derivable from any ideal.

Having an ideal pattern of life gives one interests, and the maintaining of these will shape our capacities for enjoyment. Most of modern ethics seems to have this backwards. It asks: "What do we enjoy?" and then attempts to characterize what is valuable. But with adequate ideals, a human can try to shape life in such a way that embodying the ideal should be also enjoyable. Human nature is very flexible with respect to what we can enjoy.[13]

Given what was said above about rules, we can see why these do not play such a crucial role in the alternative pattern. One cannot define an ideal in terms of rules, since the ideals are in terms of what we are and feel, and not only in terms of what we do. Having over-all aims and thus interest, hope, and acceptance is a matter of having the required capacities, and not a matter of merely following rules.

The advantage of the dominant modern ethical views is that their construal of ethics as a hierarchical pyramid of rules yields over-all coherence and consistency. The alternative pattern allows possible clashes between sensitivities, or between rules and sensitivities. Thus it does not guarantee over-all consistency. There have been, however, many writers of ethics who have questioned the claim that such coherence is attainable in human lives.[14]

The rational and objective character of ideal-formation is compatible with a pluralistic approach to desirable patterns of life. Given individual differences, within certain parameters, we cannot expect all humans to be suited for the same kind of life. But this pluralism is no more or less extensive that the corresponding pluralism in our concept of bodily health. The fact that different types of people and different age-groups realize bodily health in different ways does not show medicine to be a subjectivistic or relativistic science.

Understanding these variations in human nature should enable us to incorporate tolerance into an adequate ideal. For example, this understanding would enable a rational and cooperative person to understand why less gifted and less privileged persons might have more difficulties forming an ideal that is not self-centered and leaves room for capacities to feel for others.

But such tolerance has its limits. The limits are set by the extent to which those opting for different ideals possess characteristics that are the grounds for our respect for them. It will not do to say that the mere fact that someone belongs to the biological species *homo sapiens* should suffice for the eliciting of respect, unless it is assumed that by merely being a human biologically entails having at all times capacities for reason, cooperativeness, kindness, etc. And even on this assumption, the latter characteristics serve as the grounds for respect, and not the mere biological classification.

Keeping in mind the distinction highlighted recently by Chomsky between discovery procedures and justificatory procedures, let us sketch what the alternative pattern has to say about practical reasoning. Since it leaves open the possibility of widely differing discovery procedures—religious and secular—we shall concentrate on the justificatory process. We saw already that the first step is the formation of an ideal, i.e., a characterization of an ideal personality pattern or patterns. This is grounded in, but not deductively derivable from, a conception of human nature. The ideal will yield–to the extent that it specifies our relations to others–capacities for forming attitudes and feeling, and rules for conduct towards others. The extent to which ethics thus "falls out of" the ideals is depending on the nature of the ideal. Thus the alternative pattern leaves room for a partial autonomy of ethics.

The manifestation of the desirable attitudes and capacities for feeling as well as the following of the relevant rules yields, on the ground level, actions, manifestations of attitudes, and particular feelings at particular occasions.

Looking at it in reverse order, actions and feelings are justified in terms of the constituents of the ideal. The ideal itself does not admit of further justification[15] but is subject to rational criticism. For instance, it might be in conflict with assumptions about human nature, or be incomplete, incoherent, etc.

It is possible for people not to go through this whole justificatory process. For example, someone might have rules of ethics, follow them, but not have an over-all aim in life, in terms of ideals or otherwise. Such a person would not be unethical. But the fact that one can stop at a level beneath that of ideal-formation does not show that there is a large conceptual gap between ideals and ethics. For one can stop even earlier. One might do all of the ethically required things but have no ethical rules. Such a person would do the right thing for the wrong reasons, or for no reason at all. Is such a person immoral? The fact that we can stop at any one of the levels of the justificatory ladder does not show that there is a sharp break in the ladder conceptually at any one point.

The alternative pattern leaves only a small role for the "big rules" of modern ethics to play. Their role is merely that of a couple of items on a long check-list. Having utilized our conception of an adequate ideal, and having allowed a variety of capacities to be exercised, we come to a tentative conclusion of what we should do, or what attitude we should adopt. At this point we add: "And it should be done as fairly as possible, and in such a way as to make it as enjoyable for people as possible." Thus the big rules do not really specify the substance of how to react. They merely help at the end of a deliberative process, in case we have several equally viable alternatives, to narrow things down to a choice to be made. They have no priority over kindness, care, the development of intelligence, etc.

The difference between the modern patterns and the alternative sketched here can be shown also in terms of charts representing cognitive processes involved in practical reasoning. According to the modern frameworks, practical reasoning is basically a matter of rule-application, with sensitivity being relegated at most to the role of facilitating the application of rules to concrete situations. (Figure 1.)

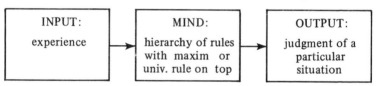

According to the alternative pattern, the input is already affected by the exercise of sensitivities. Our perception of a morally tainted situation depends partly on our inner cognitive-perceptual structure. For example, it takes sensitivity to perceive cruelty, abuse, etc. in all circumstances. The output is a judgment, action, or feeling.[16] (The sound agent need not go through the justificatory procedure in any conscious way prior to reacting to a situation in an appropriate way.) Finally, what the mind contributes to the formation of the output is not merely a set of ethical rules, but also a conception of what we called an *ideal*, i.e. a set of capacities, dispositions to feel, etc. (Figure 2.)

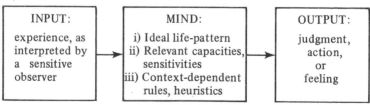

Given what we said about ideal-formation, and the relation of sensitivities to ethical rules, it follows that within the alternative pattern there is no sharp distinction between the ethical and the prudential. The ideal-formation already involves what moderns would call ethical considerations. Reacting to moral situations, concerns with health, exercise of kindness and fairness, etc. are all considered as parts of how we should live. Though there are orderings in terms of priorities, these rankings do not yield a sharp division of the useful and the obligatory.

The alternative pattern can also account for the facts mentioned at the outset that utilitarianism and deontic ethics have problems with. First, it can account for the important role that sensitivities such as kindness play in our "moral" reactions to others. For it can represent differences between humans which do not center on disagreements about rules but on lack of uniformity of kinds and degrees of sensitivity and feelings.

Thus it can also account for what was called "historical moral blindness." For it can represent the salient difference between us and those who impaled their foes on stakes as not a difference in rules to be followed, but a difference in sensitivities.

Finally, the alternative pattern can account for the case presented in the first section more adequately than utilitarianism and deontic ethics. For it can represent the difference between those who find the scene described incongruous and those who do not as a difference in sensitivity rather than in rule-systems, and it can explain how critiques of each other's sensitivities leads to comparisons of ideals, rather than to comparisons of rule-hierarchies. The fact that according to this approach, the resolution of the conflict requires a reorientation of how we should feel, and hence not merely deductive reasoning, does not make conflict-resolution any less rational.

VII

Plato and Aristotle; Realizations of the Alternative Pattern. In this section it will be shown that, though the ethics of Plato and Aristotle differ in many ways, both are examples of what was called above the "alternative pattern."[17]

"Meaning-of-life" questions concern over-all aims in life; at their best in terms of what type of a person we should will to be. Even prior to the rise of philosophic ethics, there was much discussion about over-all aims in life in Greek literature. For example, the famous debate between Neoptolemus and Odysseus in the *Philoctetes* centers on this issue. In philosophic ethics the issue is phrased in terms of over-all aims, or *teloi*, for human life. Thus even though there is no idiom in ancient Greek corresponding to the modern English idiom of "meaning-of-life," there is firm evidence for relating the "telic" speculations of the Greeks to the concern for meaning in people's lives in contemporary discussions. When the over-all aim for life is given by some Greek thinkers in terms of what kind of a person we should be, the prescription culminates in the specification of a set of excellences (*aretai*) or outstanding personality traits, which constitute the norms for a life that has a point and is worth living.

To give life meaning in terms of a set of excellences is very different from merely proposing for humans a set of possible objects of satisfaction. The mere satisfaction of desires need not lead to pride and self-esteem. But being able to live up to a set of norms specified in terms of *aretai* does have these feelings as its consequence. To live up to excellences is to meet norms for being the kind of human that we can respect and see as a valuable part of reality.

In terms of the previous section, the positing of a set of excellences can be described as the formulation of an ideal. Within an excellence-ethics the formulation of an ideal is prior to the development of the capacities for enjoyment that make the embodying of the ideal a satisfying experience. Since, however, the range of what is enjoyable and attainable is constrained by human nature, we find in Greek thought the discussions of excellences intertwined with discussions about human nature.

The key to Plato's ethics is the analogy between the relationship of health to body and the relationship of goodness to person, or "soul". (The usual translation of *psychē* as "soul" is highly misleading.) The natural tendency of a body is to function in a healthy way. Hence in such a body each of the natural constituents fulfill their potentialities. Likewise, in a life with the appropriately chosen over-all aim, the whole person and each of its constituents can fulfill their potential (*Republic* 444c-d). But just as different bodies at different stages of development might realize health in different ways (*Meno* 72d-e) so different patterns of life might fit persons with different talents.

In his discussions of health (e.g. *Gorgias* 464b ff. and 521a) Plato demonstrates that health cannot be defined in hedonistic or utilitarian terms.[18] Similar reasoning applies to the good. Since the good serves as a guideline for what we should *be*, rather than merely telling us what to *do*, it cannot be defined as a set of rules. On the other hand, nor can the good be identified with the useful or the pleasant. For the notion of self-interest—for Plato—presupposes a theory about what the self is and should be. Hence according to Plato there can be no sound conception of what the useful or really enjoyable things are apart from the formulation of an ideal. The formulation of the ideal—the set of excellences—will have in it fused what modern moral philosophers try to distinguish as the ethical and prudential. To the question "Is the good life enjoyable?" Plato would reply by asking: "Enjoyable by whom?" He goes on to argue that the good life can be enjoyed by a person who developed the appropriate capacities. Plato assumes—along lines argued in this paper in the previous section—that one must, tacitly or otherwise, commit oneself to an ideal. Hence we cannot remain "neutral" as to what and how we should enjoy. Or, to put it in another way, such "neutrality" is itself a commitment to an ideal, and a very inadequate one at that.

Full participation in the good ensures our embodying the adequate ideal. Given what we said in the previous section about the ideal, the good must combine the ethical and the prudential. Furthermore, everyone who aims at some over-all ideal for life aims at the good or some apparent good. The difficult passages about the Form of the Good (*Republic* 505a1-4, 506c-e5) should be interpreted in this light. In his recent book,[19] T. Irwin mentions the paucity of arguments by both Socrates and Plato for positing a single entity as the Good. Irwin, like other modern commentators, takes the Good to be at the top of a hierarchy of objects of satisfaction for human desires. If it were such, there would be a need for argument. It is not obvious that human desires form a monolithic pyramid in terms of priorities and end-means relations. But if the Good is what we take it to be, according to the alternative pattern of analysis, then there is no need for argument here. The Good functions as a magnet that gives orientation, and hence meaning, to human lives. There is no more reason to be surprised that Plato posits the Good without argumentation than that he posits health without much discussion.

Since the realization of the Good involves being a certain kind of a person, we would expect Plato to specify the ingredients of an adequate ideal. This is, in fact, what we find in Book IV of the *Republic*. In 437a *ff.* he describes what he takes to be the main constituents of human nature: understanding, the spirited element, and the appetites. In 441d *ff.* he outlines what it is for these constituents to function well. To be the kind of person who functions well is to be the kind of person we aspire to be. Such a person can realize the excellences in his or her life. We *value* this kind of ideal personality pattern. Hence this pattern yields *norms* for us to live up to. These are norms for what to be, and only derivatively for what to do.[20] The excellences do not yield rules of the sort that form the backbone of the dominant modern ethical theories. "Be wise!" and "Be courageous!" tell us what to be like and how to feel; hence they cannot be rules, since--as we saw--rules govern solely actions.

Given what we said about the link between the Good, ideals and the excellences, it follows that the excellences are neither independently established moral standards, nor a non-ethically established, non-moral good. Embodying them is constitutive of a life in which our nature is fulfilled, and hence a life towards which we aspire when fully cognizant of the human condition. Living such a life gives us freedom, purpose, and self-sufficiency (cf., e.g., *Lysis* 215a).

Once we see how Plato's moral theory falls within the alternative pattern, we are no longer surprised that there is very little talk in his ethical writings about rules, and that his treatment of pleasure and the good differs so much from what we find in typical modern essays on this topic.[21]

Some of the Platonic ideal bears on how we should behave towards others and what attitudes we should adopt towards our fellow human beings. For Plato takes intellectual pursuits to be the chief aim of a well-lived life. Furthermore, he construes the pursuit of wisdom to be a cooperative and non-competitive enterprise. Hence cooperativeness and non-competitiveness are already built into the ideal; we need no special ethical rules for their introduction.

The key intellectual pursuit is what Plato describes--in the *Meno* and elsewhere--as "recollection." But teaching those things of which there is genuine knowledge--by Plato's criteria--also involves "recollection." For teaching is to help the student to "recollect," and this can be done only if the teacher too "recollects." Hence the high value placed by Plato on teaching. Since every human has to some degree the capacity to learn to "recollect," everyone is a potential partner in intellectual pursuits. This forms the basis for respect of humans in the Platonic scheme. Again, since according to the ideal we all want to be teachers, there is no need for an autonomous rule of respect for humans; those embodying the Platonic ideal will have it anyway. All humans embodying the ideal will want to cooperate, since they all aspire to understanding, and can achieve this best when working with each other.[22]

Though the attitudes that are parts of the Platonic ideal yield much of what one would call ethical conduct and approach to other humans, they leave certain questions open. In particular, they say nothing about principles of distributing material goods. The possession of these, however, will be not very important to those who live according to the Platonic ideal.[23]

Thus we see how Plato starts with certain assumptions about human nature, formulates an ideal, posits this as that which can give over-all aim to our lives and hence meaning to it, and derives from the ideal a partial determination of how one should react to others. The ethics is in terms of the exercise of certain basic human capacities. Rules of action play only a secondary part in this scheme. This shows that Platonic ethics fits the alternative pattern, and that within it the ethical and the prudential are inextricably interwoven.[24]

Though different in detail, Aristotle's ethics too fall within the same pattern. In the beginning of the *Nicomachean Ethics* Book I, Aristotle examines "the good" at which actions, activities, and humans in their rational moments, aim. Contrary to the usual modern interpretations this "good" cannot be the object of all desires. It is not said to be what people desire, but what people and activities aim at. It gives an over-all *telos* to human life. Thus we should interpret it the way we interpreted the analogous Platonic claim about "the good;" and argument can be seen as unnecessary in Aristotle's introduction as well. Aristotle says that we choose (1094a15 *ff.*) and aim at (1095a15 *ff.*) this good. Having it enables us to live well-lived lives.

Thus we see Aristotle, like Plato, starting with the assumption that there should be some over-all aim in our lives; something whose attainment can give us what we would call today "meaning" to our lives and give us self-esteem.

Among the candidates for "the good" we find the unreflective life devoted to the pursuit of pleasure, the life spent in pursuit of prestige (*timē*), and the life in which we develop primarily our rational faculties and other characteristically human excellences.

The mentioning of these three items is hardly accidental. They exemplify three ways of formulating over-all aims in life: in terms of something to be *possessed* (pleasure), something to be *achieved* (prestige), and something to *be*. Aristotle opts for an ideal in terms of something *to be*. There is nothing that we can possess that would be itself make us valuable members of the world of living things, and achievements are notoriously context-dependent. The only adequate way of formulating ideals is in terms of what we should be.

In the formulation of his ideal Aristotle relies on considering what is the typical functioning (*ergon*, 1197b24 *ff.*) of humans. If he were engaged in the task of finding what is the object of everyone's desires, then this investigation of human *ergon* would be irrelevant; why should everyone desire that which represents our unique functioning? But if we look for something that makes a human valuable, then this consideration has obvious relevance. He also argues that his ideal will give us self-sufficiency. This too suggests that he wants to set an over-all aim in life for us, rather than merely spell out conditions for satisfying our desires.

The health analogy holds for Aristotle's ethics as well. Just as one discerns by reflection on the bodily functioning what health should be, so one can discern by reflection and observation of the whole functioning of a human person what the norms for being a good human and leading a good life should be.

Spelling out the constituents of a good (healthy) person (or "soul"?) is centered around the "golden mean" doctrine. In order to function well, we need to possess the desirable psychological capacities and must combine the expression of these in appropriate ways. Since the key stress is on developing certain personality traits, and learning how to manifest these successfully, there is very little talk of rules in Aristotle's ethics. His ideal, the *phronimos* or man of practical wisdom, acts more by habit than by rules. Thus to say that we should apply the mean as the *phronimos* does is not circular (1107a36 *ff.*). The *phronimos* lives the kind of life we all should aim at. Since this life involves having a certain personality structure, and exercising sensitivities, no set of rules alone could define it. The rule-component is summed up by the rather vague notion of the "mean," but the specifications of the excellences, and hence the desirable personality type, does all of the conceptual work. Given this independently given description of the ideal personality, it is not circular to say that we should aim at embodying this type.

There are many differences between the ethical systems of Plato and Aristotle. These differences affect both the ideal to be emulated and the means that enable us to live up to the ideal. But these differences do not affect the general logic of the arguments which follow what we called previously the alternative pattern. For Aristotle too the key excellences are non-competitive and cooperative. Thus here too the specification of the ideal gives a practical characterization of how we should react to other humans. Aristotle claims that humans are by nature social creatures (*NE* I:8). Therefore to be the right kind of person includes adopting helpful and cooperative attitudes towards others. One might say that for Aristotle these are the "healthy" attitudes; and they are involved in fulfilling our natural capacities. (For more on *ergon* see 1098a5 *ff.*) The person who adopts the right ideal is generous not out of a sense of obligation but because he enjoys it.

Since the formation of an ideal cannot be sorted out into ethical and prudential ingredients, and Aristotelian ethics depends on a certain ideal, therefore in this system too we cannot separate sharply moral from non-moral goods, nor the prudential from the ethical.

Aristotle's comment (1098a17 *ff.*) that a well lived life involves the successful completion of the natural process of life shows a great difference between the Greek conception of life and the one underlying typical modern ethical thought. Aristotle does not mean to say what he is often taken to be saying, namely that nobody can be called happy until he is dead. He is not talking about happiness, and he is not saying what someone is doing at the time of death. He is saying something about life as a process that allows for various modes of completion. In many modern ethical theories--and in Hellenistic ethics as well--life is just a stretch of time, to be filled with certain things and to be kept clean of others (the valuable and the immoral respectively). This view is in harmony with the consumer conception of the self (e.g. as a satisfaction-seeking mechanism) that reaches its climax with the development of industrial societies. The candidates for the "fillings" are the sorts of things that one can HAVE, POSSESS, or CONSUME (pleasure, satisfaction, happiness, goods, etc.), rather than BE.

Within the classical Greek philosophic conception life is a natural process in which each stage has its own natural place and its own possibilities for achieving excellence and enjoyment. Like the development of an acorn, life has its own rhythm and its own structure. The internal structure determines what counts as completion. Completing a life is not just passing away so much time. It is more like the completion of a race, or a work of art. Hence the emphasis, both in Aristotle and in Platonic dialogues like the *Phaedo*, on how to face death. A successful life involves facing death with dignity and without fear. In view of this conception of a human life, classical Greek ethics are much more suitable for treating problems like those of old age, growing up, etc. than the dominant modern ethical theories. It is not surprising that one finds today these problems treated more in textbooks of psychology than in philosophical texts. This is shown poignantly by current discussion of "applied ethics." The conception according to which the discussion of the modern "big rules" is pure ethics, while the discussion of how to age gracefully is applied ethics (applying what?) would strike both Plato and Aristotle as bizarre. For them ethics is the formation of an adequate ideal, and hence of a proper aim for human lives. This involves aging gracefully at least as much, if not more, than worrying about how to be fair and maximize happiness in the world. There is talk of practical reasoning in Aristotle, and in these discussions rules are mentioned. But these rules are always specific and context-bound. Their formulation and application assumes as the proper background a human with the right kind of capacities and sensitivities.

The development of Greek ethical thought shows not only changes in content but also changes in form. Virtue-ethics can be placed within a variety of cognitive structures. Homeric ethics illustrates *imitation-ethics*. Within such a framework a human, or semi-god, is singled out for others to imitate. Thus the form of the basic ethical principles is: "Be like X!" Imitation-ethics has its obvious limitations; the person to be imitated lives in a restricted context, his pattern cannot be generalized, etc. As the next stage, *rule-ethics* emerges, especially in legal contexts. But Plato is not slow to point out that rule-ethics too has its drawbacks. Rules need application, applications require sensitivity. Only in the hands of the right kind of person do rules become instruments of human flourishing.

With the rise of *philosophic ethics*, in the writings of Heraclitus, Plato, and Aristotle, we see a third type of thought about values emerging: the spelling out of the right ideal, or desirable personality structure, that makes us valuable and gives orientation to our lives. This too can involve "imitation" but only on a very abstract plane; what we imitate are abstract blue-prints and not concrete entities, real or mythical. It involves also rules, but only in the context of developed sensitivities and capacities that constitute the human potential.

Together with the form the content changes as well. The key fact about the Homeric virtues is not that they are external, behaviour-oriented, but that they are individualistic and competitive. The virtues of Plato and Aristotle are non-competitive, necessarily cooperative, and cumulative.[25] This shift in the nature of the excellences brings with it a reorientation of what is to be construed as the desirable attitudes to be adopted towards others.

The ethics of Plato and Aristotle are called at times by modern historians of ethics versions of self-realization or eudaimonism. Thus construed they are merely different answers to the same questions that dominate modern ethics. But this conception requires our viewing the excellences as either means towards the non-moral good of self-realization, or as themselves parts of this non-moral good. As we have seen, neither of these conceptions is viable. The excellences provide more than rules for conduct. As parts of a personality-structure, they are parts of an answer to questions about what our over-all aim in life should be; and this question transcends the moral vs. non-moral dichotomy.

Why did ethics become divorced from "meaning-of-life" questions? The following are merely speculative historical hypotheses. It is possible that the task of separating ethics from religion was thought--wrongly--to bring with it necessarily the separation of ethics from questions about the meaning of life. Secondly, the modern period is characterized by wide-spread scepticism concerning the possibility of objective methods for formulating what are called ideals in this essay. Thirdly, it was thought that people's aims are hopelessly varied, and that thus we need an autonomous set of ethical rules to serve as "traffic rules" to guide humans on life's stormy paths.

The only thing that recommends the "traffic rule" conception of ethics is the tolerance that is built into it. But we saw that tolerance has its limits; and limited tolerance can be built into an adequate ideal. Reacting to others involves more than following rules for action. It involves adopting certain attitudes and having certain feelings towards others. Attitudes and feelings cannot be matters of obligation. As we saw, their evaluation leads us to opting for ideals of what to be. The formulation of such ideals transcends the distinction between the moral and the non-moral since the grounds for its justification involve conception of desirable constituents for the self and desirable relations to others. The sense of 'desirable' here is basic, and cannot be reduced to moral and prudential desirability.

If the logic of this essay is correct, then humans are driven to consider ideals for themselves. Such an enterprise is no less rational or objective than the alleged enterprise of formulating and defending a set of autonomous ethical rules. The enterprise of formulating over-all aims for human lives has at least the advantage that it starts the questioning at the right place.[26]

Notes

1. The framework may be religious or secular. Again it may be pluralistic or monolithic; it can leave also more or less room for matters of individual difference.

2. Loss of interest cannot be explained by not gaining pleasure from something. Those who believe in the "pleasure-principle" have the facts backwards. It is not the case that "x loses interest in y because he no longer gains pleasure from it," but rather that "since x lost interest in y, x no longer gains pleasure from y."

3. William K. Frankena, *Ethics* (Englewood, N.J., Prentice-Hall, 1963).

4. *Ibid*. p. 6. My survey leaves out questions of distributions and rights; but those topics are not germane to the matters discussed in this paper.

5. *Ibid*. pp. 13-14.

6. *Ibid*. p. 49.

7. *Ibid*. pp. 70-75.

8. A notable exception is the moral philosophy of John Dewey.

9. Kant is difficult to interpret on this point. On the one hand he tells us that ethics is a matter of a rule of action (the categorical imperative), on the other hand he says also that the good person will do the right thing out of a sense of duty. But how can one have a *rule* about what our motives should be? If it is not a matter of moral rules, then what kinds of criteria is Kant appealing to?

10. This has implications for institutions like marriage in which both feelings and actions are important factors. If the argument presented

here is sound, then it makes no sense to promise how we will feel for the rest of our lives; we can only promise to do everything within our power to maintain certain feelings.

11. Two modern echoes of this alternative pattern are Wittgenstein's lecture on ethics, printed in the *Philosophical Review* 74 (1965) pp. 3-12; and David Wiggins, "Truth, Invention, and the Meaning of Life," Royal Society Lecture, Nov. 1976 (collected at pp. 332-378).

12. Much of what is a matter of distributing goods, and other parts of social and political philosophy, will require independent foundations, not based solely on ideal-formation.

13. In "Moral Reasons" (*Midwest Studies in Philosophy* III, 1978), p. 63, Kurt Baier writes: "...we believe that in a sound morality, each member has adequate reasons to follow its precepts even when doing so is contrary to his desires, needs and interests." But according to the alternative framework, we should not take interests, etc., as fixed antecedently to the specifications of what ideals a human life should embody. It might turn out that morality is in the "true interest" of the agent, even if this is not recognized by him at t h e outset.

14. The view that there are inevitable moral conflicts has been maintained by such traditional figures as Sidgwick, and such more recent thinkers as Wittgenstein and (in unpublished works) Martha Nussbaum and Ruth Marcus.

15. The fact that the ideal cannot be deduced from statements about human nature shows that the alternative pattern is not a version of naturalism. The fact that the ideal does not admit of further, purely factual, justification no more shows this pattern to be a version of emotivism than the analogous considerations show medicine or logic to be "emotive" theories.

16. It is not clear that judgment must be prior to action. In a paper read at Stanford, 1977, Stuart Hampshire distinguished between "geometrical" and "perceptual" models of practical reasoning. According to the perceptual model the proper reaction may precede the corresponding judgment, though the sound agent can give, retroactively, a justification of the action performed.

17. The same considerations apply to Jewish and Christian ethics. In the Old Testament we are presented with a set of taboos (most of the commandments) but also with an ideal life in terms of honoring God, and living by faith. Rules of respect, cooperation, etc. "fall out of" the

specifications of this ideal. In the New Testament passages like the Sermon on the Mount formulate an ideal to be embodied. Given this ideal, there is no need for an additional set of ethical rules. Yet it would be absurd to say that the ideal itself is purely ethical rather than prudential. Furthermore, it specifies sensitivities, not mere conduct. Hence the talk about the need to be "reborn" among Christians.

18. For details see J. Moravcsik "Ancient and Modern Conceptions of Health and Medicine," *The Journal of Medicine and Philosophy* Volume 1 (1976) pp. 337-348.

19. Terence Irwin, *Plato's Moral Theory* (Oxford: University Press, 1977), pp. 51-52 and p. 224.

20. The important distinction between norms and values was pointed out to me by my colleague Philip Rhinelander.

21. Plato's treatment of pleasure is not uniform. He, appropriately, compares different kinds of pleasures, as a physician would compare the pleasures of a healthy person to those of a drug addict. In *Gorgias* 493b *ff.* the soul seeking physical pleasure is compared to a leaky jar. The proper satisfaction of physical needs should create an equilibrium, and it cannot be healthy to be driven primarily by desires whose satisfaction leads us to an endless regress.

He seems however, to overplay his hand in *Republic* Bk.VII when he says that the guardians might have to be forced back into the cave. For his basic view is that understanding makes us into cooperative persons who want to share, learn, and teach. Hence the guardians should want to go back into the cave, without the goading of a sense of duty or external constraints.

There seems to be a flaw also in the arguments of Bk.   IX, showing the good life to be more enjoyable than the alternative. For one of the arguments relies on the testimony of a wise human who had opportunities to compare all kinds of pleasures. This argument has its echo in the writings of John Stuart Mill, who also claims that the judgment of the wise person is preferable to the judgments of those who know only physical satisfaction. But while such a move is legitimate within Mill's hedonistic system, it should have no place in Plato's argumentation. For Plato has no value-neutral sense of "enjoyment." He should argue that the good life will be enjoyed by those with the right psychological make-up, and then he should show why we should want to become persons of that type, regardless of questions of enjoyment, since that personality-type is that which is analogous to the healthy body.

22. For the epistemological underpinnings of this view see J. Moravcsik "Understanding and Knowledge in Plato's Philosophy," *Neue Hefte fuer Philosophie* 15/16 (1979), pp. 53-69.

23. The Christian ideal places less emphasis on intellectual virtues, and more stress on emotional capacities such as kindness, love, and willingness to forgive. But it too minimizes the importance of possessing external goods.

24. Nicholas White in *A Companion to Plato's Republic* (Indianapolis: Hackett Publishing Co., 1979) points out that the Form of Good embraces both what moderns call duty and what they call interest, and that thus Plato stands outside of the teleological-deontological dichotomy (pp. 56 *ff.*). But he does not emphasize the health-analogy as much as this essay, and does not spell out the "alternative pattern" within which one can interpret Plato as offering a radically different outline of practical reasoning.

25. This is one of the differences that Plato discerns between physical and intellectual pleasures. The latter are cumulative; we can build on the earlier achievements. The former make us start all over again.
The move from external to quiet and cooperative virtues is seen by A.W.H. Adkins (*Merit and Responsibility*, Oxford University Press, 1960) but he does not see Plato and Aristotle arguing within what is called here the "alternative" pattern; hence he does raise questions about the *aretai* in terms of the ethical-prudential dichotomy.

26. Earlier versions of this paper were read in 1979 for the Philosophy Departments of California State University, Fullerton, Stanford University, and for the annual Philosophy Colloquium at Chapel Hill. I am indebted to many people for helpful comments. I owe special debts to Kurt Baier, Michael Bratman, Andrea Halliday, and James O. Urmson, though I am not sure that any of these philosophers would agree with my conclusions.

MARX, HEGEL,

AND THE GREEK AESTHETIC IDEAL

PHILIP J. KAIN

In 1843 the young Marx wrote:

> Freedom, the feeling of man's dignity, will have to be
> awakened again in these men. Only this feeling, which
> disappeared from the world with the Greeks and with
> Christianity vanished into the blue mist of heaven, can
> again transform society into a community of men to
> achieve their highest purpose, a democratic state.[1]

In this passage we recognize a theme that can be found
running through the writings of many late 18th and 19th
century German thinkers–a· concern with what we might
characterize as the "myth of Greece." For many, ancient
Greece represented a lost ideal, a high point of the human
condition. What characterized this ideal, it was thought, was
wholeness of personality, spontaneity of culture, and unity
with external objects and institutions. The individual Greek
possessed a *wholeness* in the sense of an extraordinarily
complete development of his powers and capacities. As Marx

says:

> We are struck with admiration when we see among the
> Ancients the same person distinguishing himself to a high
> degree as philosopher, poet, orator, historian, priest,
> administrator, general of an army. Our souls are appalled
> at the sight of such a vast domain.[2]

The Greek was able to develop a vast array of his powers
both mental and physical; he did not limit himself to one or a
few. His development was not one-sided or fragmented. Even
more importantly the individual's rational and sensuous
faculties were in harmony. The significance of this appeared
especially in the realms of ethics and politics where this
harmony meant that principles and feelings, duty and
inclination, were in agreement, thus producing in the
individual a *spontaneity* rather than a tension or opposition.
Inclination was found to be in spontaneous natural
agreement with duty unlike, for example, the Kantian
morality, where inclination and duty are found in opposition.
With this agreement between principle and feeling the
activity of an individual Greek, his effort, appeared as an end
in itself; it appeared satisfying and enjoyable. Because of this
the Greek felt in *unity* with his object. He was in close touch,
at home, in control. The state, for example, appeared as the
product of the citizen's own energies. It was the citizen's
highest end and he felt a part of it. Likewise, the Greek felt
in unity with nature. Instead of being dominated by it he felt
in harmony with it. In both his art and in his labor the
natural environment appeared humanized; the individual was
at home with it.

The reason that many thinkers were so fascinated with
ancient Greece, by its wholeness, spontaneity, and unity, was
that these were precisely the characteristics which were
missing from their own world. In the view of the thinkers
upon which we here will focus (Marx for the most part but
also to some extent Hegel and Schiller) the fundamental
economic and political problem of their own world was

precisely the absence of the wholeness, spontaneity, and unity of the ancient world and instead of the presence of alienation and estrangement. Let me briefly explain these last two concepts.

At the political level the state is and should appear as the product of the activities and energies of its citizens, but in the modern world the political state has come to appear separate and independent; it has taken on a life of its own distant from the citizens and out of their control. It has become alienated. This situation has even reached the point where the state has turned upon its creators as a hostile and oppressive force. It has become estranged. Thus, in this realm the unity of the ancient world has been lost as well as the possibility of spontaneous agreement between general and particular interest, between duty and inclination.

At the social or economic level we also find separation, opposition, and hostility similar to that at the political level. The individual has become separated from the object, from the product, the world of nature which is transformed through labor. The individual is not in control of his product, rather the product, determined by the economic laws of the market, controls the individual. Given this domination, the individual's laboring activity cannot put him into unity with his world. Instead activity results in objects which confront the individual as an independent, hostile, and estranged power. Besides this, the individual's laboring activity under modern industrial conditions (e.g., in the factory) has become limited, one-sided, and mechanical--thus producing a loss of wholeness and scope in the development of the individual's powers and capacities.

What was it then that destroyed the ancient world's unity and harmony and brought about alienation and estrangement? All of our three thinkers at one time or another in their thought felt that it was the development of the division of labor that was responsible. With the development of the division of labor the individual's activity was restricted to a narrow realm. Specialization required that one develop a single capacity to the exclusion of others, destroying the possibility of wholeness, of the many-sided development of the individual. With specialization, mental was separated from physical activity and these distinct sorts of activities now devolved upon different individuals. Classes developed and became rigidly separated. The state became alien, distant from the citizens, out of their control--unity and spontaneity were lost. The division of labor did make for material progress and development but at the same time a great spiritual price had to be paid.

The question then that faced these three thinkers was how to get back the wholeness, spontaneity, and unity--the freedom--of the ancient world without loss of the results of material development. One of the things they did was to develop a model which derived from ancient Greek culture and from modern aesthetic principles. Let me give a brief outline of this model.

At the level of the individual, the first necessity is to overcome the sort of activity in which the individual only develops a single isolated capacity and in which mental and physical capacities are separated. Even in the sort of labor found in the modern world the individual must bring all of his powers, fully developed, into play equally and harmoniously. They must work together as a totality. What is also necessary is a harmony between the individual's rational capacities and sensuous external nature. (Along these lines Schiller speaks of a harmony between sense and reason, Hegel of a harmony between spirit and nature, and Marx of a harmony between consciousness and sensuous activity.) A harmony is required between the self and the external object, whether this object be nature, the product or activity of labor, or the political state. Here, what is important is that the individual not be dominated or oppressed by the object, nor on the other hand can the individual have turned away from the object, withdrawn into himself, and lost touch with the object as, it was thought, man withdrew from the external world into the realm of spirit with the rise of Christianity. The individual must be able to contemplate the object as an end in itself as it freely confronts him.

This is an aesthetic ideal. After the individual has been able to satisfy his basic material needs and desires, to free himself from these cares, only then, can he take a step back from his object, distance himself from it, so as to be able to contemplate it freely and appreciate it aesthetically. Because he has made the external object his object, because he forms it, works on it, controls it, it can no longer dominate him. Thus the individual need no longer have a grasping, need-driven relationship to the object, a relationship which makes aesthetic appreciation impossible. At the same time the individual has not withdrawn into himself, has not turned away from the external object towards something higher or deeper (this would also make the aesthetic relationship impossible). He is still in close touch with the object. Thus at the same time that he is active he contemplates; he forms and appreciates. The individual's physical and mental capacities operate together, harmoniously, as a totality. The individual's relationship to the object is thus an aesthetic relationship because even though actively engaged in labor, labor has been transformed (it is no longer need-driven) and thus the individual is left free to contemplate, appreciate the object (now under his control) as an end in itself. Schiller expects to realize this aesthetic model in the modern world by remaking the subject, by an aesthetic education of the individual. Marx expects to bring about the aesthetic relationship by changing the object, by remaking society and labor.

All of these thinkers at one point or another in their writings agreed that this model, which we might call the Greek-aesthetic model, could indeed be the model for wholeness, spontaneity, and unity in the modern world. By now you are no doubt wondering about the naïvete of this ideal. How can the Greek model serve a much more complex modern world? What about the historical accuracy of this model itself? What about Greek slavery? Indeed, for none of these thinkers did the model provide an adequate solution. In each of them we find at a certain point a definite shift (or at least, as with Schiller, a certain tension[3]) away from the original model in the direction of some alternate model. In the case of Hegel and Marx the original model was eventually given up (or transformed in the case of the later Marx).

In this paper, therefore, I propose to explore to what extent Marx employed the Greek-aesthetic model as an ideal for remaking the modern world, and to what extent due to its inadequacy he had to shift away from this model toward another solution. For lack of time, I will refer to Hegel and Schiller only where this will help to understand Marx.

Let us begin with Marx's views on labor. The young Marx of 1844 fits into the tradition which we have been describing, the tradition of reconciling sense and reason (or as Marx puts it, sensuous activity and consciousness) aesthetically. This reconciliation will take place after the overcoming of alienated labor and as a part of an ideal sort of labor in the new society. Work, for Marx, will become an activity enjoyable as an end in itself. Through work one will develop to the fullest *all* of one's essential powers. This will constitute the individual's freedom, an aesthetic freedom. There will be no need, for example, for a separation between labor and leisure–the ideal condition will be found in labor itself.[4]

In speaking of this future reconciliation, Marx says in the *1844 Manuscripts* that nature must appear as man's work, his reality. Man objectifies himself in reality through his labor. Having formed his world, he will, Marx says, be able to contemplate himself in a world he has created, a humanized world.[5] For man to be able to be in a contemplative relationship to a humanized world, two things are necessary. First, he must be in control of the object upon which he works. It cannot be under the control of another or determined by a power alien to him--by the capitalist or by the laws of the market. In other words, the worker must not be confronted by an alien, hostile, objective world, the result of his labor, but a result which is out of his control and before which he is helpless. Second, in man's relation to the object, he himself must be whole. His work must be gratifying, enjoyable, an end in itself. He must not be dominated, driven by need, such that his labor is reduced merely to the means of meeting those needs, the means merely to gaining a wage. A contemplative attitude is incompatible with a need-driven existence. The work itself must be enjoyable as an end in itself. Given these two conditions, man can freely contemplate his world as the result of his own activity. Man can, Marx says, create according to the laws of beauty. The individual's relation to the object need no longer be one of grasping, possessing, or having. The senses will have been emancipated such that they appreciate, contemplate, the object (a person or thing) for its own sake. The individual will have a free aesthetic relationship to his world.[6]

Hegel in his *Aesthetics* presents a view of labor which in certain ways is very similar to Marx's. In the ancient world, according to Hegel, work for the epic hero was a pleasant activity that put him into a harmonious relationship with his surroundings. The hero interpenetrated the external world with his volitions and humanized his environment. (Think for example of Odysseus constructing his own marriage bed.) Through pleasant work, nature was made to satisfy man's needs and was unable to dominate him.

Hegel contrasts this ancient model of labor to labor in the modern world. Here labor is mechanical, fragmented, abstract, and unpleasant–it does not put man into unity with his world. Besides, we find two classes of men, one class which labors but is in poverty and another class which has wealth but does not labor. Modern labor does not accord with the ideal because wealth, satisfaction of needs, on the one hand, and labor, one's own accomplishment, on the other, are separated. This division of labor makes the ideal impossible. For the ideal, man himself must labor and his labor must be satisfying both in the sense that it be enjoyable as an activity and that it provide for his needs. This puts man into a harmonious relationship to his world.[7] Hegel's view in general is that the ancient world was characterized by an aesthetic harmony. In Greece spirit and nature were in balance thus bringing about an age of beauty.

But for Hegel, aesthetic reconciliation will not occur again in the modern world. Here Hegel disagrees with Schiller and the young Marx. In Hegel's later political theory the two classes of the modern world are not reconciled. The division of labor is seen as a necessary constituent of modern society and is left intact. Further, Hegel argues that the modern world of machinery, factory made products, and a scientific outlook independent of all personal views, is incompatible with ancient man's vital connection with nature. The external world is not humanized through such mechanical work; man cannot leave the stamp of his individuality upon the external world.[8] Thus the aesthetic model is relegated to the past; it represents a stage in spirit's development--the ancient world. It is not an ideal for the modern world as it is for Schiller and the younger Marx.

I say the *younger* Marx because the later Marx, in his Introduction to the *Grundrisse,* echoes these pessimistic passages from Hegel's *Aesthetics.* Marx seems to agree with Hegel that certain ideal characteristics of the ancient world *are* lost. Marx argues that developed industry and factory production are incompatible with Greek mythology--the grasping and shaping of the natural world through the artistic imagination. He argues that the epic hero, epic conditions, and indeed, it seems, man's vital connection with the natural world are all impossible in an industrially developed society; they are only possible in an undeveloped one. Thus, just as for Hegel, there existed in the ancient world a beautiful unity that can never return.[9] It is true that Marx is here talking primarily about art, the epic, but if an artistic or aesthetic unity with the natural world is incompatible with modern industry, factory production, and division of labor, then the question that we must deal with, in turning to the later Marx's ideal of labor, is whether the overcoming of alienated and estranged labor can be of the same sort as earlier in 1844, that is, whether it can any longer be based on the Greek-aesthetic model.

It is clear that the later Marx's goal, communist society, is still to be a society without commodity exchange, private ownership, and thus without fetishism (which is to say without alienation and estrangement). Besides this, the goal of communist society would be to overcome the division of labor, especially class division of labor and the division between mental and physical labor, and generally to overcome all exploitative and inhuman working conditions. The goal is a free association of persons and the free social and intellectual development of the individual.

But the fundamental change from 1844 is that the highest development of the individual is no longer expected to occur in and through the activity of labor. Instead it will now occur outside of labor in leisure time. The goal of communist society will be to increase the productivity of labor and to shorten the work day in order to provide this leisure time--free time to be devoted, for example, to education in the arts and sciences (as Marx himself suggests in the *Grundrisse*).[10]

Marx says explicitly in the third volume of *Capital* that the true realm of freedom begins only where labor which is determined by necessity and mundane conditions ceases; it thus lies beyond the sphere of material production. Within the sphere of material production there can be a limited form of freedom; it can consist only in socialized man, the associated producers, rationally regulating their interchange with nature and bringing it under their control, instead of being ruled by it. But it nonetheless still remains a realm of necessity. Beyond it in leisure time begins that development which is an end in itself, the true realm of freedom which can blossom forth only with this realm of necessity as its basis. The shortening of the working day is its prerequisite.[11]

Even if the factory process becomes automated, as Marx foresaw that it would, with work becoming merely the overlooking of machines (more a scientific than a physical activity), and even granting that this would involve a certain degree of satisfaction and development, even so, real enjoyment, real development, would still have to take place in leisure. The overlooking of machines could at times just be boring. Besides as Marx says in the third volume of the *Theories of Surplus Value* the labor of material production is always dominated by the pressure of an external purpose.[12] Thus it could never be an end in itself.

What we can say is that Marx in his later life (when through study of economics he had gained a more thorough grasp of what the real possibilities are in the process of production) still felt that the negative aspects of the labor process could be overcome. Labor will no longer be a painful, inhuman sacrifice. The factory will be run by the freely associated workers. Conditions in general will be improved. But the hope of an aesthetic character for labor, which originated more, perhaps, from Marx's philosophical reflections than from economic ones—this aspect of Marx's vision of 1844 is dropped—or rather transferred to the realm of leisure.

The sort of freedom that can be found in material production is now thought to be of a quite different sort. One might say that it is now closer to a rational sort of freedom. Nature will be subordinated to reason, to science, to a purpose decided upon by the workers themselves. And not only external nature, but also (during labor time) the worker's own inclinations must be subordinated to this self-determined purpose. This activity will involve a definite form of satisfaction and freedom--the self-determination of the workers. But labor will not be an end enjoyable in itself; labor will not have been transformed such that the worker could have an aesthetic or contemplative relation to his object. Feeling will not have been brought into equal balance, into harmony, with reason. Rather, it is to be subordinated to reason.[13]

Let us now turn to Marx's view of the state.

The goal of Marx's political writings (from 1843 on) is to overcome the alienation and estrangement of the state. His aim is to overcome the opposition and indeed the difference between civil society and the political state. The state should no longer stand over society, dominating it as a separate, independent power out of the control of the citizens. The goal, suggested in Marx's *Critique of Hegel's Philosophy of Right* and elsewhere, is to revive the unity of the ancient Greek state. The governing element should appear as the result of the citizen's own powers. Public concerns should be the real private concerns of the citizen.[14] The state as an independent power should (to use Engels' later phrase) wither away.

As Marx's political views develop, he comes to propose a two stage transition from the existing estranged state to the ultimate withering away of the state. Stage I he called the dictatorship of the proletariat (it has also been called the socialist stage). Stage II is full communism--the state having withered away. Marx makes this distinction most clearly in the *Critique of the Gotha Program*, but it can also be found if one reads carefully, in the *Communist Manifesto*.[15]

A certain problem arises here. The problem is whether or not, for Marx, stage I is a society which has already overcome alienation and estrangement.

In the *Gotha Program* stage I is a controlled or modified exchange economy. Goods are exchanged, the workers use money (certificates for contributed labor time) to purchase these goods, and the workers earn these certificates in proportion to the work they contribute. In the *Manifesto* stage I, the society described by the ten demands at the end of section II, is even more clearly an exchange society. Rents are still paid on land and there is an income tax. If there are incomes to be taxed there will obviously be goods to exchange income for. In stage II, full communism, there would be no exchange and no money--goods would be distributed not according to contribution but simply according to need.

If there is exchange, there should be alienation--at least according to Marx's general argument. In Chapter 1 of Vol. 1 of *Capital* and even as early as Marx's "Comments on Mill's *Elements of Political Economy*" (in 1844) it is not merely capitalism but exchange itself that causes alienation; any sort of extended exchange even under socialism, it would seem, should cause alienation.[16] Alienation occurs because the economic laws of the market come to control the producers--a relationship between things (the products on the market) controls the relationship between persons (the producers), instead of the other way around. Even in a socialist exchange economy (a society without rent, interest, or profit) the laws of the market could, it seems, come to control the producers. So there should be alienation in stage I, the socialist stage, because there is still exchange present. The problem is that Marx denies that there is alienation present.

In Chapter 1, Vol. I of *Capital* Marx describes the fetishism of commodities—which is what we have just described as alienation in exchange. Exchange relations (independent, uncontrolled laws of the market) control the producers.[17] Marx contrasts this sort of society in which fetishism occurs to four other models or societies in which alienation or fetishism is not present. In the first three there is no fetishism simply because there is no exchange. But the fourth of these unalienated societies is a socialist exchange society. Goods are distributed here (just as in stage I in the *Gotha Program*) according to labor time contributed.[18] We would assume that there would be labor certificates to exchange for goods. If there is exchange, there ought to be alienation. Why is Marx claiming that there would be no alienation here?

The answer, I suggest, is that the exchange that exists in this society is not allowed to control the producers. The workers are associated, production is cooperative not independent, and production is consciously directed according to a social plan. The workers consciously and collectively control their exchange relations instead of being controlled by them.

If we move back to the *Manifesto* we can find (now that we are looking for it) a somewhat more extended description of how exchange can be controlled. We have said that if the producers control their exchange there will be no fetishism or alienation at this level. But to do this controlling, according to the *Manifesto*, requires a powerful state standing over society to direct this exchange. However, a powerful state standing over society would mean estrangement at the political level. The state here, Marx says in the *Manifesto*, is a class state, the proletariat organized as the ruling class; this state will have a political character, which means the organized power of one class for oppressing another. The state will act in a hostile relation to society. It will stand above society. It will, for example, have an exclusive monopoly on credit, capital, communications, and transportation–all centralized in the hands of the state. One might want to argue that the goals of this state are in the interest of the majority, are more humanitarian, equalitarian, etc. But nevertheless, as Marx says in the *Manifesto*, until a later period (which would be stage II) when classes have disappeared and when production has been transformed into an association of the whole nation, the state power will not lose its political character.[19] Until then society will have to be regulated from above.

However, the socialist stage of the *Manifesto* (with the powerful state we have described) does not match our unalienated socialist society from Chapter 1, Vol. I of *Capital*. In the *Manifesto* the regulation of society from above is to cease when class distinctions have disappeared and when the means of production are finally held in common. In the socialist exchange society of *Capital* as well as in the *Gotha Program* the means of production are already held in common. There is no evidence of the existence or the effect of classes. Even further, nothing is said of a state standing over society. What is the explanation of this difference?

The explanation I suggest is that Marx has shifted away from the view held in the *Manifesto*. He has decided here already in *Capital* that a state standing over society is not necessary even in the transitional stage, stage I. This change of views is made explicit later in the *Civil War in France* and in the 1872 Introduction to the *Manifesto*. Based on the experience of the Paris Commune (the worker's government which lasted for little over two months in Paris in 1871) Marx decides that as in the Commune, which is considered an example of stage I or the dictatorship of the proletariat, there need not be a state standing over society. Such state power is in fact to be destroyed.[20]

The explanation of how one can have a dictatorship of the proletariat which would not be a state standing over and dominating society is not perfectly clear in Marx's own writings. Dictatorship would seem to imply state domination. However, in commenting on Marx's political views, Lenin (in *State and Revolution*) suggests a possible answer to this problem. Lenin argues that if the proletariat in stage I forms the majority of the population then there will no longer be a state in the proper sense, the Marxian sense, of the word. There will be no state in the sense of an organized force (possessing a monopoly of the means of violence) for the suppression of a majority by a minority. If the workers form the majority, little force or suppression will be necessary. The government will be democratic and the withering away of the state will already have commenced.[21] This democratic character would be insured, following Marx's suggestions in the *Civil War in France*, if government representatives were elected only for very short terms, if they were bound to their constituents by a direct mandate, and if the standing army (the monopoly on the means of violence) attached to the state were eliminated and replaced by a militia which could protect the citizens from a government which might try to stand over and dominate society.

To conclude: we saw that in his views on labor Marx started with the Greek-aesthetic model but later changed his mind, deciding that it was incompatible with a developed economy. In his views on the state (after 1842), however, Marx doesn't change his mind. He continuously struggles to work out a theory of how to overcome the opposition between state and society and to bring about a state which at least in this respect is like the ancient Greek state.

It might seem odd that Marx would accept the Greek-aesthetic model at one level but not at another. Hegel, however, did something much the same. For a moment let us look back again at the "Greek Ideal." If we read Hegel carefully, we can see that there were really two ideal periods of Greek life. In the *Philosophy of History* the "perfect bloom of Greek life" was the period of the Athenian city state, the sixty years between the two wars. On the other hand, in the *Aesthetics* there is another ideal period, that of the heroic age described by Homer. It is clear that this earlier period, for Hegel, is the source of the ideal of labor, the labor of the epic hero. And this ideal, for Hegel, is incompatible with the later period of the Athenian city state, where (just as in the modern world) there is a division of labor between those who work and those who have a pleasant form of existence but do not work. And even further, as Hegel argues, the epic and epic conditions are incompatible with an established state, its laws, institutions, and division of labor. A hero cannot be subordinate to an authority like that of a state or its laws. The hero himself, the personal volition of the individual, can be the *only* authority.[22] On the other hand it is clear that the ideal of the state, where the state appears as the result of the citizen's own efforts, where the state is not alien or abstract, this ideal derives not from the epic age where there was no state and could be no state, but from the period of the Athenian city state. Thus, even in the ancient world, for Hegel, one must choose between two incompatible ideals, that of labor or of the state. Hegel's goal for modern society (I would argue if I had time) is to drop the ideal of labor, but to maintain as much as possible of the city state ideal.

The later Marx's position is something like this. He decides that the ideal of labor cannot be realized in full in the modern world. So instead he introduces a separation between labor and leisure. If one were to look for an ideal model for the separation of labor and leisure one could find it in the Greek city state where the man of leisure, at least as Aristotle has it, concerns himself with higher intellectual activities and with political activity (of course Marx's goal is to provide leisure for all).[23]

In the leisure time of communist society one develops oneself, educates oneself in the arts and sciences, and involves oneself, just as the Greek citizen did, in political and social affairs. The purpose of labor time, no longer resembling the model of the heroic period but now resembling the model of the city state period, is to provide the material means for each and all to take part in leisure activities which are ends in themselves. In other words the ideal of labor is not simply dropped as it was for Hegel.

In *Capital* Marx considered the view of Aristotle to be a dream contradicted by capitalist society, but a dream, we can now see, which can come true in a socialist society. Marx quotes Aristotle's *Politics*:

> If...every tool, when summoned, or even of its own accord, could do the work that befits it just as the creations of Daedalus moved of themselves, or the tripods of Haephaestos went of their own accord to their sacred work...then there would be no need of apprentices for the master, or of slaves for the lord.[24]

By increasing production through technology and by reducing the work day Marx tries to find a place for labor within a model resembling that of the city state period. Here labor is not an end in itself but it nevertheless plays an important role in contributing the material means to the individual's development and to the enriching of leisure activities. The labor ideal is thus subsumed under and unified with the city state ideal; only in this way can something of it be preserved.

As Marx says in the *Grundrisse*, the ancients were never concerned with which form of property created the greatest wealth. Rather they always asked what form of property created the best citizen. This conception of things, Marx says, is much more exalted than that of the modern world. For the ancients, man always appeared as the aim of production rather than production and wealth being the aim of man.[25] The ideal society of the later Marx, though changed, is still based on the model of the ancient world.

Notes

1. *Writings of the Young Marx on Philosophy and Society (WYMPS)*, ed. L.D. Easton & K.H. Guddat (New York: Doubleday, 1967), p. 206; and for the German, *Marx Engels Werke (MEW)* (Berlin: Dietz, 1972ff.), I, 338-9.

2. K. Marx, *The Poverty of Philosophy* (New York: International, 1963), p. 144 and *MEW*, IV, 157.

3. See my article "Labor, the State, and Aesthetic Theory in the Writings of Schiller", forthcoming in *Interpretation*.

4. "Comments on Mill's *Elements of Political Economy*" in *WYMPS*, p. 281 and *MEW*, Erg. I, 462-3.

5. K. Marx, *Economic and Philosophic Manuscripts of 1844 (EPM)*, ed. D.J. Struik (New York: International, 1964), p. 114 and *MEW*, Erg. I, 517.

6. *EPM*, pp. 108-14, 138-42 and *MEW*, Erg. I, 512-17, 539-43.

7. G.W.F. Hegel, *Aesthetics*, trans. T.M. Knox (Oxford: Clarendon, 1975), I, 181-5, 257-61; and for the German, *Saemtliche Werke (SW)*, ed. H. Glockner (Stuttgart-Bad Cannstatt: Frommann, 1965ff.), XII, 251-5, 345-52.

8. *Aesthetics*, II, 1053 and *SW*, XIV, 342-3.

9. K. Marx, *Grundrisse (G)*, trans. M. Nicolaus (London: Allen Lane, 1973), pp. 110-1; and for the German, *Grundrisse der Kritik der politischen Oekonomie (GKPO)* (Frankfurt: Europaeische Verlagsanstalt, n.d.), pp. 30-1.

10. *G*, pp. 706, 708, 612n and *GKPO*, pp. 593-4, 595-6, 506n. See also K. Marx, *Capital*, ed. F. Engels (New York: International, 1967), I, 530 and *MEW*, XXIII, 552.

11. *Capital*, III, 820 and *MEW*, XXV, 828.

12. K. Marx, *Theories of Surplus Value*, ed. S. Ryazanskaya (Moscow: Progress, 1963), III, 257 and *MEW*, XXVI, part 3, 253.

13. *Capital*, I, 178 and *MEW*, XXIII, 193. *Capital*, III, 82 and *MEW*, XXV, 828. *G*, pp. 611-12 and *GKPO*, p. 508.

14. K. Marx, *Critique of Hegel's Philosophy of Right*, trans. A. Jolin and J. O'Malley (Cambridge: Cambridge University, 1970), pp. 29-33, 121 and *MEW*, I, 231-4, 326-7.

15. K. Marx, *Communist Manifesto* in *Birth of the Communist Manifesto*, ed. D.J. Struik (New York: International, 1971), pp. 111-2 and *MEW*, IV, 481-2. K. Marx, *Critique of the Gotha Program* (New York: International, 1938), pp. 8-10, 18 and *MEW*, XIX, 19-21, 28. For a more extended treatment of the issues which follow see my

article "Estrangement and the Dictatorship of the Proletariat in the Writings of Karl Marx", forthcoming in *Political Theory*.

16. "Comments on Mill," pp. 272-5 and *MEW*, Erg. I, 451-4. *Capital*, I, 82 and *MEW*, XXIII, 97.

17. *Capital*, I, 72-3 and *MEW*, XXIII, 86-7.

18. *Capital*, I, 76-80 and *MEW*, XXIII, 90-4.

19. *Manifesto*, pp. 111-2 and *MEW*, IV, 481-2.

20. K. Marx, *Civil War in France* in *Writings on the Paris Commune*, ed. H. Draper (New York: Monthly Review, 1971), pp. 70-4 and *MEW*, XVII, 336-40. *Manifesto*, p. 130 and *MEW*, XVIII, 96.

21. V. I. Lenin, *Selected Works* (Moscow: Progress, 1970), II, 352-3.

22. G.W.F. Hegel, *Philosophy of History*, trans. J. Sibree (New York: Dover, 1956), p. 265; and for the German, *Vorlesungen ueber die Philosophie der Weltgeschichte*, ed. G. Lasson (Hamburg: Felix Meiner, 1968), II-IV, 641. *Aesthetics*, I, 180-5 and *SW*, XII, 250-5.

23. Aristotle, *The Basic Works of Aristotle*, ed. R. McKeon (New York: Random House, 1941); *Politics*, pp. 1183, 1279, 1288-9; *Metaphysics*, p. 690; *Nicomachean Ethics*, pp. 1104-5.

24. *Capital*, I, 408 and *MEW*, XXIII, 430. *Politics*, p. 1131.

25. *G*, pp. 487-8 and *GKPO*, pp. 387-8.

A REPLY TO PROFESSOR KAIN

CSUF STUDENTS

This panel[1] would like to note that it does not consider its role to be an adversary one. By graciously submitting his work to us well in advance of today's discussion, Dr. Kain has made it possible for us to come to a fuller understanding of Marx's relation to the Greeks and the Greek Aesthetic Ideal.

Dr. Kain opens by noting that the "myth of Greece" is a persistent theme found in late eighteenth century and early nineteenth century German thinkers. There are two dimensions to this "myth". First, as opposed to the modern bureaucratic state, political life in classical Greece was thought to be a reflection of the citizen's own vital interests, and a product of his own energies. Secondly, although economic life in *classical* Greece clearly involved a division of labor, specialization and separation between mental and physical activity, those propounding the "myth" found in an earlier "Heroic Age" described by Homer an ideal for productive man.

It is against this background that Dr. Kain examines the development of Marx's view of labor. He finds, in general, that the early works accord with the Heroic Ideal, much influenced in this respect by Schiller. In the later Marx, however, Kain finds support for Hegel's view that the "heroic" harmony between the sensuous and necessary aspects of labor cannot be revived in a modern world. The world of machinery, factory production and a scientific outlook has severed man's vital connection with nature sufficiently for this more integral view of production to be forever related to the past.

Dr. Kain supports this view by passages in the *Grundrisse* in which Marx discusses the application of historical materialism to developments in art. The epic is said to have arisen from simple productive conditions. Thus its expression of those productive conditions in an Heroic Ideal is not transferable to a world with more complex productive conditions. The panel wishes to question, however, whether Marx's central concern in these passages is to deny what seems obvious: that the Greek Aesthetic Ideal can ever be literally regained. There are aspects in these same passages which suggest that Marx is more concerned to challenge modern man to reproduce on a modern, technological plane what is first clearly *expressed* in the beautiful art of the Greeks. Marx writes:

> The difficulty is not in grasping the idea that Greek art and *epos* are bound up with certain forms of social development. It lies rather in understanding why they still constitute for us a source of aesthetic enjoyment and in certain respects prevail as the standard and model beyond attainment.... A man cannot become a child again unless he becomes childish. But does he not enjoy the artless ways of the child, and must *he not strive to reproduce its truth on a higher plane?* (panel's italic)[2]

The panel agrees that the Greek world and its experience cannot be expected to be recreated in a modern industrial setting. It does not, however, agree that the experience to which the myth refers--the grasping and shaping of the actual world, the imposition by man of form onto matter--is necessarily incompatible with industrial society. It is still a productive ideal, and an aesthetic one. In a socialist context, advanced modes of production are the means for the universal as opposed to the sporadic and isolated realization of this ideal. The charm that Greek art holds for us can thus be *explained* as expressing an ideal which we definitively and powerfully feel in its childhood form, but which we are driven to *realize* in an adult form, in stable, institutionalized and planned conditions. Nonetheless, the panel acknowledges the burden of explaining how this would be possible, and what precisely it would mean.

There is, in fact, as Dr. Kain points out, a greater stress in Marx's later works on the distinction between necessary labor time and free time. Does this distinction, however, entail that Marx has forsaken his earlier ideal? The panel finds certain shortcomings in this dichotomy. First, we are not forced to conclude that the early Marx considered *all* labor time, especially that which he later explicitly called "necessary," to be ideally or possibly self-expressive. Secondly, in the *Critique of the Gotha Program*, a mature work, Marx writes:

> In a higher phase of communist society, after the enslaving subordination of the individual to the division of labor...has vanished; after labor has become not only a means of life, *but life's prime want*, after the productive forces have increased with the all-around development of the individual...only then can the narrow horizon of bourgeois right be crossed.[3]

These remarks do not seem to betoken an abandonment of the aesthetic ideal of work. Third, Marx's concept of the "leisure time" which lies beyond necessary labor rejects a passive, consumer-oriented conception of leisure. It can and properly should, then, be designated by terms which connote work, labor, production—an artistic conception of leisure. Accordingly, we can see necessary labor as, in some respects, continuous with leisure activity (as work) rather than as severely contrasted with it as Dr. Kain would have it.

Necessary labor might be seen as a necessary condition for free-time activity, and so in some sense a component of the productive ideal itself.

The panel recognizes that its view presupposes that the necessary labor in question can lose its alienated character. Dr. Kain too is at pains to inquire why even his own less integrative theory of socially necessary labor time does not open the door to alienation within socialism itself. The hypothesis that suggests itself here, both to Dr. Kain and to the panel, is that the "Classical Political Ideal" can come to the rescue of the "Heroic Productive Ideal." So far forth, Marx is following Hegel. For according to Dr. Kain Hegel's recognition that the Heroic Ideal cannot be reconciled with a modern division of labor leads him to forfeit this ideal in deference to a later city-state or political ideal.

In Marx's use of this idea, though each citizen when acting in the realm of socially mandated labor time would subject his creative will to the production decisions of the majority, this would not be alienating. For social and communal persons would be subject, even in the realm of necessary labor, only to decisions that they, as public persons, have themselves made. This would be alienating only if non-alienation presupposed a "free time" in which individuals pursue self-objectification in a "private" time and space which they jealously guard and that the collectivity is eager to snatch away. But this is not the case. The person who realizes his individuality is, for Marx, precisely the same person who defines himself communally as a "species being." Moreover, necessary labor, under these conditions, is not at all the same as forced labor. If it does not directly express man's highest creative capacities, it nonetheless does directly express his capacity for communal decision making; and it leads to the fulfillment of creative capacities precisely because the principle of action adopted by the collectivity is focused on developing these.

Dr. Kain recognizes, as do we, that any such solution must fail, however, if the alienation in question is a function not of a loss of political autonomy, but is more deeply rooted in certain economic arrangements, especially those involving large-scale production and distribution. Dr. Kain takes up this side of the problem by considering Marx's views about the relation between alienation and exchange economies, and in particular socialist exchange economies. Dr. Kain holds that for Marx exchange *as such* invariably results in alienation. Thus any sort of extended, systematic exchange, even under socialism, will at the very least tend toward this result. Consequently Marx's first stage of socialism, according to Dr. Kain, requires a powerful state to counteract these tendencies. Unfortunately, however, this state will itself produce political estrangement. Thus, according to Dr. Kain, only with the "withering away" of the state is alienation, or its shadow, conquered, precisely because only under this condition is exchange completely eliminated.

The panel believes, however, that for Marx there is such a strong connection between alienation and exchange only in the case of capitalist exchange, and in general exchange should be treated at most as a possible symptom of alienation rather than its essence. In the *Grundrisse*, and in the early comments on James Mill, Marx in fact describes an "original" type of exchange, not of market values but of productive activities themselves as determined by communal needs and aims.[4] (Anthropologists have subsequently made us aware in detail of this sort of exchange.) This unalienated exchange might even be ascribable to Greek society, where capital is held in common; and to socialist society. For in the latter case, with a presupposition of commonly owned means of production, exchange loses its profit motive and market valuation. In such a system exchange becomes a "social musilage," a means by which the individual recognizes and expresses himself and others. Communally-owned property, one of the aims of socialism, would thus preserve and extend the Greek ideal of individual development and social unity in a way that gives scope to the political ideal.

In Dr. Kain's view, however, the *natural* tendencies of exchange toward alienation require a powerful state apparatus to damp down these tendencies. The estranging effects of such a state entail that only with the "withering away" of this state is alienation truly overcome. And if Dr. Kain is right this occurs only with the elimination of exchange properly so-called itself. If, however, the panel is right, even in "stage one" of socialism alienation as such is eliminated, through the communal ownership of the means of production and the elimination of private property. The villain is private property, not exchange as such. There seems no reason to assume that Marx is compelled by his later views to withdraw what he wrote in 1844: "The positive abolition of private property and the appropriation of human life is therefore the positive abolition of all alienation..."[5] Consequently a less dictatorial state apparatus would seem to be required. And *its* "withering away" would signal not so much the transcendance of exchange, but the transition to a state of plenty rather than scarcity, requiring consequently less administrative domination in a world in which it is possible that we may give to each according to need.

Notes

1. The following students, majors in philosophy and in political science at California State University, Fullerton, contributed to the preparation of these edited remarks: William Douglas, Kurt Haunfelner, Mark Haunfelner, Daniel Jones, Christoph Kotowski, and Sam Sotoodeh.

2. *Introduction* to the *Grundrisse,* trans. D. McLellan, in D. McLellan (ed.) *Karl Marx: Selected Writings* (Oxford: Oxford University Press, 1977), p. 360.

3. *Critique of the Gotha Program,* in McLellan, *op. cit.,* p. 569.

4. *Grundrisse,* in McLellan, *op. cit.,* p. 361: "The exchange orginally found in production–which is an exchange not of exchange values, but of activities determined by communal needs and communal aims–would from the start imply participation of individuals in the collective world of products." Cf. also *On James Mill,* in McLellan, *op. cit.,* p.120.

5. *Economic and Philosophic Manuscripts of 1844,* in McLellan, *op. cit.,* p. 89.

ARISTOTLE AND NIETZSCHE:

"MEGALOPSYCHIA" AND

"UEBERMENSCH"

BERND MAGNUS

I

The title of my paper is "Nietzsche and Aristotle: *Megalopsychia* and *Uebermensch.*" *Megalopsychia,* in the context of interest to us, is the term employed by Aristotle in the *Nicomachean Ethics,* Book IV, Chapter 3, 1123b-1125b,[2] in connection with his discussion of virtues concerned with honor. The Greek expression *megalopsychia* consists of the stem *psychia,* familiar to us from *psyche,* psyche; i.e., soul, mind, spirit, to which the prefix *megalo* is added. *Megalo, megas,* or *megalou* can be translated as "great" or "large". *Megalo,* therefore, is a combining form meaning "large", "great," or "powerful": as in "megalomania," for example. Indeed, megalomania, in the sense of a mental disorder which is characterized by delusions of grandeur, may be viewed as the *pathological* counterpart of *megalopsychia. Megalopsychia,* in Greek, carries with it no pejorative connotations. Far from it. The term is commonly translated "greatness of soul."[3] *Megalopsychia* has been translated as "high-mindedness";[4] it has also, and quite interestingly, been translated as "self-respect."[5] However, the

260

term *megalopsychia* is without question best known to English speaking persons under the translation "pride". It is in fact translated that way in the widely used McKeon collection of Aristotle's writings.[6] Translating *megalopsychia* as "pride," as W. D. Ross does on that occasion, may seem strange to some, but the strangeness is mitigated when one recalls that Aristotle's discussion of *megalopsychia* occurs as he attempts to apply to concrete cases of virtues and vices his definition that virtue is a disposition to choose the mean between excess and deficiency, defect. Thus viewed, *megalopsychia,* "pride," is the mean which lies between vanity (which is excessive) and humility (which is deficient). On this reading, pride is a virtue; humility is a vice--as is vanity.

A second term in the title of my paper is *Uebermensch,* a word no doubt somewhat more familiar. It is Nietzsche's word, translated into English either as "superman" or "overman".[7] In what follows, I will continue my habit of using the German *Uebermensch* instead of "superman" or "overman", but not simply for reasons of pedantry. "Superman" seems to me to have been forevermore preempted by Clark Kent (and Lois Lane); and I cannot for the life of me see Nietzsche's *Uebermenschen* leaping tall buildings with a single bound. "Overman," on the other hand, adds the paltry prefix "over" to the stem "man" and conveys few of the superlatives which are so super when we use the prefix "super."[8] "Overman," incidentally, never found its way into common usage, as "superman" did, despite the fact that it is more than seventy years old, for Kaufmann merely adopted Thomas Common's use, from the earliest English translation of Nietzsche. The "over" prefix works well, it seems to me, for "overhearing," "overlooking," "overpassing," "overworking" and "oversleeping"; but it still seems jarring when used in connection with descriptions of praiseworthy qualities of persons. Finally, I prefer to use the German *Uebermensch* for two additional reasons: as a quasi-technical expression--much as the German word *Dasein* is now an English commonplace, as in *Daseinsanalysis*--and because the word is non-sexist in German. It is perhaps ironic that Nietzsche, who is often viewed as an arch-misogynist, should use the term *Uebermensch,* since it can apply with equal force to men and women alike.[9]

The connection between Aristotle's conception of pride, greatness of soul, and Nietzsche's *Uebermensch* has been frequently mentioned. Walter Kaufmann, in particular, has made interesting claims for a connection between some of Aristotle's and Nietzsche's views. He has suggested, for example, that "Aristotle's conception apparently made a tremendous impression on Nietzsche, whose opposition to Christianity can scarcely be seen in proper perspective apart from Aristotle's ethics...."[10] Kaufmann argues, further, that "many of the provocative ideas he [i.e., Aristotle] expresses so unprovocatively and dryly are fashioned into polemical arrows in Nietzsche's works, especially in *Zarathustra.* Nietzsche's debt to Aristotle's ethics is thus considerable, and it is quite unjustifiable to infer from Nietzsche's disagreement with Aristotle's theory of tragedy that Aristotle meant little or nothing to him....."[11] These are interesting and important points Kaufmann makes. We may be able to extract at least four claims from these quotations. Kaufmann suggests (1) that Aristotle made a tremendous impression on Nietzsche and that he is therefore indebted to Aristotle, particularly to his ethics; (2) that many of Aristotle's ethical notions resurface as transmogrified polemics in Nietzsche's works; (3) that Nietzsche's critique of Christianity can scarcely be understood apart from Aristotle's ethics; (4) and, finally, that his rejection of Aristotle's theory of tragedy does not imply that Aristotle meant little or nothing to Nietzsche.

Thesis (4) expresses a virtually logical truth; for we do not rail against those who mean nothing to us. One point of this paper, regrettably perhaps, is to suggest that the remaining three of Kaufmann's four claims may be misleading, if they are pressed very hard. I shall argue in what follows that Aristotle's ethics--even his conception of pride--has *very* little to do either with Nietzsche's moral philosophy, or with his conception of *Uebermenschen.* That is, I believe the comparison with Aristotle is quite superficial; it has no greater force, I think, than repellent comparisons of Nietzsche with fascism, antisemitism, or any other number of "isms" to which he has been assimilated. If I am right in what I claim, it will follow that Kaufmann's thesis (3) is mistaken, that Nietzsche's critique of Christianity *can* be quite well understood without reference to Aristotle's ethics. Indeed, there is no hidden agenda here to quibble about Walter Kaufmann's considerable scholarship. My purpose, rather, is to underscore the point that Nietzsche's attempted transvaluation of values is dominated by his understanding (or misunderstanding) of Plato and Socrates: not Aristotle. Understanding Nietzsche's critique of Plato is the problem, therefore, not Nietzsche's alleged assimiliation of Aristotle's ethics.

I divide what follows into four parts. The first part is, quite simply, Aristotle's description of pride, of the great-souled man, as that description is appealed to by Kaufmann and others. Part two of this paper is a brief attempt to outline relevant parts of Aristotle's *Nicomachean Ethics,* in order to place his dicussion of *megalopsychia* in its proper setting. Part three is a truncated sketch of Nietzsche's moral philosophy, on the one hand, and his *Uebermensch,* on the other hand.[12] Finally, part four of this paper will suggest that we can better get our proper bearing in studying Nietzsche by grasping his thesis that Plato inaugurated what I have called a systemic hierarchical dualism, which Nietzsche took to be the origin and inner logic of nihilism itself. Nietzsche thought that Platonism conditioned Western thought, speech, and behavior as nothing else before or after it has done. In that context, Christianity is merely Platonism for the masses for Nietzsche; moreover, he took it to be his task to effect a transvaluation of this systemic hierarchical dualism, primarily as expressed in the doctrine of eternal recurrence.[13]

II

What follows is a very abbreviated quotation from the *Nicomachean Ethics,* Book 4, Chapter 3, in which pride and the proud man are examined:

> A person is thought to be proud if he claims much and deserves much.... He that claims less than he deserves is humble...the truly proud man must be a good man.... Pride seems...a crowning ornament of all the virtues.... Great honours accorded by persons of worth will afford [the proud man] pleasure in a moderate degree: he will feel he is receiving only what belongs to him, or even less, for no honour can be adequate to the merits of perfect virtue, yet all the same he will deign to accept their honours, because they have no greater tribute to offer him. Honour rendered by common people and on trivial grounds he will utterly despise, for this is not what he merits.... He therefore to whom even honour is a small thing will be indifferent to other things as well. Hence proud men are thought to be haughty.... The proud man is justified in despising other people--his estimates are correct; but most vain men have no good ground for their pride.... He is fond of conferring benefits, but ashamed to receive them, because the former is a mark of superiority and the latter of inferiority. He returns a service done to him with interest, since this will put the original benefactor into his debt in turn, and make him the party benefited. The proud are said to have a good memory for any benefit they have conferred, but a bad memory for those which they have received (since the recipient of a benefit is the inferior of his benefactor, whereas they desire to be superior).... It is also characteristic of proud men never to ask help from others, or only with reluctance, but to render aid willingly; and to be haughty toward men of position and fortune, but courteous toward those of moderate station...and to adopt a high manner with the former is

not ill-bred, but it is vulgar to lord it over humble people.... He must be open both in love and in hate, since concealment shows timidity; and care more for the truth than for what people will think.... He is outspoken and frank, except when speaking with ironical self-depreciation, as he does to common people. He will be incapable of living at the will of another, unless a friend, since to do so is slavish. He does not bear a grudge, for it is not a mark of pride to recall things against people, especially the wrongs they have done you, but rather to overlook them. He is...not given to speaking evil himself, even of his enemies, except when he deliberately intends to give offense.... Such then being the proud man, the corresponding character on the side of deficiency is the humble man, and on that of excess the vain man.[14]

Pride is one of the so-called seven deadly sins in the Christian tradition; the others are lust, sloth, anger, envy, gluttony, and avarice. One can certainly understand from the above how Aristotle's characterization of pride is far removed from initial Christian perception of this matter. It is equally plain, moreover, that many of Nietzsche's deliberately anti-Christian moral observations bear a striking but superficial family resemblance to some of Aristotle's observations on the nature of pride. The danger, therefore, is the temptation to convert this elective affinity--or family resemblance if you prefer--into the claim that there exists a *causal* relationship in which Nietzsche's philosophy is made accessible through Aristotle's. I believe that Kaufmann and others may have yielded to this temptation.

III

Aristotle begins the *Nicomachean Ethics* in characteristic fashion: "Every art and every inquiry, and similarly every action and pursuit, is thought to aim at some good; and for this reason the good has rightly been declared to be that at which all things aim."[15] Since there are many goods, in the sense in which many things are good *for* something else, what we seek is something which is good for its own sake, something we desire for its own sake and do not desire as a means to something else. Insofar as the good is, for Aristotle, something we in fact aim at, the good for man--if there *is* one overarching good--is something we by nature *do* seek; and Aristotle is persuaded that what we all seek is *eudaimonia,* happiness. Happiness is that for the sake of which all our other undertakings are undertaken, and it is never desired as a means to something else. However, since some people identify happiness with pleasure, or wealth, or honor, we must see which activity is peculiar to man, in the hope of finding that the good for man--his *eudaimonia*--consists in the fulfillment of his function. Neither growth, reproduction, nor sensation are peculiar to man: however, reason is. Hence, if human happiness is to consist of the fulfillment of our distinctive function, then it must consist of the activity of reason itself or it must consist in activity according to reason.

Our distinctive function, reason--our virtue or excellence--has both a moral and an intellectual aspect, therefore, and action which is virtuous is activity in conformity with reason. Thus far, then, Aristotle has identified the good for man, in Book I, as happiness; he has defined happiness with reference to man's characteristic function, which, in turn, results in a division of virtues into intellectual and moral.

Books II-V, then, give a detailed account of moral virtue; Book VII discusses continence, incontinence and pleasure; Books VIII and IX discuss friendship; and Book X again discusses pleasure and happiness, this time from the perspective of the ideal life, the life of contemplation.

It is in Book II that Aristotle argues that moral virtue, like the arts, is acquired by repetition; that it is a state of character whose *differentia* is the disposition to choose the mean between excess and deficiency. Excess and defect are vices either with respect to a feeling or an action, Aristotle maintains. Thus moral virtue is :

a state of character concerned with choice, lying in a
mean, i.e., the mean relative to us, this being determined
by a rational principle, and by that principle by which
the man of practical wisdom (*phronēsis*) would
determine it.[16]

Thus courage is said to be the mean between rashness (which
is excess) and cowardice (which is deficient); temperance is
the mean between self-indulgence and "insensibility";
liberality is said to be the mean concerning money-matters,
where prodigality and meanness are said to be vices.

A few further matters deserve our attention in this hurried
gloss. First, not every action or passion admits of a mean:
Spite, envy, adultery, theft and murder, for example, are
themselves bad *simpliciter*:

> The goodness or badness with regard to such things does
> not depend on committing adultery with the right
> woman, at the right time, and in the right way, but
> simply to do any of them is wrong.[17]

Secondly, there is no mean within vices. There is no
moderate excess, deficient excess, excessive excess; there is
no moderate deficiency, deficient deficiency nor excessive
deficiency. Thirdly, there is no vice within the mean, i.e.,
there is neither excess nor deficiency of a mean. Finally, just
as there are inherently base things, there are, on the other
side of this coin, inherently great things. And one of these,
for Aristotle, is honor. I mention this now because Aristotle's
discussion of *megalopsychia*, pride, occurs in the context of
virtues concerned with honor. Indeed, pride, according to
Aristotle, "is concerned with honor on the grand scale."[18] If
we do not wrench Aristotle's description of pride entirely
from the context in which Nietzsche no doubt found it, a
slightly different picture emerges from our earlier one:

> Pride seems even from its name to be concerned with
> great things; what sort of great things, is the first

question we must try to answer. It makes no difference whether we consider the state of character or the man characterized by it. Now the man is thought to be proud who thinks himself worthy of great things, being worthy of them; for he who does so beyond his deserts is a fool, but no virtuous man is foolish or silly. The proud man, then, is the man we have described. For he who is worthy of little and thinks himself worthy of little is temperate, but not proud; for pride implies greatness, as beauty implies a good-sized body, and little people may be neat and well-proportioned but cannot be beautiful. On the other hand, he who thinks himself worthy of great things, being unworthy of them, is vain.... The man who thinks himself worthy of less than he is really worthy of is unduly humble, whether his deserts be great or moderate, or his deserts be small but his claims yet smaller. And the man whose deserts are great would seem most unduly humble.... The proud man, then, is an extreme in respect of the greatness of his claim, but a mean in respect of the rightness of them; for he claims what is in accordance with his merits, while the others go to excess or fall short.... Honours and dishonours, surely the greatest of external goods, therefore, are the objects with respect to which the proud man is as he should be.... *Now the proud man, since he deserves most, must be good in the highest degree; for the better man always deserves more, and the best man most. Therefore the truly proud man must be good. And greatness in every virtue would seem to be characteristic of a proud man.... Therefore it is hard to be truly proud; for it is impossible without nobility and goodness of character....* Vain people, on the other hand, are fools and ignorant of themselves, and that manifestly; for, not being worthy of them, they attempt honourable undertakings, and then are found out; and they adorn themselves with clothing and outward show and such things, and wish their strokes of good fortune to be made public, and speak about them as if they would be honoured for them. But undue humility is more opposed to pride than vanity is; for it is both commoner and worse.... Pride, then, is concerned with honour on the grand scale, as has been said.[19]

IV

One of the first things Nietzsche would have us understand and overcome if we are to understand and overcome nihilism, Nietzsche's archenemy, if we are to recover from its alleged sustaining grip upon our lives, is the origin and nature of moral valuations. Nietzsche would have us abandon altogether any metahistorical ground, any ultimate justification for particular moral sanctions. Universality is, for Nietzsche, interesting pretense. Instead, we will be required to talk about the utility of morality, where "utility" is construed as usefulness to the survival and welfare of the community. For whatever else morality may be, "morality is primarily a means of preserving the community in general and warding off destruction of it,"[20] for Nietzsche.

Conformity of behavior is initially compelled, historically speaking, if that is required by the community's interests. Conduct is made conformable through coercion, through compulsion, as in the debtor/creditor relationship sketched in *The Genealogy of Morals.* Compulsion is merely an early, rudimentary form of behavior modification and control, however. "Custom" soon replaces compulsion as a coercive force: One behaves as one is expected to behave. At a still later level of refinement, subtlety and social organization, the voice of the community is rendered authoritative and internalized in the form of "conscience." Internalization of the community's tacit valuations is the critical notion here, for obedience to one's conscience may now be felt by the pliant "subject" as something noble, even pleasant. The coercive-compulsive threat may be lost altogether in this subtle internalization of society's dictates. Our "conscience" is no less our nature for being a second nature, as it were.

Paralleling the interiorization of society's dictates is the extension of what is considered morally praiseworthy or blameworthy. Moral valuations, moral judgments are now extended beyond actions to cover intentions as well. An agent's intentions now become matters of praise and blame, not only his actions. The notion of virtue has its origins in this extended universe of moral discourse, Nietzsche reminds us, opening up mental states to "moral" inspection--as does the notion of the virtuous man.

As we look more closely at this Nietzsche portrait of the rise of moral valuations, he also paints a "twofold early history of good and evil."[21] This theme of Nietzsche's--that there is such a twofold early history of morals and two fundamentally opposed moral perspectives which correspond to and arise out of this history--is at once basic to him and insightful. Only its surface can be exposed in this discussion, however.

Mention of the two primary types of morality which he has discovered was made explicit by Nietzsche in *Beyond Good and Evil*. He calls them "master morality and slave morality."[22] Keep in mind that Nietzsche's characterization is not intended, at least not initially, for purposes of invidious comparison. The characterization is, rather, connected to Nietzsche's genealogical methodology.[23] A certain moral outlook originates with slaves, he would argue, another presumably with their masters. Echoes of their respective conditions can be heard as rationalized in their moral perspectives. Nevertheless, all advanced civilizations display a mixture of both moral outlooks--those of slave morality as well as master morality--and elements of each moral framework are generally simultaneously active in one and the same individual. The distinction between master and slave morality is neither primarily historical nor linear therefore; it is typological primarily, on this reading. Accordingly, the morality of the aristocrat, master morality, identifies "good" and "bad" as expressions ascriptive of persons rather than actions. To say that X is "good" is much the same as to say X is "noble." To say that X is "bad" is much the same as to say X is "base," "despicable." And again, masters judge the baseness of persons, and their actions only derivatively.

Those who are base, those who are slaves, are essentially weak and powerless by contrast. Nietzsche maintains, therefore, that among the powerless the moral standard is that which is useful or beneficial to the community *simpliciter*. In further consequence, slave morality extols qualities such as sympathy, kindness and humility, all of which have high utility for the community. By way of contrast, independent, strong individuals come to be regarded with suspicion. They are a threat, and, accordingly, are judged "evil." Thus we come full circle. The person judged "good" (i.e., "noble") by the standards of master morality is judged "evil" precisely for those traits by the standards of slave morality. The "good" man becomes "evil" in this scenario. The relationship is symmetrical. The "good" man in slave morality terms is "base" in terms of master morality.

Nietzsche characterized this slave morality, often in strident tones, as herd-morality. The moral valuations and standards of "slave morality" are to be read as expressions of the needs of the herd (i.e., the community).

This bare sketch of master and slave moralities is filled in in *The Genealogy of Morals*. The concepts are deepened and rendered more systematic there. For one thing, the notion of resentment, *ressentiment*, is given prominent display and functions just precisely as the sort of explanatory tool which Nietzsche needs to account for moral attitudes and beliefs. The concepts of resentment and sublimation are then also used to explain why Christianity is slave morality sanctioned and incarnate.

We began with two types, the aristocratic master, the servile slave. The master is and his morality extols autonomy, independence, power, self-control, pride, spontaneity and passion. The self-directed master derives his value not from the community, not from "the herd," but from the abundance of his own life and strength. The slave, however, fears the strength and power of the master. He despises him. He is dependent, powerless, without self-direction or self-control. To seize control over his own psychic destiny, the slave must curb and tame his master. He must displace him in a sense. And the method of "overcoming" the master and his morality, the means to his displacement, is to render the values of the herd absolute and universal: "The revolt of the slaves in morals begins with resentment becoming creative and giving birth to values."[24] The revolt of the slaves in moral matters is indeed creative and resentful. Powerless to effect a fundamental change in his condition, he wreaks vengeance against the master by converting the master's attributes into vices. And while master morality sanctions coexistence with inferior types and morals--so long as the baser ones keep their valuations to their own kind--the resentment of the slave yearns for universality. Nothing may escape its moral clutches alive. Nietzsche does not of course suggest that the slave's resentment of and revenge against the master is either direct or conscious: far from it.

It is in this context, in the context or moral-psychological imperialism, that the slave's resentment is to be understood. Since the slave cannot displace the master in reality, he avenges himself symbolically, mythically. Enter the religion of the slave--Christianity.

Whatever else Christianity may be for Nietzsche--and we should not forget that it *is* many things besides--it is first the ideology of slave morality. It expresses the slave's resentment against the attributes of master morality, by vilifying them. The virtues of the master become "sin." In place of power, it is said that the meek are to inherit the earth. Pride is sin. Humility is virtue. Charity, chastity and obedience eclipse self-reliance, spontaneity and autonomy. And it is said that it will be easier for a camel to pass through the eye of a needle than for a "rich" man to pass into the kingdom of heaven.

The resentment of slave morality which finds expression in Christianity is at once virulent and fateful. Virulent, because its moral imperialism is of unprecedented scope. Its "moral" dictates are meant to cover all persons at all times. Denied the actual gratification of supremacy over the master, it condemns him symbolically--but for eternity. He is

condemned to hell. The scope of the sanction is "eternity."
Apart from its virulence, Christian slave morality is fateful;
fateful in that it introduces into the Western psyche
something virtually ineradicable--consciousness of sin and
guilt.[25]

Since the slave suffers his dependent condition, he
construes his suffering in terms of sin and guilt. But more
fateful still he (falsely) construes *existence* itself as guilt and
sin. Existence becomes punishment and expiation, in
short:[26]

> Because there is suffering in those who will...willing and
> all life were supposed to be a — punishment!

> And now cloud upon cloud rolled over the spirit, until
> eventually madness preached "Everything passes away;
> therefore everything deserves to pass away!

> "And this too is justice, this law of time that it must
> devour its children." Thus preached madness.

> "Things are ordered morally according to justice and
> punishment. Alas, where is deliverance from the flux of
> things and from the punishment called existence?" Thus
> preached madness.

> "Can there be deliverance if there is eternal justice? Alas,
> the stone *It was* cannot be moved: all punishment must
> be eternal too!" Thus preached madness.

> "No deed can be annihilated: how could it be undone
> by punishment! This, this is what is eternal in the
> punishment called existence, that existence must
> eternally become deed and guilt again!"[27]

The innocence of existence, its topic neutrality, is
abolished in the triumph of slave morality *qua* Christianity.
Christianity is the fruit of resentment. As a confession of

weakness it represents the decline of life, decadence, degeneracy, in contrast to the exuberant ascent of life which seeks expression in master morality. And so it also follows for Nietzsche that Christianity severs body and soul, that it deprecates the human body, impulse, instinct, passion, beauty, sensuality, the uninhibited exercise of the mind, and aesthetic values generally.

It would be a mistake to infer, however, that recent apostasy from Christianity is a sufficient condition for overcoming nihilism. Nietzsche's analysis is at once more complex and subtle. For Nietzsche, "the true world" has already been abolished; its abolition, however, is a part of the problem of nihilism, not a solution to it: "The greatest recent event--that 'God is dead,' that belief in the Christian God has become unbelievable--already begins to cast its first shadows over Europe."[28] To be sure, apostasy from Christianity may be a necessary condition for the eclipse of nihilism; but it is not enough.

Nietzsche is the philosopher of the *Uebermensch* in the popular mind. Yet the teaching itself is confined to *Thus Spoke Zarathustra* and the portrayal of the ideal is very slim indeed. Much of this is unavoidable, since *Uebermenschheit* cannot be prescribed.[29] There is no formula which results in an *Uebermensch*. Nevertheless, in the light of what has already been said about master morality the contours should not be difficult to discern.

The elective affinity, family resemblance, between *Uebermensch* and master is plain enough. His type represents ascending life, self-overcoming, self-possession, autonomy and is to be contrasted with decadence, decomposition, dependency and weakness. The *Uebermensch* bears a striking family resemblance to an embodied representative of master morality, albeit idealized, while Nietzsche's famous "last man" resembles embodied slave morality in striking ways.

The "last man" is the antipode of the *Uebermensch*. His goal is happiness. He derives his perceptual set from "the herd." He understands his will-to-power in terms of the will-to-power of the "other." He is other directed in Riesman's sense. Even his attempts at excellence, his strivings, are understood in the context of and in terms of the achievements and valuations of others. He competes, when he competes, against the anonymous others: the "they," *das Man* in Heidegger's sense. He values as "they" value. He hopes as "they" hope, fears as "they" fear, prizes and praises as "they" prize and praise. He dreams the dreams of the other. But the "last man" is not some specific person. Rather, he is everyone and no one. He is the last man in each of us. He is what is to be overcome; the torpor and sloth of average everydayness.[30] But it would be a mistake to view this privative mode of being-in-the-world simply as impoverishment, simply as a regrettable accident. Rather, average everyday existence is the norm, just as the unexamined life is the norm; it *is* average and everyday. And while Plato has Socrates say in the *Apology* that the unexamined life is not worth living, the examined life cannot be lived by everyone, nor even by the few at all times. Average everydayness permeates the exceptional life, too.

If the last man is cousin of the slave, in Nietzsche's genealogical sense, then he is slavishness, conformity to the dictates and standards of the crowd. He is everyone. He is no one in particular.

I have said that Nietzsche's man is the conceptual-genealogical cousin of the "slave" and that *Uebermensch* is cousin of the. master. In consequence, *Uebermensch* must be what is extraordinary, rather than average, exceptional rather than everyday, rare rather than commonplace and common. When the last man's life is shrouded in ambiguity, the life of the *Uebermensch* is focused. Authentic self-possession replaces conformity to tacit cultural values. Thought and articulate speech replace idle curiosity, nosiness, and chatter. Informed concern may replace gossip.

Master morality extols autonomy, independence, power, pride, spontaneity, intelligence, beauty and passion, I have said earlier. And unsurprisingly, the *Uebermensch* also will have to exhibit traits of autonomy, traits of self-possession, given Nietzsche's own preference profile.

If will-to-power, for example, is form-giving, shaping, articulation, then the *Uebermensch* forms and shapes the will-to-power which he himself is. It is not a question of mastering others, of overcoming the herd by overpowering it. The herd to be overcome is the herd in ourselves. Mastery and overcoming are to be understood as self-mastery and self-overcoming primarily. So the will-to-power shapes *itself* in the case of the *Uebermensch* by rooting out vestiges of "the last man" within. And since giving form to one's life in this instance cannot be a question of conforming to the form given by others, the *Uebermensch* is self-forming, in a certain sense--even when the form given appears superficially to conform. This form-giving which is self-overcoming may properly be characterized as the transformation of life into art-form.

As an idealized type (which may be Nietzsche's own idealization), one may view the *Uebermensch* as the highest possible integration of intelligence, strength of character and will, autonomy, passion, taste, and perhaps even of physical prowess.[31] Think of it as instinct spiritualized to avoid the unfortunate extreme effort which this characterization suggests. For, lastly, while Nietzsche's "higher men" may try to impose art upon their lives, their labors suggest too much effort, too much exertion, to be authentic *Uebermenschen.* So we are to think of *Uebermenschen* as distinguishable even from the higher men to whom we point with pride. Being an *Uebermensch* is presumably effortless. *Uebermenschheit* is to be understood as the expression of ascending life, overfullness and effortlessness.

It is admittedly difficult to think of "the Roman Caesar with Christ's soul"[32] without conjuring up an image of extreme effort. It is indeed difficult even to imagine such an *Uebermensch* without imagining at the same time a veritable spiritual background, without imagining at the same time a tremendous dramatic tension. And yet Nietzsche asks us to form just such an image.

Zarathustra's celebrated first speech "On the Three Metamorphoses"[33] may be particularly helpful in this

connection. Zarathustra tells us straightway that he will tell
us about three metamorphoses of the spirit. He will tell us
how the spirit became a camel; how the camel became a lion;
and how the lion, finally, became a child. Note that we are
dealing with the transformation of spirit, not of body.
Accordingly, the metamorphoses, the transfiguration of
camel to lion to child, should not be viewed as a "natural"
process in any biological sense. Not everyone's spirit is
transfigured or, indeed, can be transformed.

The (spirit of the) camel is a beast of burden. It demands
of itself what is difficult, indeed what is most difficult:
"There is much that is difficult for the spirit, the strong and
reverent of spirit would bear much: but the difficult and
most difficult are what its strength demands." The camel's
excellence is a function of the load it is able to bear, how
much it can carry. And the camel-spirit excels to the extent
that it too is able to understand, internalize and appropriate
the values of its culture. The camel-spirit kneels down
"wanting to be well loaded." And through the load it wishes
to carry it wishes to exult in its own strength. This
camel-need is a *bona fide* need to excel. But the terms of the
competition, the norms and standards for the competition
and for excellence, are not of the camel's own making.

Each cultural activity defines its own competition. For the
scholar whose camel-spirit would bear much, for example,
there are the obvious "tools" to acquire--languages (the more
the better), literatures (the more the better), histories (the
more the better), methodologies (the more the better). And
the scholar who would bear much knows the weight of his
burden; the iron discipline, the pleasures deferred, the genteel
poverty. He knows all too well the musty odor of books
within dank library walls while children laugh and celebrate
life on sun-drenched lawns outside. And he is no stranger to
"feeding on acorns and grass of knowledge and, for the sake
of truth, suffering hunger in one's soul." It is thus in every
discipline to which the camel-spirit subjects itself. Its reverent
spirit excels according to the burden it can bear. For
Nietzsche's would-be Christian, for example, this may include

"loving those who despise us," which is often spoken of but seldom achieved.

The camel-spirit is a paragon of its culture, the embodied highest standards and achievements of its own crowd. For many, perhaps for most, that is the aim of life. For some, however, the camel's burden once assumed plummets into the vortex of reflection. What has become second nature, habit, is brought to full consciousness, to self-conciousness. Then the dark night of this spirit begins and like the camel that, burdened, speeds into the desert, thus the spirit speeds into its desert."

The second metamorphosis occurs in the isolation of reflection, in the soul's interior dialogue with itself:

> In the loneliest desert, however, the second metamorphosis occurs; here the spirit becomes a lion which would conquer its freedom and be master in its own desert. Here it seeks out its last master: it wants to fight him and its last god; for ultimate victory it wants to fight with the great dragon.

The lion is the spirit of negation: rage, destruction. Its willful self-assertion, however, remains dependent. Negation is umbilically connected to, dependent upon, that which it would negate. So the lion is the dialectical negation of the camel. And in order to defeat the camel in itself, the lion-spirit must isolate the camel's sustaining and informing source: the great dragon. And the great dragon, we have suggested earlier, expresses the values, standards, in terms of which the camel-spirit once understood its burden, its task, itself. The lion must negate the values of the camel:

> Who is the great dragon whom the spirit will no longer call lord and god? "Thou shalt" is the name of the great dragon. But the spirit of the lion says, "I will." "Thou shalt" lies in his way, sparkling like gold, an animal covered with scales; and on every scale shines a golden "thou shalt."

Values, thousands of years old, shine on these scales; and thus speaks the mightiest of all dragons: "All value of all things shines on me. All value has long been created, and I am all created value. Verily, there shall be no more 'I will.' " Thus speaks the dragon.

Notice also that the canvas has been enlarged, stretched as it were. The lion must negate the values of the camel, to be sure. But now the lion rejects not merely one set of values among others. It does not merely reject one camel in a flock. The dragon now becomes values *simpliciter:* All value! The dragon represents the value-positing activity itself--valuing--which alone makes possible particular imperatives. Each imperative sparkles like the scales of the dragon which *is* value-positing, *is* valuing. That is why all values shine upon the dragon; that is why all value has long been created; that is why the dragon will tolerate none of the lion's self-assertiveness.

But if the dragon represents all values hitherto and the value-positing impulse itself,

My brothers, why is there a need in the spirit for the lion? Why is not the beast of burden, which renounces and is reverent, enough?

To create new values--that even the lion cannot do; but the creation of freedom for oneself for new creation--that is within the power of the lion. The creation of freedom for oneself and a sacred "No" even to duty--for that, my brothers, the lion is needed. To assume the right to new values--that is the most terrifying assumption for a reverent spirit that would bear much. Verily to it it is preying, and a matter for a beast of prey. It once loved "thou shalt" as most sacred: now it must find illusion and caprice even in the most sacred, that freedom from its love may become its prey: the lion is needed for such prey.

So the lion, the spirit of negation, can create nothing new, we are told. The lion cannot create new values. But it can create that freedom which is a precondition for the creation of new values. It emancipates from the old--and that is terrifying for the camel-spirit. Without negation there can be no affirmation here.

> But say, my brothers, what can the child do that even the lion could not do? Why must the preying lion still become a child? The child is innocence and forgetting, a new beginning, a game, a self-propelled wheel, a first movement, a sacred "Yes." For the game of creation, my brothers, a sacred "Yes" is needed: the spirit now wills its own will, and he who had been lost to the world now conquers his own world.

The child presumably "sees" the world anew. The vision of the child is the creation of new value in just the sense that its pristine innocence is unburdened by the perceptual set which informs the vision of the camel and the lion. One must see beyond the moral and metaphysical fetters which bind our vision, in the sense of no longer seeing through them. It is a matter of surpassing, going beyond the tradition: *not* by ignoring it but by overcoming it.

That last point is important. The spirit cannot begin as a child. New values are *not* created by ignoring or remaining innocent of old ones. While it is possible to be merely a camel-spirit, or a camel-spirit become lion-spirit, it is not possible to achieve the new vision of a child without having passed through the camel and lion stages. The only way out of the tradition is *through* it. This point is often overlooked, particularly by the impatient and by the young. One cannot become a great composer without first submitting to the discipline of music, for example. Great art does not arise *ex nihilo* either.

What is required for new values is the same thing that is required for all genuine creation: A memory that knows how to forget.[34]

We are now in a better position, perhaps, to grasp the sense in which Nietzsche thought that being an *Uebermensch* was in some sense to be effortless. Like the child of the three metamorphoses, the integration of intelligence, strength of character and will, autonomy, passion, taste and prowess, have become *natural* in the *Uebermensch.* The form he has given his life now *is* his life. And again, as in the case of the child, the form of life which the *Uebermensch* is is not burdened by derivation from the lives of others. He lives his life in authentic self-possession.

V

I said at the outset of this paper that Nietzsche's view of Plato, not Aristotle, is decisive to him. While I cannot here explain that thesis in the detail it deserves, I can at least begin that discussion. Perhaps the best way to start is with Nietzsche's own, highly compressed "history" of philosophy, as it appears in *The Twilight of the Idols:*

How the "true world" finally became a fable: *history of an error.*

1. The true world; attainable for the sage, the pious, the virtuous one–he lives in it, *he is it.* (Oldest form of the idea, relatively clever, simple, persuasive. Circumlocution for the sentence, "I, Plato, *am* the truth.")

2. The true world; unattainable for now, but promised for the sage, the pious, the virtuous one ("for the sinner who repents"). (Progress of the idea: it becomes more subtle, deceptive, incomprehensible--*it becomes female,* it becomes Christian...)

3. The true world; unattainable, indemonstrable, unpromisable, but the thought of it–a consolation, an obligation, an imperative. (The old sun at bottom, but penetrating through mist and skepticism; the idea has become elusive, pale, nordic, Koenigsbergian.)

4. The true world unattainable? At any rate, unattained. And as unattained, also *unknown*. Consequently, also not consoling, redeeming, or obligating: to what could something unknown obligate us? . . . (Gray morning. First yawn of reason. Cockcrow of positivism.)

5. The "true world"--an idea which is no longer useful for anything, not even obligating--a useless idea, an idea become superfluous, consequently, a refuted idea; let us abolish it! (Bright day; breakfast; return of *bon sens* and cheerfulness; Plato's embarrassed blush; pandemonium of all free spirits.)

6. The true world we have abolished: Which world remained? The apparent one perhaps?. . . But no! *With the true world we have abolished the apparent one as well!* (Noon; moment of the briefest shadow; end of the longest error; high point of humanity; INCIPIT ZARATHUSTRA!)[35]

The error begins with Plato, we are told. The true world is attainable for the pious, for the virtuous, for the sage. If Nietzsche's general strategy is to be applied in this case , then we must see the Platonic thrust as a symptom of the decline of life, as itself a symptom of nihilism. And while it may strike us as odd to see the Socratic-Platonic achievement negatively, to see the sense in which it is symptomatic of a distressed condition, it must nevertheless be seen in this light (also) if we are to understand Nietzsche's thesis:

This irreverent thought that the great sages are *types of decline* first occurred to me precisely in a case where it is most strongly opposed by both scholarly and unscholarly prejudice: I recognized Socrates and Plato to be symptoms of degeneration, tools of the Greek dissolution, pseudo-Greek, anti-Greek (*Birth of Tragedy*, 1872). The consensus of the sages--I comprehended this ever more clearly--proves least of all that they were right in what they agreed on: It shows rather that they themselves, these wisest men, agreed in some *physiological* respect, and hence adopted the same negative attitude to life–*had to* adopt it. Judgments, judgments of value, concerning life, for it or against it, can, in the end, never be true: they have value only as symptoms; in themselves such judgments are stupidities. One must by all means stretch out one's fingers and make the attempt to grasp this amazing finesse, *that the value of life cannot be estimated.* Not by the living, for they are an interested party, even a bone of contention, and not judges; not by the dead, for a different reason. For a philosopher to see a problem in the value of life is thus an objection to him, a question mark concerning his wisdom, an un-wisdom. Indeed? All these great wise men–they were not only decadents but not wise at all?[36]

Important notions are mentioned here. Among these is Nietzsche's opinion that the value of life cannot be estimated and that judgments about life are therefore to be viewed reflexively, viewed primarily in terms of the attitude of the person doing the judging.[37] Further, Nietzsche here expresses the view that the sages of all ages seem to agree virtually physiologically with respect to their negative judgment, their negative attitude toward life. Their judgments are therefore to be viewed as symptoms. Consider:

Concerning life, the wisest men of all ages have judged alike: *it is no good.* Always and everywhere one has heard the same sound from their mouths--a sound full of doubt, full of melancholy, full of weariness of life, full of resistance to life. Even Socrates said, as he died: "To live--that means to be sick a long time: I owe Asclepius the Savior a rooster." Even Socrates was tired of it. What does that evidence? What does it evince? Formerly one would have said (--oh, it has been said, and loud enough, and especially by our pessimists): "At least something of all this must be true! The consensus of the sages evidences the truth." Shall we still talk like that today? *May* we? "At least something must be *sick* here," *we* retort. These wisest men of all ages--they should first be scrutinized closely. Were they all perhaps shaky on their legs? late? tottery? decadents? Could it be that wisdom appears on earth as a raven, inspired by a little whiff of carrion?[38]

So an essentially negative attitude toward life typifies philosophers generally, Socrates (and Plato) in particular, [39] and inspires visions of a "true world" to redeem the painful "apparent" one. So, again viewed merely negatively, the philosopher's quest for a world *meta ta physika* is equivalent to the spiritualization of the plebs' revolt against his condition. In this particular instant case

Socrates' decadence is suggested not only by the admitted wantonness and anarchy of his instincts, but also by the hypertrophy of the logical faculty and that *sarcasm of the rachitic* which distinguishes him. Nor should we forget those auditory hallucinations which, as "the *daimōnion* of Socrates," have been interpreted religiously. Everything in him is exaggerated, *buffo,* a caricature; everything is at the same time concealed, ulterior, subterranean. I seek to comprehend what idiosyncrasy begot that Socratic equation of reason, virtue, and happiness: that most bizarre of all equations, which, moreover, is opposed to all the instincts of the earlier Greeks.[40]

In the Socratic identification of reason with virtue (*aretē*) and happiness, a transvaluation of traditional Greek values had occurrred. *Psychē* is valued, *doxa* is devalued:

With Socrates, Greek taste changes in favor of dialectics. What really happened there? Above all, a *noble* taste is thus vanquished; with dialectics the plebs come to the top. Before Socrates, dialectic manners were repudiated in good society: they were considered bad manners, they were compromising. The young were warned against them. Furthermore, all such presentations of one's reasons were distrusted. Honest things, like honest men, do not carry their reasons in their hands like that. It is indecent to show all five fingers. What must first be proved is worth little. Wherever authority still forms part of good bearing, where one does not give reasons but commands, the dialectician is a kind of buffoon: one laughs at him, one does not take him seriously. Socrates was the buffoon who *got himself taken seriously*: What really happened there? [41]

What really happened in the triumph of dialectics, asks Nietzsche?

Is the irony of Socrates an expression of revolt? Of plebian *ressentiment?* Does he, as one oppressed, enjoy his own ferocity in the knife-thrusts of his syllogisms? Does he *avenge* himself on the noble people whom he fascinates? As a dialectician, one holds a merciless tool in one's hand; one can become a tyrant by means of it; one compromises those one conquers. The dialectician leaves it to his opponent to prove that he is no idiot: he makes one furious and helpless at the same time. The dialectician renders the intellect of his opponent powerless. Indeed? Is dialectic only a form of *revenge* in Socrates? [42]

Viewed negatively, Socrates represents the triumph of baseness, represented by the ascent of Greek rationalism, and the corresponding repudiation of noble instinctuality. The agonistic victory of reason over honor and fame may even be veiled vengeance (*Rache*) against the established Greek universe of discourse, Nietzsche suggests. But surely that is only half the story. After all, the unrelenting Socratic method is neither more nor less an expression of will-to-power than is the Periclean. In the case of Socrates, the form-giving which the will-to-power is, is reason. And what makes the "problem" of Socrates so interesting is that he is a destiny. In him reason is exaggerated. In him it overcomes. Through him the character of reason is deified:

> He saw *through* his noble Athenians; he comprehended that his own case, his idiosyncrasy, was no longer exceptional. The same kind of degeneration was quietly developing everywhere: old Athens was coming to an end. And Socrates understood that all the world *needed* was him--his means, his cure, his personal artifice of self-preservation. Everywhere the instincts were in anarchy; everywhere one was within five paces of excess: *monstrum in animo* was the general danger. "The impulses want to play the tyrant; one must invent a *counter-tyrant* who is stronger." When the physiognomist has revealed to Socrates who he was--a cave of bad appetites--the great master of irony let slip another word which is the key to his character. "This is true," he said, "but I mastered them all." *How* did Socrates become master over *himself*? His case was, at bottom, merely the extreme case, only the most striking instance of what was then beginning to be a universal distress: no one was any longer master over himself, the instincts turned *against* each other. He fascinated, being this extreme case; his awe-inspiring ugliness proclaimed him as such to all who could see: he fascinated, of course, even more as an answer, a solution, an apparent *cure* of this case. [43]

The "cure" Socrates embodies consists of the rejection of warring impulses, the coronation and canonization of reason. The cure is to turn reason into a tyrant:

> When one finds it necessary to turn *reason* into a tyrant, as Socrates did, the danger cannot be slight that something else will play the tyrant. Rationality was then hit upon as the savior; neither Socrates nor his "patients"

had any choice about being rational: it was *de rigueur*, it was their last resort. The fanaticism with which all Greek reflection throws itself upon rationality betrays a desperate situation; there was danger, there was but one choice: either to perish or--to be *absurdly rational.* The moralism of the Greek philosophers from Plato on is pathologically conditioned; so is their esteem of dialectics. Reason-virtue-happiness, that means merely that one must imitate Socrates and counter the dark appetites with a permanent daylight--the daylight of reason. One must be clever, clear, bright at any price: any concession to the instincts, to the unconcious, leads *downward*.[44]

So the will to truth finds extreme expression in and as Socrates. Socrates and Greek rationalism generally become *"absurdly rational,"* Nietzsche asserts. Note again that it is not reason *per se* of which Nietzsche wishes to dispose. It is rather, to be *absurdly* rational. What is "absurd" about fanatical rationalism is that it inevitably severs mind and body, *psychē* and *soma*, and vilifies the senses. It is a caricature of intelligence. It is, curiously enough, an extreme exaggeration. Socratic-Platonic rationalism lacks measure, balance, from this perspective.

To return to our discussion of the "true world," then, it is indeed attainable for the "sage, the pious, the virtuous." The virtuous wise man counters the allure of impulses and sensations "with a permanent daylight": Reason. Rationality at any price, and away with instinct! The true world--he lives in it, he is it.

I have given to understand how it was that Socrates fascinated: he seemed to be a physician, a savior. Is it necessary to go on to demonstrate the error in his faith in "rationality at any price"? It is a self-deception on the part of the philosophers and moralists if they believe that they are extricating themselves from decadence when they merely wage war against it. Extrication lies beyond their strength: what they choose as a means, as salvation, is itself but another expression, but they do not get rid of decadence itself. Socrates was a misunderstanding; *the whole improvement-morality, including the Christian, was a misunderstanding.* The most blinding daylight; rationality at any price; life, bright, cold, cautious, conscious, without instinct, in opposition to instincts--all this too was a mere disease, another disease, and by no means a return to "virtue," to "health," to happiness. To *have* to fight the instincts--that is the formula of decadence: as long as life is *ascending,* happiness equals instinct.[45]

Nietzsche's attitude toward Plato and Socrates was understandably ambivalent. On the one hand Socratic-Platonic rationalism is itself spiritualized will-to-power. Its will to truth *is* the will-to-power itself: "To *stamp* the character of being upon becoming--that is the highest will-to-power."[46] The Platonic will to truth can be conceived as articulated will-to-power, in which order is imposed upon the world and upon the turbulent, disquieting, passions of the individual as well. Conceived merely as articulated will-to-power, Platonism is the highest will-to-power imaginable, for it not only has given form to becoming by placing it under the yoke of reason, but being, the "true world" which the world really is, assumes the character of the Platonic dialectic. The "true world" is a circumlocution for the sentence, "I, Plato, *am* the truth," we are told.

On the other hand, extrication from "appearances," extirpation and the positing of a "true world" are still to be understood as symptoms of distress. They are still to be understood as expressions of decadence. For, as Nietzsche says, the formula for decadence is precisely to *have to* fight the instincts. Contrast, if you will, the effortlessness captured by the metaphor of the child, as opposed to either the metaphor of the camel or the lion. In a certain sense, Socratic vision is new creation, to be sure, but it is not the expression of ascending life, the pristine vision of the child. It is not yet *natural*. Socratic-Platonic rationalism may even be heroic, but "all that is good is instinct--and hence easy, necessary, free. Laboriousness is an objection; the god is typically different from the hero. (In my language: light feet are the first attribute of divinity.)"[47]

In this context, Aristotle's ethics--however interesting it may be in its own right--is but another version of Platonic rationalism for Nietzsche, Kaufmann notwithstanding. It must be recalled, after all, that Aristotle's *Nicomachean Ethics* culminates in a discussion of the moral life which argues that philosophic activity, the exercise of the contemplative faculty, constitutes perfect happiness. It could just as easily have been written by Plato, in spirit:

> If happiness is activity in accordance with virtue, it is reasonable that it should be in accordance with the highest virtue; and this will be that of the best thing in us.... That this activity is contemplative we have already said. For, firstly, this activity is the best thing in us, but the objects of reason are the best of knowable objects; and, secondly, it is the most continuous, since we can contemplate truth more continuously than we can *do* anything. And we think happiness has pleasure mingled with it, but the activity of philosophic wisdom is admittedly the pleasantest of virtuous activities.... And this activity alone would seem to be loved for its own sake; for nothing arises from it apart from the contemplating, while from practical activities we gain more or less apart from the action.... If reason is divine, then, in comparison with man, the life according to it is divine in comparison with human life.... That which is proper to each thing is by nature best and most pleasant for each thing; for man, therefore, the life according to reason is best and pleasantest, since reason more than anything else *is* man. This life therefore is also the happiest.[48]

From this perspective, Aristotle's ethics scarcely represent a radical departure from the Platonic rational ideal which so preoccupied Nietzsche. That may also help to explain why Nietzsche nowhere in the published writings expressly addresses himself to Aristotle's ethics, while his references to Aristotle's esthetics abound throughout his *corpus*.

There *is* one reference to Aristotle's ethics--not only to his theory of tragedy--available in published writings, however; and in its tone, its mood, in its point--in its pathos, in short--it captures admirably Nietzsche's indifference toward Aristotle's ethics, and much else besides; it is note number 198 of *Beyond Good and Evil*; it is the note which motivated this paper, and on which I should like to conclude it:

> All these moralities that address themselves to the individual, for the sake of his "happiness" as one says--what are they but counsels for behavior in relation to the degree of *dangerousness* in which the individual lives with himself; recipes against his passions, his good and bad inclinations insofar as they have the will to power and want to play the master; little and great prudences and artifices that exclude the nook odor of old nostrums and of the wisdom of old women; all of them baroque and unreasonable in form--because they address themselves to "all," because they generalize where one must not generalize. All of them speak unconditionally, take themselves for unconditional, all of them flavored with more than one grain of salt and tolerable only--at times even seductive--when they begin to smell over-spiced and dangerous, especially "of the other world." All of it is, measured intellectually, worth very little and not by a long shot "science," much less "wisdom," but rather, to say it once more, three times more, prudence, prudence, prudence, mixed with stupidity, stupidity, stupidity--whether it be that indifference and statue coldness against the hot-headed folly of the affects which the Stoics advised and

administered; or that laughing-no-more and weeping-no-more of Spinoza, his so naively advocated destruction of the affects through their analysis and vivisection; *or that tuning down of the affects to a harmless mean according to which they may be satisfied, the Aristotelianism of morals....This, too, for the chapter "Morality as Timidity."* [49] [My italics]

Notes

1. This paper was presented, in slightly modified form, at the Ninth Annual CSUF Philosophy Symposium, "The Greeks and the Good Life," March 6-9, 1979. I want to thank the Fullerton Philosophy faculty and its students for their kind invitation. I want particularly to thank Professors David Depew and John Cronquist for organizing the conference; Professor J. Michael Russell and his student panel for their thoughtful reactions to my work. Finally, I am once again indebted to the Riverside campus Academic Senate Research Committee for its continuous support and assistance.

2. All references to the *Nicomachean Ethics* will be to the specific Book, Chapter and Greek text-line. The exception will be the case in which I wish to call attention to one particular translation or other.

3. See for example, The Loeb Classical Library, vol. XIX, *The Nicomachean Ethics,* tr. H. Rackham (Cambridge: Harvard University Press; London: William Heinemann, 1926), pp. 213-227 (hereafter simply "Rackham").

4. See for example, The Library of Liberal Arts, *The Nicomachean Ethics,* tr. Martin Ostwald (Indianapolis, New York: The Bobbs-Merrill Co, Inc., 1962), pp. 93-99. The following footnote (No. 18) is of special interest for this discussion:

> *Megalopsychia* literally means 'greatness of soul' and was translated into Latin as *magnanimitas,* from which English 'magnanimity' is derived. However, since, as this chapter will show, the connotations of *megalopsychia* are much wider than the modern meaning of 'magnanimity,' 'highmindedness' seems better suited to rendering the pride and confident self-respect inherent in the concept.

5. Sir W. David Ross translates it this way in his *Aristotle* (Methuen, 2nd edition, 1930); yet in his own translation of the text he seems to prefer the more commonly used "pride."

6. See *Ethica Nicomachea,* tr. W. D. Ross, in *The Basic Works of Aristotle,* ed. by Richard McKeon (New York: Random House, Inc., 1941), pp. 991-995. Ross also prefers "pride" to his own "self-respect" in volume 9 of the Oxford Text Series, *Ethics* (Oxford University Press, 1925); and in his translation, *Nicomachean Ethics of Aristotle,* Worlds Classics Series (Oxford University Press, 1954).

7. Compare, for example, the translations of *Thus Spoke Zarathrustra* by Walter Kaufmann (New York: Viking Press, 1956), Marianne Cowan (Chicago: Regnery-Gateway, 1957), H. J. Hollingdale (Baltimore, Md.: Penguin, 1961) and Thomas Common (in *Complete Works of Friedrich Nietzsche,* ed. Oscar Levy, vol. XI, 1909-1911).

8. Consider only a few: "superhuman," "supernatural," "superlunary," "superego," "supereminent," "supergiant," "superliner," "supernova," "superstar," "superpower," "supersubstantial," "supersubtle."

9. I hasten to add that when I use the term "man" throughout this paper--as in the "great-souled man," for example--I wish it to be understood as neutral with respect to gender, as a synonym for "person" or "human being."

10. Walter Kaufmann, *Nietzsche: Philosopher, Psychologist, AntiChrist.* (Princeton, New Jersey: Princeton University Press, Fourth edition, 1974), p. 382.

11. Kaufmann, p. 384.

12. Most of what is said in part IV is a slight revision of remarks made in my *Nietzsche's Existential Imperative* (Bloomington and London: University of Indiana Press, 1978. Studies in Phenomenology and Existential Philosophy).

13. The notoriously difficult *Wiederkunftslehre* will remain a mere mention in this paper. It is treated elsewhere in detail.

14. This is Rackham, with an important exception. I have substituted "pride" and "proud" for "great-souled" throughout.

15. Book I, Chapter 1.

16. Book II, Chapter 6.

17. Book II, Chapter 6.

18. Book IV, Chapter 3.

19. Book IV, Chapter 3.

20. KGW IV$_3$, p. 211; Schlechta I, p. 900. An explanatory note: Several German editions of Nietzsche's works are used and cited here. The best is the (still-in-progress) Colli and Montinari *Kritische Gesamtausgabe der Werke* (Berlin: De Gruyter, 1967 ff.); it is referred to as "KGW," following the current convention. A second, complete edition sometimes cited here is the *Grossoktavausgabe* (Leipzig: Kroener, 1901-1913); it is referred to as "GOA." Karl Schlechta's three volume *Werke in drei Baenden*–hereafter simply "Schlechta"–is a convenient but inadequate reference source. Finally, I sometimes refer to "Kaufmann" as well; such references will be to his translation of *Nachlass* materials under the title *The Will to Power.*

21. KGW IV$_2$, p. 65; Schlechta I, p. 483.

22. KGW VI$_2$, p. 218; Schlechta II, p. 730.

23. Nietzsche's approach to moral issues consists of several strands which he seldoms disentangles. Sometimes he seems to argue from linguistic usage considerations alone, as if a "meaning is use" formula were to apply to his analyses of words: such as *gut* (good), *schlecht* (bad) and *boese* (evil), as well as to their etymological surrogates and ancestors. Sometimes the linguistic genealogy is a tacit etiology; it tells us what caused words to be used as they were/are used, to have the meanings they had/have. Sometimes he argues that all these considerations are preliminary, that what counts is a certain typology which the linguistic and etiological discussions merely serve to illustrate. Although these three sets of considerations require different evidence and arguments, I believe they can be made consistent. This, however, is not the place to try.

24. KGW VI$_2$, p. 284; Schlechta II, p. 782.

25. That guilt is a mechanism by which the powerless attempt to assert themselves has become a cliche since Nietzsche (not Freud) first discovered this phenomenon; think of a mother's putative guilt-manipulation (e.g., *Portnoy's Complaint*), or the often cited "liberal's" guilt, when it becomes ripe for manipulation by the disinherited of the earth.

26. In this case, the generality of the guilt engulfs everyone, including the slave. Like a pebble cast into a limpid pool of water, its ripples touch everything.

27. KGW VI$_1$, pp. 176-177; Schlechta II, pp. 394-395.

28. KGW V$_2$, p. 255; Schlechta II, p. 205.

29. This point is not sufficiently appreciated. On the one hand, no specifiable set of traits or characteristics or preferences follows from Nietzsche's characterization of *Uebermenschlichkeit*; on the other hand, Nietzsche had some clear trait, characteristic and preference preferences of his own. Conflating *Uebermenschlichkeit* with Nietzsche's preference-profile is a common source of confusions. Compare what follows here with my *Nietzsche's Existential Imperative*, especially pp. 142-146, for example.

30. The analogy with Heidegger's *Being and Time* is deliberate. The resemblance between *das Man* and Nietzsche's last man strikes me as useful. It is merely suggested here. It could and perhaps should be fleshed out. Spelling the resemblance out would also support the contention that *Uebermenschlichkeit*–the antithesis of "the last man"–does not baptize specific qualities of persons; rather what it captures is a certain attitude toward life and world–one which finds them worthy of *infinite* repetition.

31. Remember the earlier caution; nothing in the conception of an *Uebermensch* entails or implies this set of characteristics.

32. KGW VII$_2$, p. 289; Kaufmann 493 (p. 513).

33. KGW VI$_1$, pp. 25-27. The quotations which follow will be from this aphorism, unless otherwise indicated. This discussion also appears, in slightly different form, in *Nietzsche's Existential Imperative*.

34. The compelling illustrations derive from the fine arts. When Rubinstein plays Beethoven's "Moonlight Sonata," for example, he must in a certain sense remember his entire musical training, from scales to rote learning of the sonata itself. His hands enlist his memory in their service. But it cannot be only memory. When Rubinstein performs the sonata "creatively", as we like to say, he forgets everything in a certain sense. The rote memorization, the indicated phrasing, tempo, etc., dissolve in virtuosity. Or consider Picasso approaching paint and canvas, or Faulkner "forgetting" the constraints of grammar. In each such case, you will find what I am calling a memory that knows how to forget.

35. KGW VI$_3$, pp. 74-75; GOA VIII, 82.

36. KGW VI$_3$, pp. 61-62.

37. The notion that philosophical positions can function diagnostically is important, particularly for the doctrine of eternal recurrence and the attitude which is characteristic of *Uebermenschen*.

38. KGW VI$_3$, p. 61.

39. For a more comprehensive discussion of Nietzsche's complex attitude toward Socrates (and Plato) see W. Dannhouser's *Nietzsche's View of Socrates* (Ithaca: Cornell University Press, 1974.)

40. KGW VI$_3$, p. 63.

41. KGW VI$_3$, p. 63-64.

42. KGW VI$_3$, p. 64.

43. KGW VI$_3$, p. 65-66.

44. KGW VI$_3$, p. 66.

45. KGW VI$_3$, pp. 66-67.

46. GOA *Nachlass XVI*, 101; Schlechta III, p. 895; Kaufmann 617 (p. 330).

47. KGW VI$_3$, p. 34.

48. Book X, Chapter 7.

49. *Basic Writings of Nietzsche*, translated and edited by Walter Kaufmann. (New York: Random House, Inc., 1968), pp. 299-300. Although all translations of Nietzsche--save this last one--are my own, I have taken advantage of Walter Kaufmann's excellent ones throughout, sometimes modifying them only slightly. All English-speaking Nietzsche scholars are indebted to Kaufmann. His translations are elegant and the project's scope has been massive. Finally and in addition, were it not for Walter Kaufmann's pioneering monograph (mentioned in note 10), Nietzsche's rehabilitation in the English-speaking world would surely have been delayed still another generation.

ABOUT THE CONTRIBUTORS

GEORGIOS ANAGNOSTOPOULOS is Associate Professor of Philosophy at the University of California, San Diego. He publishes on topics in ancient philosophy.

EUGENE GARVER studied and taught at the University of Chicago, and is currently Associate Professor of Philosophy at California State College, San Bernardino. His articles and reviews have appeared in *Ethics, Journal of the History of Philosophy,* and *Philosophy and Rhetoric.*

DAVID K. GLIDDEN is Assistant Professor of Philosophy at the University of California, Riverside. He has studied at Princeton University, and recently in Germany as a Humboldt Fellow. He publishes on Plato and topics in Hellenistic philosophy.

PHILIP J. KAIN is Assistant Professor of Philosophy at the University of California, Santa Cruz. His book *Schiller, Hegel and Marx* will appear shortly. He is completing a book on Marx's method and epistemology.

BERND MAGNUS is Professor of Philosophy, and Chair of the Philosophy Department, at the University of California, Riverside. He is the author of *Nietzsche's Existential Imperative* and *Heidegger's Metahistory of Philosophy.* He is co-editor of *Cartesian Meditations,* and a frequent contributor to many professional journals.

JULIUS M.E. MORAVCSIK is Professor of Philosophy at Stanford University. He has written over the past two decades many papers dealing with the philosophies of Plato and Aristotle, and is the editor of several anthologies.

MERRILL RING is Professor of Philosophy at California State University, Fullerton. He studied at the University of

Washington and has taught at the University of California, Santa Barbara. He writes and publishes mainly on epistemological topics.

GERASIMOS SANTAS is Professor of Philosophy at the University of California, Irvine. He is the author of *Socrates: Philosophy in Plato's Early Dialogues,* and is now at work on a book comparing the theories of love of Plato and Freud.

STEVEN SMITH is Associate Professor of Philosophy at Claremont Men's College. He studied at Harvard University. He is the author of *Satisfaction of Interest and the Concept of Morality* and is currently preparing a book of readings on the good life.

CHARLES M. YOUNG is Associate Professor of Philosophy at Claremont Graduate School. He is the author of several articles on Plato and Aristotle, and is currently working on a book on Plato's ethics.

DAVID J. DEPEW is Associate Professor of Philosophy at California State University, Fullerton.